TOWARD TRANSLINGUAL
REALITIES IN COMPOSITION

TOWARD TRANSLINGUAL REALITIES IN COMPOSITION

(Re)Working Local Language Representations and Practices

NANCY BOU AYASH

UTAH STATE UNIVERSITY PRESS
Logan

© 2019 by University Press of Colorado

Published by Utah State University Press
An imprint of University Press of Colorado
245 Century Circle, Suite 202
Louisville, Colorado 80027

All rights reserved

 The University Press of Colorado is a proud member of the Association of University Presses.

The University Press of Colorado is a cooperative publishing enterprise supported, in part, by Adams State University, Colorado State University, Fort Lewis College, Metropolitan State University of Denver, University of Colorado, University of Northern Colorado, University of Wyoming, Utah State University, and Western Colorado University.

ISBN: 978-1-60732-903-9 (paperback)
ISBN: 978-1-60732-904-6 (ebook)
DOI: https://doi.org/10.7330/9781607329046

Library of Congress Cataloging-in-Publication Data

Names: Bou Ayash, Nancy, author.
Title: Toward translingual realities in composition : (re)working local language representations and practices / Nancy Bou Ayash.
Description: Logan : Utah State University Press, [2019] | Includes bibliographical references and index.
Identifiers: LCCN 2019014747 | ISBN 9781607329039 (pbk.) | ISBN 9781607329046 (ebook)
Subjects: LCSH: English language—Rhetoric—Study and teaching (Higher) | English language—Social aspects—Lebanon—Beirut. | English language—Social aspects—Washington (State)—Seattle. | Academic writing. | Language and culture.
Classification: LCC PE1404 .B668 2019 | DDC 306.44/6—dc23
LC record available at https://lccn.loc.gov/2019014747

Cover photographs: ramifications of banyan tree transplanted in Beirut © Hasan Nisr (*top right*), urban translingualism © Nancy Bou Ayash (*top left, bottom*).

For Riad,
May you continue to find joy in and grant me knowledge about the playfulness of language and translation.

CONTENTS

List of Illustrations   ix
Preface   xi
Acknowledgments   xv

Introduction   3

1 Language Ideologies in Teaching Writing: A Language Representations and/as Practices Perspective   20

2 Working Translingual Language Representations and/as Practices   41

3 Unpacking Local Language Representations and/as Practices: Portraits of Postmonolingual Tensions from Beirut   63

4 Unpacking Local Language Representations and/as Practices Continued: Postmonolingualism in Seattle   103

5 Translingual Activism: Turning up the Volume of Critical Translation in Writing Pedagogy   140

Conclusion: Lessons on Thinking and Doing Translinguality *with* Beirut and Seattle   174

Appendix A: An Ethnography of Language Representations and/as Practices   186
Appendix B: Profiles of Featured Participants   195
Appendix C: Student Interview Protocol   196
Appendix D: Teacher Interview Protocol   198
Notes   201
References   213
About the Author   227
Index   229

ILLUSTRATIONS

FIGURES

1.1.	Archipelago model of language-in-use and language relations	31
2.1.	Wire madness in cityscapes	48
3.1.	Translingual practice in Lebanese license plates	68
3.2.	Experimenting with design practices and functions	84
3.3.	A memoir of urban explorations	85
3.4.	Graphic narrative for a major course project	85
4.1.	Translingual practice on restaurant walls in Seattle	106
5.1.	Summary of writing-translation connections sequence	147

TABLES

1.1.	Distinction among mono-, multi-, and translinguality in writing instruction	25
A1.1.	Characteristics of research contexts	187

PREFACE

In a book that seeks to make visible the dynamic negotiations of language-ideological tensions that characterize much of contemporary social, cultural, and literate life, it is worth highlighting some of the productive challenges I myself have grappled with throughout the conception and development of this project.

The book you are about to read takes you on a journey from Beirut, overlooking the Mediterranean Sea in Lebanon, to the large urban center that is the Pacific coast city of Seattle in the United States, uncovering the multiple and contesting language ideologies that are circulating and at play in the complex language and writing ecologies young writers in those locations inhabit. Needless to say, the diverse and varied data from the study I conducted in Lebanon for my doctoral dissertation could have easily filled the entire pages of this book and even carried me into another book project. But it wasn't long before I realized that embarking on a whole new study in a new setting was necessary for analytically broadening and theoretically refining my own (and I hope my readers') understanding of the complexity of translingual realities in superdiverse literate contexts. As I was just beginning to develop my own take on the young paradigm of translingualism that I apparently advance, I became dissatisfied with the current directions of translingual scholarship in composition studies, most notably a limited preoccupation with (1) critiques of powerfully entrenched monolingual assumptions about language and language relations in the study and teaching of writing at the expense of more deliberate translingual-oriented pedagogical interventions and enactments grounded in rigorous, systematic, and self-reflexive qualitative research from various parts of the world; (2) actual translingual/translanguaging/code-meshing strategies in writing at the expense of the complex interaction of language representations and practices in specific local ecologies at both macro and micro levels that make the successful negotiation and implementation of such strategies possible in the first place; and (3) the creation of meaning and negotiation of language difference among writers proficient in multiple languages or varieties of a language when writers to whom English is the one and only language are indeed co-collaborators in its reworking and translation in light of varying identities, values, and socio-ideological interests. Hence, the intellectual genesis of this book and its multi-sited/*sight*ed approach.

Pulling together the various perspectives on and experiences with confronting language-ideological tensions and contradictions in teaching and learning college English writing on opposite parts of the globe into a coherent narrative was far from straightforward. I must confess to feeling overwhelmed by my ambitious ethnographic engagements, which entailed moving flexibly—both physically and intellectually—between and across languages, language varieties, cultures, epistemologies, localities, and institutions and coming to terms with all the chaos, complexity, and unpredictability that labor demanded. Despite these challenges, it certainly has been an enlightening and a sobering experience to start noticing the broader, fundamental intersections in the management of linguistic and cultural difference in massively divergent writing program infrastructures and ecologies.

As this book entered its stages of revision and rewriting, it was equally challenging to move the manuscript more efficiently and smoothly through a large amount of conceptual, theoretical, and empirical material. Meeting reader expectations for clarity, transparency, efficiency, and uninterrupted meaning transmission when dealing with a range of issues, conceptual and analytical tools, super-diversifying locations, and ecologies that only brought about further layers of complexity, ambiguity, and 'thickness' proved to be tedious and cumbersome. While I've made a conscious attempt to trim down some of my twelve-line-long sentences and unpack dense passages, I remain convinced that an appropriate dose of labor for the reader is necessary and valuable to stimulate a translingual thinking and reading experience that forces one to slow down, linger, pause, and think more carefully and critically about: one's own practices with and assumptions about language and language difference in writing; the current state of language relations in one's local sociolinguistic, classroom, and program ecologies; what it really means to start viewing and putting language into work as translingual; and how to best proceed accordingly at both the individual and collective levels. As such, I remind the reader that there will be a few moments in this book—starting from the complexity and opacity I deliberately maintain in my own language and writing practices to the positioning of chapter 2, which I dedicate for a theoretical discussion of my own particular take on translingualism—where I make deliberate attempts to push you to sustain the kind of intellectual exercise I'm urging you to take responsibility for in your research, teaching, and administrative practices in light of your expertise, workload, and available resources. As the title of this book suggests and as the detailed description within its pages will point us toward, the degree to which the work we do at the level of both language representations and practices continues to contradict with sociolinguistic realities and young writers' desires needs to be taken seriously and can no longer be sidestepped or ignored. It is my hope that you would join my ongoing efforts to develop a richly textured and more useful translingual understanding of and labor with language and language difference in composition studies for the sake of better serving our communities, our students, and their literacy learning processes.

ACKNOWLEDGMENTS

A demanding research project such as this that spans a number of years and different geographic locations would not have been possible without the thoughtful and generous support of countless individuals. It would be futile to even attempt to list those without unintentional omissions, but I wish to at least acknowledge the following for the direct and indirect ways they have contributed to this book in its ever-changing forms.

For their contributions to the progress of this project when I was still conceptualizing its framework and current direction, I wish to thank both Bruce Horner and Min Zhan Lu. I owe a special debt to Bruce, who has regularly supported, stimulated, and challenged me in so many ways to become a better scholar, and to Min for believing in me way back when I was still testing the waters in a new cultural and disciplinary context and sticking with me ever since. Throughout our deliberations, whether by phone or email, over home-cooked or restaurant meals, during trips to the farmers market or shared cab rides, in the busy lobbies or hallways of conference hotels, they have both challenged me to constantly keep my own language representations and practices in check and to raise the kinds of critical questions about the study and teaching of academic writing in local and global contexts that lie at the heart of this book. Min was the very first to recognize, but more important, to help *me* recognize the value of the various resources I carried with me from other language- and literacy-related disciplines, cultures, languages, and worldviews when I had fallen into the habit of dismissing them as irrelevant. She has taught me more than she realizes and more than I can actually say here about the importance of and possibility for thinking, languaging, researching, teaching, writing, and living "against the grain." Thanks to her unique way of leading by example, I intend to do the same with my current and potential mentees. She has been an invisible presence during the composition of these pages.

And here I also wish to thank Suresh Canagarajah, who I was very fortunate to meet for the first time during my first Conference on College Composition and Communication (CCCC) meeting in Louisville, Kentucky. I didn't know who he was back then and only realized the next morning that I had met the scholar of the highest standards whose name

I couldn't properly pronounce but whose scholarship first inspired me to attempt to straddle the worlds of language and composition studies. I have benefited immensely from both his inspiring work and one-on-one conversations on the challenges and pleasures of creating new knowledge in educational practice and policy through traversing diverse linguistic, cultural, national, and disciplinary boundaries. I am grateful to him for agreeing to be an external reader on my dissertation committee despite his many other responsibilities, for his thoughtful questioning and intellectual generosity were instrumental in urging me to adopt a more activist stance in chapter 5 and throughout the book. To this very day, I remain amazed by and highly respect his unique humility and his generosity with his guidance and already limited time, especially with graduate students and junior scholars.

I have for several years now tried to explore past and contemporary theories and ideologies of language and their effects on various aspects of the study and teaching of writing, and this book is an extension and deepening of earlier attempts. Portions of chapter 3 draw from my essays "U.S. Translingualism through a Cross-National and Cross-Linguistic Lens" (in *Reworking English in Rhetoric and Composition*, ed. Bruce Horner and Karen Kopelson [Carbondale: Southern Illinois University Press, 2014], 116–30 [© 2014 by Nancy Bou Ayash. All rights reserved]), "Hi-*ein*, Hi بين or بين Hi? Translingual Practices from Lebanon and Mainstream Literacy Education" (in *Literacy as Translingual Practice*, ed. Suresh Canagarajah [New York: Routledge, 2013], 96–103 [© 2013 by Taylor and Francis. Reprinted with permission]), and "Conditions of (Im) Possibility: Postmonolingual Language Representations in Academic Literacies" (*College English* 78 [6]: 555–77 [© 2016 by the National Council of Teachers of English. Reprinted with permission]). I would like to thank Taylor and Francis Group, LLC and NCTE, for permission to reproduce parts of that material. Every effort has been made to trace and contact copyright holders of the video *La France au Liban "Taxi"* by Laser Films and obtain permission for the use of the extracts appearing in this book, but without success.

This work has benefited enormously from productive exchanges with a wonderful community of scholars equally invested in language and literacy matters, whom I've been lucky to meet and from whom I continue to learn: Christiane Donahue, Bronwyn Williams, Tatjana Soldat-Jaffe, David Martins, Kate Vieira, Amy Wan, LuMing Mao, Jonathan Hall, Rebecca Lorimer Leonard, Jerry Won Lee, Paul Kei Matsuda, Jay Jordan, Brooke Schreiber, Ligia Mihut, Esther Milu, Tika Lamsal, Hem Paudel, Carrie Kilfoil, Brice Nordquist, Vanessa Kraemer, Amy Lueck,

Jennifer Marciniak, Megan Bardolph, Michael Sobiech, Shyam Sharma, Suzanne Blum Malley, Alanna Frost, Tom Lavelle, Rasha Diab, Keith Lloyd, Tim Dougherty, and many others. Prior to the publication of this book, I had the chance to try out some of the ideas I include in the discussion on translingual-oriented metaphors in chapter 2 and on critical writing-*trans*lation connections in chapter 5 at the 2014 and 2015 CCCC meetings through the panels consecutively entitled "Rethinking Difference in Composing Composition: Language, Translation, Genre, and Modality" (with Bruce Horner, Anis Bawarshi, Juan Guerra, and Cynthia Self) and "Writing as Translation, Translation as Writing" (with Bruce Horner, Christiane Donahue, and Laura Tetreault). I wish to thank the other panelists and all those who attended the sessions for their tough questions and insights that have sharpened my thinking and analyses. Thanks also to the various participants from around the world at the 2014 and 2016 CCCC Workshop on International Exchanges about Higher Education Writing Research and its co-chairs, Christiane Donahue and Cinthia Gannett, for the stimulating conversations and responses to my work.

I also owe many thanks to my wonderful colleagues at the University of Washington for their lively support and intellectual stimulation, namely Juan Guerra, Habiba Ibrahim, Anis Bawarshi, Candice Rai, Suhanthie Motha, John Webster, Gary Handwerk, Brian Reed, Sandy Silberstein, Gillian Harkins, Jessica Bernstein, Carolyn Allen, Jeff Knight, Juliet Shields, Karam Dana, Priti Sandhu, Collete Moore, Charles LaPorte, Gail Stygall, Joe Butwin, Carrie Mathews, Michelle Liu, Elizabeth Simmons-O'Neill, and Katie Malcom. I am particularly grateful to Anis Bawarshi for following this book's trajectory from its initial uncertain steps to its final form. He kindly read and commented extensively on various drafts from the proposal stage onward. The informed and critical feedback he offered on the original manuscript was instrumental in pushing me to develop and sharpen the book you are now reading. In addition to his mentorship and encouragement through moments of healthy self-doubt and intellectual struggles, I have come to admire his passion, selflessness, spiritual authenticity, and incredible talent—a very rare combination these days in both academia and the outside world. A special thanks to Juan for all his support and heartfelt advice, to Suhanthie for her generous backing and constant reassurance, to John for pushing me to further pursue this line of research by productively disagreeing with my views, to Candice for reading and commenting on my work and parts of this project when she didn't have to, and to Sandy for her generous batches of soup that kept me going during a seemingly endless string of dreary and wet days. For their invigorating discussions and thought-provoking questions that continue to push my own thinking about translingualism in different directions, I thank members of my graduate seminars "Translation in Translingual/Transnational Writing" (Fall 2014), "Cross-Disciplinary Perspectives on Translation: Politics, Theory, and Practice" (Winter 2018), and "Language Ideologies, Policies, and Pedagogies in Composition" (Winter 2017), particularly Lise Lalonde, Allison Cardinal, Holly Shelton, Judy-Gail Baker, TJ Walker, Gust Burns, Dino Kladouris, Qingran Wang, Molly Staumbugh, Sara Lovett, Sumyat Thu, Anthony Warnke, Daniel Weller, Fatema Musazay, Ian Sherman-Youngblood, Jacqui Pratt, Erin Bird, Shane Peterson, Julie Michel, Joshua Guernsey, Patrick McGowan, Merzamie Cagaitan, Lubna Alzaroo, Ainiwar Abdumutailifu, Zhenzhen He, Yan Wang, Mandy Macklin, and Shauna Searcy. Thanks to the UW Royalty Research Fund for making all of this possible by providing funding and much-needed release time. I am also thankful to Holly Shelton and Patrick McGowan for providing valuable assistance with transcriptions and to Carolyn Busch for helping make that support possible. In addition, I want to acknowledge all the hard behind-the-scenes work of the English department staff, especially Karla Toft, Rob Weller, Janie Worm, Annie Fisher, Kathy Mork, Ali Dahmer, and Carolyn Busch.

I would also like to express my thanks to mentors and colleagues in Lebanon at the American University of Beirut, Lebanese American University, and Notre Dame University–Louaize for their early transcontinental support of my work, namely Kassem Shaaban, Lina Choueiri, Amy Zenger, Rula Baabaki, Rima Iskandarani, Dany Badran, Rula Diab, Assad Eid, and the late Juheina Yakzan and Boulos Sarru', whose untimely deaths I still mourn.

At Utah State University Press, I thank Michael Spooner for believing in this project early on and Rachael Levay for taking the reigns and for her enthusiastic support from beginning to end. I was especially gratified by the strong praise and encouraging comments by two anonymous reviewers as well as their perceptive and probing feedback, which helped shape the current manuscript. One reviewer's extensive suggestions were particularly useful in pushing me to craft a more polished and readable (I hope) final version while still preserving the complexities and entanglements inherent in the subject matter and the local ecologies with which I engage. The phenomenal production and marketing team at the press was a pleasure to work with, most especially Laura Furney, Beth Svinarich, Cheryl Carnahan who took on the challenge of copyediting a translingual manuscript with great professionalism, and Daniel Pratt who skillfully executed the book cover design.

I will be forever thankful to all the university writing students, teachers, and program administrators in both Beirut and Seattle who have been magnanimous with their time and exciting stories. The enthusiasm and great interest they've shown in the idea behind this project while sharing the specificities of their literate lives and work have made the long, tedious process of working on this book a deeply enjoyable experience. I am unable to mention any specific names because of ethical considerations, but they know who they are.

I have been very lucky in my friends and companions outside my academic circles whose continued interest in the evolution of this project as I coped with chronic illness has meant a lot to me over the past few years. A warm thank you to three remarkable women who have become part of my extended family and have made Seattle feel like home, Diane Guerra, Amy Feldman-Bawarshi, and Janan Ghazal, for their dear friendship and moral support. On the other side of the Atlantic, I am heavily indebted to Zeina Abdallah, a faithful sister and dearest friend, who constantly checked in from afar to inquire about my book's progress and assisted immensely in finding the best Beiruti translanguaging spots to capture on camera. A special thanks to her and Hasan Nisr for the stunning photograph of the banyan tree that appears on the cover of this book. I am also incredibly thankful to my brother, Nizar, for attempting to make sense of the ideas I presented him with and for blending and altering elements from various images (from iStock by Getty Images) to produce the language-island model that appears in chapter 1. The biggest thank you must go to my supportive neighbor, yet another Nizar, for taking risks to help snap the images that bring home some of the arguments I make and help keep the traffic of information moving even in Beirut's so-called security zones but mostly for thinking on his feet when that was spotted on surveillance camera networks.

I have inherited the characteristics of boundless curiosity and fearlessly pursuing one's dreams from my parents, Amin and Sawsan (Iris) Bou Ayash, who provide unending inspiration for a strong work ethic, the spirit of adventure, and ambition. None of this, however, would have been imaginable without the love, care, and encouragement I've received from my lifelong partner and soulmate, Riad (Roy) Bou Sleiman, especially through some of the harder times. I will always cherish the unmatched patience he showed when I had to interrupt our weekend getaways and summer vacations (and, sadly, our honeymoon) to address various book-related issues or when I woke up frantically in the middle of the night to write down a seemingly brilliant thought or stopped (sometimes illegally) at the side of roads and highways for a quick snapshot of languaging-in-action. The fact that he tolerated all the mood swings and tirades, provided management of our daily household responsibilities while I completed my work, and came to my defense every time I was shamed by family members and close friends for becoming "antisocial" (at least according to Lebanese standards) and increasingly cherishing quiet time with my work and ideas really helped bring this book to a successful completion. Most of all, I thank him for his incredible heart, dedication, and humorous support throughout this wild ride. Habibi toi, shhedti feek 3atoul majrou7a. Merci beacoup encore et encore.

Just as important, for unknowingly exposing me to translingualism and its workings far before I even had the language to talk about it and what it really entailed, I remain fortunate to be surrounded by both Iris and Roy, who always find the courage to claim English as their own, unconcerned whether they get things right. When I make a joke of it, they laugh with pride in their abilities to live in and through translation and to keep the language alive. When I have foolishly urged them to learn it properly, they have persistently argued and demonstrated that successfully communicating with the rest of the world is not a one-way street. This book is the gift I give back to them after many years of giving very little credit for their dynamic language competence. They continue to be my best-loved examples of working and reworking English and the language we use for describing it, both an inspiration. I look forward to many more years of learning and translating together in and out of the multiple language resources we share.

TOWARD TRANSLINGUAL
REALITIES IN COMPOSITION

INTRODUCTION

We discussed whether it was correct before we ran it. It's grammatical, if you think about what we're trying to say. It's not think the same, it's think different. Think a little different, think a lot different, think different. "Think differently" wouldn't hit the meaning for me.

(cited in Isaacson 2011, 330)

I know that most conventional academic American readers expect me to explain my main argument at the beginning of my essay. However, as a writer who was educated in an eastern culture and whose writing is inspired by the work of an established Chinese writer Xun Lu, I choose to write this essay following a Chinese writing style that keeps the main argument at the end of a writing piece. Due to the complexity and richness of my experiences [with language], readers of my essay need to be a patient because my deep feelings [about language] that have changed over time cannot be captured by a single statement or two. I hope this decision would encourage my readers to focus more on my personal experiences and collaborate with me in order to grasp my conclusion about the power of language in expressing one's feelings and emotions and bringing different writing styles and cultures together.

(Ruijia, freshman English student, Fall 2013)

Despite prolonged deliberations with a team from a large multinational advertising agency and his in-house editors about the grammaticality of the "*Think Different*" slogan the company chose for its 1997 brand image campaign, Steve Jobs, the late co-founder and CEO of Apple, Inc. at the time, insisted on adopting the now famous line and sticking to the ungrammatical usage of "different" rather than its adverbial form "differently." Selling a large number of electronic devices to schools and college students nationally and across the globe, Jobs and his team "wrestled with the language" and feared that the grammatically incorrect slogan might cause "English teachers to break out in hives" (Blumenthal 2012, 192). As Jobs explained in his authorized biography,

DOI: 10.7330/9781607329046.c000b

he intentionally chose to use the word *different* as a noun, as in "think victory" (cited in Isaacson 2011, 330), "think vision," or "think genius." Through the term *different*, he also wanted to capture a sense of colloquialism, as in the popular mantra "think big or go home," which echoed American society's attitudes toward enterprise, boldness, and success (Isaacson 2011, 330). In addition to manufacturing and distributing what was "inside the boxes" consumers used to accomplish their daily tasks ("Apple Confidential" 2013), Jobs in an internal meeting described his strong desire to (re)build Apple's identity and purpose as inspiring and empowering people to think and get "outside the box" in the same way the different-thinking figures honored in this brand marketing campaign, as the ad puts it, have "push[ed] the human race forward" (Isaacson 2011, 329).[1] Recounting the genesis and architecture of the "Think Different" campaign and the "different" thinking behind its ungrammatical slogan, Jobs, as illustrated in the above quotation, argued that the standardized grammatically correct phrase "think differently" couldn't capture the full range of social meanings of significance to his vision and to what he described as the company's "core values" of "tak[ing] risks," defying the status quo, and ultimately "chang[ing] the world" by doing things in a different way ("Apple Confidential" 2013; cf. Isaacson 2011). Imbued with a sense of fluidity, malleability, and change, the idiosyncratic phrase "think different" projected an intention to place in the spotlight not what computer products could do in terms of "processor speed or memory" but, more important, "what creative people could do with" them (Isaacson 2011, 328). In other words, the strategic language design in the "Think Different" campaign was intended to encourage consumers to reimagine and reconstruct their own identities as "creative, innovative rebels" by utilizing Apple products over time and across space (Isaacson 2011, 331–32).

One might claim that such a view of language as mobile and fluid and the subsequent practice of strategically shaping it for particular ends is (1) made possible thanks to Jobs's privileged status and power to "play by his own set of rules" (Isaacson 2011, 117), given his mainstream sociocultural identity and possession of high cultural and economic capital; (2) meaningful and relevant for the kind of attention-getting or thought-provoking marketing and advertising practices necessary in the corporate world; but (3) not authorized in other social spheres, especially the educational realm where various gatekeeping and policymaking mechanisms are often uncompromising in their firm expectations that all language and literate usage abide by the dominant culture's standardized norms and conventions. For those reasons combined, I have presented the second excerpt, which demonstrates how Ruijia, a Chinese student in one of my first-year writing courses, chose to revise her introduction in response to my suggestions that she rework and narrow her ideas to a clear, concise statement of her main argument, customarily appearing early on in academic texts.

Ruijia seemed fully aware that conventional academic readers, including myself and her peers, would demand that student writers thoroughly "explain" their position "at the beginning" of a text. Interestingly, she still made an informed choice of refusing to sidestep her sense of what truly mattered to the specificity of the rhetorical situation in which she was writing and what more fully captured, as she stated, the "complexity and richness" of her diverse linguistic and cultural experiences. Rather than blindly conform to the conventions of English academic writing as I had suggested in my written comments, thereby constructing her identity into a passive, unquestioning role, Ruijia reconfigured and reconstituted conventional teacher-student/reader-writer relationships by moving into the more active role of a negotiator. In her individual literate negotiations, for instance, she acknowledged her readers' expectations and clearly articulated what she was willing to offer them and the type of engagement she expected from them in return for more successful communication and meaning creation (in this case, what she described as favorable dispositions of patience, accommodation, and collaboration). The very act of her entering into a give-and-take dynamic of negotiations with a clearly articulated goal of making deals with her readers about reconsidering the social value, validity, and effectiveness of the nonconventional rhetorical traits of her English written discourse is suggestive of Ruijia's strong authorial voice and presence. I will revisit Ruijia's writing selection in chapter 5 to make a case for reimagining academic English writing as dynamic negotiation and translation across asymmetrical relations of power and difference.

Whether we glorify or vilify Jobs's and Ruijia's semiotic ways of composing and negotiating meaning in writing, of prime interest to this book is that such difficult, often risky decisions surrounding language use in writing are inextricably linked to much broader "regimes of language" (Kroskrity 2000, 3), the ideas language users/learners from different walks of life have about (and act in relation to) language and various ways of using it in particular communicative situations and contexts, that is, their *language ideologies*. However explicit or covert they may be, language ideologies in literate contexts, as we shall see in subsequent chapters, are never singular or homogeneous and do not operate in a simple manner but are rather "unmarkedly" multiple and complex (Kroskrity 2000, 12). In the particular case of the teaching and learning of writing in the United States, for instance, we have been witnessing a serious investment in the key features, manifestations, and practical effects of conspicuously contradictory language ideologies of dominant monolingualism and emergent "translingualism" (Horner, Lu, Royster, and Trimbur 2011; Canagarajah 2013b). While a perennially forceful English-only monolingualist ideology posits a unitary view of English-language standards as irrevocable givens and universal signs of high-quality, correct language usage in writing, a counterhegemonic translingual ideology defines and engages with written English as both adaptable and adapting its shape and meaning(s) under diverse sociocultural contexts and fluctuating power relations.

For English-language users like Jobs and Ruijia, attempts to reconcile these conflicting ways of thinking about and treating language and language use as they emerged in written communication were by no means free of tensions or occurring in smoothly running trajectories. For instance, after his firm's big economic crisis, to sync up with his message to global and local markets that "Apple is still alive," Jobs chose to actively resist the restrictiveness of dominant standards of usage and instead put language, in this case English, into work as "living" and socially produced through acts of identity (Isaacson 2011, 328). However, upon his own confession, he still had to deal with a "not-so-small problem" of debating the acceptability of the idiosyncratic language usage in the ad's tagline and accompanying narrative for promoting his company's devices and services with skeptical others among his clientele and on his own team who possessed more established ideas of what counted as acceptable or aesthetically pleasing about language-in-use (Blumenthal 2012, 192). In a similar vein, drawing on the range of cultural and linguistic resources in her repertoire, Ruijia felt compelled to justify the specific conditions under which her non-standardized language and rhetorical practices emerged in her writing and under which her readers will have to, in turn, recognize the fluidity of her language usage in relation to the changing rhetorical situation and its demands. I am interested centrally in this book in the material effects of similar complex negotiations of diverse ideologies of language, which generate the particular ways various literate individuals conceive of and treat the status, functions, and meanings of language and language-in-use in their local situations while engaging in a range of social relationships (personal, civic, academic, and professional).

These "classic" tensions between conflicting yet coexisting language ideologies and their unique and complex negotiations, both inside and outside the Anglo-American sphere, have always been present in various literate situations and evident in a considerable body of language- and literacy-related research (to name a few, see Pratt 1987; Lu 1994; Pennycook 1997; Ivanič 1998; Canagarajah 1999; Harwood and Hadley 2004; Janks 2004). However, the unprecedented, distinctive speed, surge, and complexity of the transcultural and transnational flow of people—and therefore of their language and communicative repertoires and the particular ideas surrounding them—across time, spaces, borders, and communities in an era of globalization have heightened the presence of such tensions and their notable impact on literate individuals, their local language and writing practices, and ultimately their future iterations of such practices (see Kroskrity 2004; Stevenson and Mar-Molinero 2006; Arnaut et al. 2016). It is precisely these complex disjunctures, contradictions, and clashes in the ideologies of language underpinning the act of writing and its teaching and learning in the United States and other parts of the world that the current book further explores, "not by rising above them or going around them or trying to erase [or dissolve] them but by entering" (Pratt 2002, 33) and working through their powerfully flowing traffic. In doing so, subsequent chapters in this book draw out the unexpected linkages in tension-ridden literate negotiations of such language-ideological differences and their reverberations across the divides of location, institution, program, language, culture, and identity. Taking us to the heart of these lived tensions at two urban university campuses in two different cosmopolitan cities, namely Beirut, the capital of Lebanon, and Seattle, the largest city in Washington state in the United States, *Toward Translingual Realities in Composition* explores some of the complexity and messiness involved in the way various undergraduate student writers think about and utilize their diverse language and semiotic resources to negotiate and renegotiate their literate life and work amid relations of power, authority, and difference. As significantly diverse and distant as these two institutional settings are in their size, geographic location, language-ideological histories, sociolinguistic makeup, and sociopolitical agendas and missions (see appendix A for a detailed comparison), they intersect in their shared preoccupations with managing intensified degrees of language and sociocultural diversity and difference and sensitively grappling with the ensuing binds, paradoxes, inconsistencies, and compromises that come their way. The transnational ethnographic perspectives I share in this book, drawn from over five years of fieldwork, reveal the daunting nature of the challenges these young writers face to strike a balance between preserving their diverse language and semiotic resources and still producing successful academic writings in the eyes of their teachers and other key gatekeepers.

In its reflections on and multilayered analyses of the workings and impacts of conflicting language ideologies in specific literate situations, *Toward Translingual Realities in Composition* looks into the many different manifestations of diverse linguistic-ideological orientations in daily sociolinguistic realities, local language and language-in-education policies, and the design of writing pedagogies and curricula in both contexts. Giving voice to the lived experiences of student writers from diverse language and cultural backgrounds, this book brings into visibility the sticky, messy materiality of their negotiations of language-ideological tensions in academic language and literacy learning amid various historical, sociocultural, (geo)political, and economic considerations in Beirut's and Seattle's cityscapes. As I will reveal in chapters 3 and 4, monolingual and translingual linguistic-ideological orientations shaping existing understandings and usages of language are juxtaposed and coexistent yet operating in a constant tug-of-war, together creating what Yasemin Yildiz (2012) productively terms a "postmonolingual" ideological condition for the urban localities under study here and their writing program ecologies.[2] In more precise terms, a postmonolingual reading of the language-ideological tensions my participants continue to grapple with is a powerful reminder of one of this book's arguments that the multiplicity and contestation in these young writers' understandings of and practices with language get managed and often complicated by a network of invested literate actors in their immediate surrounds who position themselves differently vis-à-vis complex sociocultural and political-economic forces not of their own making. I turn next to some brief remarks on this project's design, with a much fuller description of the specific procedures of data collection and analysis and of the research sites and participants provided in appendix A for interested readers.

ON RESEARCH DESIGN

Toward Translingual Realities in Composition is a multi-sited critical ethnography that adds not only a critical edge but also a dimension of intervention in linguistic-ideological hegemonies in the teaching and learning of university-level writing.[3] Taking us away from the conventional ethnographic trope of intensive investigation and participation that privileges single-site locations across and within social and geographical spaces, this ethnography of the push and pull of language ideologies in academic literacy learning and development combines perspectives from and seeks to uncover a web of possible connections between apparently disconnected locations like Lebanon and the United States. The multi-sitedness of such fieldwork, however, does *not* simply "add together" interpretations from two discrete national-cultural sites of inquiry in arithmetic terms (1st site + 2nd site = multi-sited research)[4] but rather offers nuance, "multi-*sighted*[ness]" (Coleman and von Hellermann 2013, 10), and the "potential to force us to change perspective" (Coleman and von Hellermann 2013, 6) and practice after examining our ways of constructing categories like language and its literate doing(s) in the first place (cf. Marcus 1995; Hannerz 2003). As Leonard, Vieira, and Young (2015, vii, viii; emphasis in original) argue, of great significance in doing transnational research is "not what researchers look at but *how they look*" at relationships of movement and difference "*across space, time, and communities.*" In this sense, by embedding the study and teaching of postsecondary-level writing in the context of the globalization and pluralization of English and the transnational circles of contact and flow among English(es) and other language resources, *Toward Translingual Realities in Composition* reveals how, why, and toward what effects such varied complexes of language resources are represented, framed, negotiated, taken up, and put into work in disparate or intersecting ways in the context of shifting economic, (geo)political, socio-historical, and ideological constraints and possibilities.

With an increased interest in various transnational perspectives on the cultural politics of academic writing and reinvigorated commitments to "internationalizing" writing instruction in higher education (Schaub 2003; Donahue 2009; Lillis and Curry 2010; Martins 2015), it is worth bringing to our immediate attention the fact that these cross-border exchanges (national, cultural, and linguistic) in US composition have a tendency to remain "largely export-based" (Donahue 2009, 214) and still haven't fully expanded into a systematic, reciprocal, and "mutually transformative relationship" (Hall 2009, 34). With that in mind, *Toward Translingual Realities in Composition* goes against such dominant economies of global intellectual exchange and research that dictate waves of inquiry "*about* other countries" (Ninnes and Hellstén 2005, 3; emphasis added), institutional contexts, and literate individuals or communities, hence suggesting that nothing worthwhile is to be presumably learned or gained in return unless driven by national security motives (Wible 2009) or the advancement of economic and geopolitical self-interest. Contesting such "narrow, local, privileged, Western" flows of knowledge (Martins 2015, 5) about writing research, instruction and program administration, *Toward*

Translinglual Realities in Composition forces us to slow down and listen intensely with the intention to actively learn *with* and not only *about* less immediately relevant, hence easily overlooked, non-US sites like Lebanon. Such a counterhegemonic engagement, as Christiane Donahue (2009, 214) reminds us, necessitates recognizing "blind spots" (2009, 214) in our local ecologies and "peeling back taken-for-granted practices and beliefs" (Ninnes and Hellstén 2005, 4) involving language and language difference in the interest of self-reflexivity, self-revision, and transformation.

Throughout my description and analysis of the specific orientations to and practices with language and their ideological underpinnings in writing program ecologies at both research sites, I adopted a concurrent mixed method[5] of data gathering composed of sociolinguistic landscaping materials, textual analysis of national-/state-level language policy, various institutional and programmatic documents as well as instructional course materials, classroom observation notes, focus group discussions with writing students, semi-structured qualitative interviews with first-year writing (FYW) students and teachers, and stretches of intensive talk surrounding students' academic written work. Though the names of the cities and neighborhoods discussed in this book are real, all the names I adopt to refer to the institutions and research participants are pseudonyms. Below is a summary of the data collection methods, time frame, and the number of participants recruited in each research site:

1. Beirut University (BU), Fall 2006/2007–Summer 2012
   - Linguistic landscaping data
   - National language and language-in-education policy texts
   - Institutional and programmatic documents
   - Individual teaching materials
   - Focus group discussion
   - Forty-one FYW student interviews (one to two hours long each)
   - Focused communication around academic texts with eight students
   - Fourteen writing teacher interviews (one hour long each)
   - Descriptive field notes (five–six observation hours per week during one semester; based on one FYW course and three translation courses)

2. University of Seattle (UOS), Fall 2013/2014–Spring 2017
   - Linguistic landscaping data
   - Federal- and state-level language policy discourse and/or texts
   - University-wide and program-specific documents
   - Instructional materials
   - Fifty FYW student interviews (one to two hours long each)

- Focused conversations around texts with seven students
- Eleven writing teacher interviews (one hour long each)

A far from neutral, linguistically motivated, and politicized project like *Toward Translingual Realities in Composition* demands a critical interrogation of my own ideological affiliations, commitments, and subject positionality. It's worth emphasizing to my readers at the outset the impossibility of researching and writing about a thorny and complicated topic like language ideologies in the teaching and learning of writing without an opinion about their desirability or deleterious material effects on various social actors and local writing ecologies. As a US-trained compositionist with a non-mainstream sociocultural identity, navigating—just like my research participants—an often tension-filled path between competing language ideologies and their associated representations, practices, and discourses in my own field of study and other diverse life-worlds, I adopted multiple roles in composing this book. My main goal was to rigorously understand, explore, and explain the multiple and often contradictory roles, manifestations, and workings of the local language ideologies that are vibrant and constantly circulating among and around my participants. At times, I took the role of what Karen Lundsford (2012, 221) describes as an "information broker," constantly translating and shuttling new knowledge, discourses, and underlying assumptions between national and international research networks. More important, enacting the same calls I make in this book (as echoed in the title of and discussion in chapter 5), my additional role as a translingual activist was also emphasized by deliberately intervening in dominant language ideologies, which strive to "tidy up" the superdiverse sociolinguistic realities in local institutional, writing program, and classroom ecologies through various diversity-stripping and boundary-mapping practices. In fact, the frequent movement and flow of language resources, ideas, information, and insights within the national-cultural sites I explore in this book "lends a character of activism" that is "quite specific and circumstantial to the conditions of doing" multi-sited writing research itself (Marcus 1995, 113). It would be pointless to deny that my own analytical and descriptive research and writing practices in developing this book manuscript themselves constitute an intervention into the current nature and state of language relations in the study and teaching of writing in the United States and elsewhere with the hope that they will encourage us all to identify, question, modify, and alter them considerably.

Necessarily and inevitably, working across national, linguistic, and cultural boundaries, I enjoyed close ties with members of the urban institutional cultures I researched in both locales. Born and raised in Lebanon and a once insider at the particular institution under exploration in this project, as I was both schooled and held a teaching position there, I experienced high in-group solidarity and affiliation. Currently pursuing my career in Seattle, I was a relatively novice ethnographer still discovering and learning about this research community and had to locate my own information brokers in order to delve deeper into the specific historical, social, cultural, and political contexts that have shaped local assumptions about and responses to language and its difference. Though enjoying different levels of insider/outsider statuses did not automatically grant me expertise in the language politics, policies, and practices I describe in both locales, it gave me a vantage point from where I could be more cognizant of the nature of the explicit and tacit language assumptions and representations structuring, informing, and at times constraining my participants' labor with and on language.

A translingual stance toward language and decisions on its actual and observable use, which this book advocates, is meant to acknowledge and bring out the very fluid, emergent, and unpredictable character of language itself and all communicative practices involving language (as I discuss more thoroughly in chapter 2). With that in mind, I hope my readers approach the outcomes of this project as warrantable, illuminative, yet provisional, unfinished insights and renderings that can contribute to our understandings of how writing students in linguistically and culturally diverse urban institutions of higher education are actually talking and thinking about language generally and English specifically and how that might be influencing—knowingly or not, individually and collectively—what they are (or wish to be) doing with and to English in their academic literacies work. Constantly reminding myself of this, and I hope my readers would do the same, serves to highlight the need to keep working and reworking our ongoing explorations of the translingual understandings and doings of language amid powerful linguistic-ideological tensions in our ever-changing and complex local ecologies.

ON NAMING PRACTICES

Scholarly conversations and contributions surrounding language issues in composition studies and other complementary language- and literacy-related fields, including the book you are now reading, are getting increasingly populated with an almost dizzying collection of neologisms,[6] which seek to step outside of traditional terminologies and descriptions we've inherited from a dominant monolingual paradigm and offer a more nuanced understanding of the dynamic, fluid, and emergent nature of linguistic creations and interactions. This vibrant terminological landscape suggests that dominant ways of describing, talking, and thinking about the nature of language and its doing(s) in an era of globalization, enhanced access to the internet and new communication technologies, and ever-changing sociolinguistic realities and mobility patterns in modern urban life are becoming, at best, theoretically and practically "unsustainable" (Lillis and McKinney 2013, 429). As there are no coherent, agreed-upon labels or even definitions[7] for the same emerging concepts within or across specific language- and literacy-related fields, an explication of the terminology I employ in the present book is necessary.

I have particularly chosen the descriptor "superdiversity" coined by social anthropologist Steven Vertovec (2007) and further qualified in contemporary critical studies in sociolinguistics[8] to make visible the dynamic emergence of linguistic and sociocultural diversity in ways that supersede anything both developed and developing countries, like the case of the United States and Lebanon examined in this book, have experienced before—particularly in terms of acceleration, intensity, spread, complexity, and multi-layering of language contact and change. More specifically, the notion of superdiversity marks the complex heterogeneity of and within the kind of language and cultural diversity lived and experienced on a daily basis in today's cityscapes on the streets, at home, and in various academic and nonacademic institutions. By adopting the notion of superdiversity throughout this book as a cover term more tuned to the complexity, unpredictability, and messiness of the dynamics of language and cultural difference in urban language landscapes,[9] I attempt to escape from the simplistic arithmetic multiplicity tied to traditional conceptions of "multilingualism," which have both unwittingly fed and been fed by dominant monolingualist ideologies of language (for more, see chapter 1).

By the term *monolingualism* in this book, I refer to the current-day dominant language ideology and epistemology that can be traced back to eighteenth-century European-based thinking about language and communication and not to the mere presence of one (standard) language as is commonly used to define nation-states or individuals. By the same token, I do not use the term *multilingualism* to refer to different linguistic phenomena involving two or more language resources but rather to alternative language ideologies that have emerged in response to dominant monolingualism and have only superficially overcome its epistemological framework and effects. As I demonstrate in chapter 1, multilingual orientations to language in teaching writing have rendered observable moments of language difference contingent to a numerical representation of languages, cultures, and identities as nameable, countable, and definable entities and have ultimately constrained the possibilities of seeing and understanding language, the identities of its users/learners, and their literate practices in more dynamic terms as emergent, always varying and variant, "always deferred, always in process but never arriving" (Hopper 1998, 155).

In adopting the notion "translingual" (sometimes featuring the suffixes "-ist," "-ism," and "-ity"), which is currently receiving much zeal and attention from US compositionists, I align with a critical "linguistics of contact" that places at the center of its intellectual engagement the workings and reworkings of language "*across* lines of social" relatedness, difference, and domination (Pratt 1987, 60; emphasis in original). My own approach to translingualism throughout this book, which I will briefly introduce in the next chapter and discuss more extensively in chapter 2, synthesizes two intersecting yet different senses of the term employed to date in composition studies scholarship. The first constitutes a branch of translingualism that can be detected in work that theorizes the realization of general performative translingual competence in texts that are obviously written differently, in that they employ the more readily visible rhetorical practice of "code-meshing" or the strategic blending of home and school identities, language and literate practices, conventionally perceived as separate and discontinuous (see Canagarajah 2011; Young et al. 2014). The second sense of translingualism involves a preoccupation with less noticeable, hence easily disregarded, moments of language and cultural difference conveyed by the wealth and breadth of sociocultural and historical meanings available within and across language resources and practices (for instance, see Kramsch 2006; Pennycook 2010; Lu and Horner 2013). In this second sense, translingualism brings attention to the centrality of "translation" as a necessary and constant characteristic of the everyday language and literacy labor of all language users/learners, readers, and writers (see Pennycook 2007, 2008; Lu and Horner 2012; Horner, Necamp, and Donahue 2011).

Rather than present it as a satisfactory, flawless, stable, and enduring concept, I adopt and conceive of the term *translingual* in this book as timely and useful, at least for the time being, for several reasons.[10] First and foremost, the prefix *trans-* doesn't come with the kind of baggage of numerical plurality the existing prefixes bi-, multi-, and pluri- carry.[11] More specifically, it draws attention away from the quantification of immobile, bounded languages—as ideologically and institutionally understood and idealized—into the qualification of mobile language resources, the actual and multiple ways of doing language locally in various communicative contexts and domains of life. In addition, its relatively recent emergence in composition scholarship with only a handful of theoretical, methodological, and direct pedagogical reflections (Horner et al. 2011; Canagarajah 2013a, 2013b; Donahue 2013; Horner and Tetreault 2017) surrounding the kind of labor and active engagement it entails suggests that our ongoing (re)conceptualization and (re)working of the notion of "translingualism" can and should gradually and continually be molded and even sharpened. Marking a turning point in US compositionists' ways of thinking about, teaching, and studying language and its practice in writing, a dynamic construct like translingualism can potentially provide a particular point of entry into critical questions surrounding the increasing complexity of language difference and language-in-use in literacy learning situations: How do our writing students get socialized into or out of particular ways of understanding and treating language, its use, and users? What exactly do they do (or desire to do) with the wide array of language and semiotic resources and practices in their repertoires? What do they choose to make of and with what they do in which writing situations? What sociocultural relations and meanings do they strive to construct, maintain, problematize, or resist through their doing(s), with what investments, and at what cost(s) and what value(s) do they attach to them and the language-based ideologies that surround them? And finally, as the prevailing, sanctioned things we say about and do "within" language in writing, its study, and its teaching have become pervasive and pervasively naturalized in educational landscapes, how do we bring ourselves and encourage our students and one another to start thinking about and engaging within and across socially constructed language boundaries in a transformed translingual lens? This book goes some way to address these and a number of other related questions in later chapters. *Toward Translingual Realities in Composition* is therefore an invitation to us all—writing program administrators, teacher-scholars, and students alike—to launch and sustain this long overdue intellectual exercise.

In this book, I borrow the term *postmonolingualism* introduced in Yasemin Yildiz's (2012) work when referring to the current state of affairs in teaching writing on both sides of the Atlantic, with the side-by-side coexistence of colliding and competing ideologies of language and language relations. However, the significance of the prefix "post-"[12] in "postmonolingualism" rests not only in its inherent temporal dimension in the sense of *after* the emergence of monolingualism and its hegemony in various spheres of society and public life. Like other "posts" dominating our intellectual landscape, the term *postmonolingualism*, as deployed in this book, carries a critical, altering potential in that it marks uneasy back-and-forth vacillations and transactions between the simultaneous continuity of and "active rupture (*coupure*)" (Berger 2003, 5; cf. Hirsch 2012, 6) with a dominant ideology of monolingualism and its far-reaching consequences and workings. Understanding and studying language and language use in literate contexts through the fresh, flexible lens and dynamics of postmonolinguality, I will argue, has the potential to shift our focus as writing teacher-scholars and program administrators away from a categorical, dichotomous thinking about whether particular practices with language in academic writing—including practices of describing and evaluating them—are either monolingual, multilingual, or translingual. Rather than focus on one or the other pole, this book brings into sharper focus the actual local conditions of writing instruction (especially in the writing program ecologies explored) as caught up in postmonolingual tensions produced by the cohabitation of the competing local language ideologies of dominant monolingualism, alternative multilingualism, and counterhegemonic translingualism as continually in each other's presence, absence, and contact. I deal with each of these linguistic-ideological orientations and their coexistence (though not as equal partners) in subsequent chapters.

BOOK ORGANIZATION

In chapter 1, rather than treat the key concept of "language ideologies" in writing instruction as indicative of abstract, *in vitro*, amorphous, and elusive forces, as is commonly understood, I give special emphasis to how diverse language ideologies of dominant monolingualism, alternative multilingualism, and counterhegemonic translingualism are made manifest in the pairing of language *representations* and *practices*, that is, the *in vivo* ways of thinking and acting on situations involving language and its literate learning and use. From this perspective, I survey past and more contemporary approaches to teaching writing amid language difference while highlighting the way these approaches emerge from competing and at times overlapping representations and treatments of language, language relations, and language usage in written texts. More specifically, by tagging the three major language-ideological orientations circulating and informing work in composition onto the concretized notions of "representations" and "practices," this chapter brings into sharper focus how the key tenets of each ideological orientation are anchored in actual situated practices of designing writing curricula, pedagogies, and assessments in response to inter- and intra-linguistic and cultural difference.

Organized on an entirely different footing from that which drives dominant monolingualism and traditional multilingualism, a nascent translingual orientation to language as constantly in process and therefore emergent in relation to its social, material performativity is the topic of chapter 2. In this chapter and throughout the book, I draw on critical perspectives in linguistics and sociolinguistics, which have highlighted the crucial role of a complex, evolving view of language generally and English particularly in terms of the fluidity and movement of its use and reuse across time, space, and (real or imagined) borders and the exigency for more dynamic discursive practices in representing such an ideological orientation. In view of all this, I elaborate on an alternative set of images, metaphors, and corresponding vocabulary, which can assist in bringing out the intrinsically and perpetually translingual character of language and the necessary labor of movement within, between, and across available language resources and practices in the literate negotiation and production of meaning and difference—which have remained invisible under dominant monolingual and traditional multilingual ideological and epistemological stances. In this chapter, I also suggest that successfully adopting an emerging translingual framework in teaching writing necessitates not only reworking and reconstituting the notion of language itself but also and especially a series of now-classic concepts closely linked to it and to each other. I conclude this chapter by calling into question and reworking the established meanings and associations of some of these constructs pertaining to our and our students' work with language in the teaching and learning of writing—namely, language competence, language standards and conventions, language errors in writing, writerly agency, and the nature of writer-reader relationships amid moments of language difference.

Chapters 3 and 4 further contextualize the linguistic-ideological tensions highlighted and discussed in the preceding chapters in the specific urban sociolinguistic and educational landscapes of present-day Beirut and Seattle. I specifically devote chapter 3 to a detailed analysis of document- and interview-based data on the nature and workings of language ideologies in the case of BU, while the ethnographic fieldwork at UOS comprises the core of chapter 4. The perspectives I offer in these two chapters are in a sequence that begins with macro-level analyses of three primary sites of linguistic-ideological (re)production and intervention—that is, sociolinguistic landscapes, nation-state and institutional language policies, and writing pedagogies and assessment practices. I then move to a more focused exploration of the nature and salience of first-year writers' representations and rationalizations of language and language difference and how they are supported and impeded in complex ways by those sites of using, managing, and learning languages in relation to each other and their environment. Intriguingly, while the cultural, linguistic, socioeconomic, and (geo)political forces influencing and influenced by institutional and programmatic ecologies of writing and writing instruction at each location are massively divergent, chapters 3 and 4 afford a closer look into some of the intersections between the complex negotiations of student writers in both localities in that they must always and inevitably engage the shifting friction points of monolingualism, multilingualism, and translingualism—hence their postmonolingual character in learning academic English writing.

In chapter 5, I argue that there has to be an activist dimension to translingualism in writing pedagogy, which involves a deliberate intervention in taken-for-granted monolingual and multilingual language representations and practices in the FYW classroom in strategic and well-grounded ways. Contesting approaches to teaching writing that legitimate and propagate the view and use of English in writing in its own presence and outside the bodies, identities, histories, and contexts that bring about its translation and transformation, I report on an ongoing project that explores the possibilities and challenges manifest in reconciling translingual writing and critical translation practice on firmer ground for the years to come. Given the continuing intellectual and sociocultural pressures of dominant English-only monolingualism and its powerful resonance in teaching academic writing in the United States and beyond, I invite my readers to collaborate on further refining this much-needed bridge between translation and translingual writing theory.

By formulating contemporary language-ideological debates and tensions in terms of linkages and contestations in representations of and practices with language in academic reading and writing, transnational ethnographic accounts like those in *Toward Translingual Realities in Composition* can help open up not only new understandings of but also new potentialities for intervention in the postmonolingual dynamics of the teaching and learning of university/college English writing in the United States as well as the rest of the world. Bringing together the various studies featured in individual chapters, I conclude this book by offering insights into how writing teacher-scholars and writing program administrators, through actively and persistently reworking the design and enactment of their curricula, pedagogies, assessments, teacher training programs, and campus-wide partnerships, can more productively intervene in local postmonolingual tensions and contradictions at the level of language representations and practices.

1
LANGUAGE IDEOLOGIES IN TEACHING WRITING
A Language Representations and/as Practices Perspective

Of direct relevance to the close explorations of postmonolingual conflicts of language ideologies in university-level writing, its teaching, and its learning that the current book undertakes is a long scholarly tradition, particularly in linguistic anthropology, that recognizes that the particularly uneasy notion of language ideologies[1] does not concern "just language" alone (Blommaert 1999, 429; cf. Woolard and Schieffelin 1994, 55–65; Schieffelin, Woolard, and Kroskrity 1998, 3; Woolard 2004, 58). In fact, language ideologies always "envision and enact" the complex linkage and intersection of language with fundamental social conceptualizations of "identity, power, aesthetics, morality and epistemology" (Woolard 1998, 3). This take on language ideologies[2] that I adopt throughout this book's analyses—as underpinning and mediating strong connections between language structure and form and the wider sociopolitical and sociocultural forces of domination among individuals, communities, or institutions—is useful in capturing the rootedness, embeddedness, and spatio-temporal locatedness of language. Studying language ideologies from this perspective, therefore, brings to light the nature of local[3] understandings and conceptions of language and its use as firmly situated in time and space and inseparable from the particular identities, contexts, histories, hierarchies, and injustices that bring them into being and grant them their particular significance.

Looking at language ideologies through a locally sensitive lens, this book does not cast them as autonomous, totalizing entities, as commonly perceived, but rather seeks to project them as having tangible material effects—although not always the kind of desired effects envisioned generally by those in positions of power—in their own local ecologies. Put differently, this book reveals the impact of different local language ideologies on everyday language negotiations in the teaching and learning of university-level writing not so much as clearly defined intellectual properties of individuals, communities, or academic

DOI: 10.7330/9781607329046.c001

institutions or as transcendental ideas and metaphysical forces creating in and of themselves particular effects on literate individuals and their immediate practices[4] but rather as socioculturally situated, construed, and embodied sets of rationalizations about language and language-in-use. In fact, it is part of this book's goal to emphasize a dimension of human agency, intervention, and activism (as we shall see further in chapter 5) in its explorations of the nature and consequences of the ideologies of language, its use, and literate learning that circulate locally at diverse institutions of higher education and their writing programs in the United States and other parts of the world.

Bringing out both the sociality of language and language-ideological matters and the attendant potential for change in linguistic realities, French linguist Louis-Jean Calvet (2006, 243) observes that the notion of languages and the ideologies that construe and determine their specific connections to broader sociocultural processes and structures do not exist in a vacuum like "real, tangible objects." Instead, they are social "abstraction[s]", which "rest on the regularity of a certain number of facts, of features, in the products of speakers" (Calvet 2006, 241) and learners or, say, their concrete *practices* as well as the way they come to think of and imagine them in every interaction, namely, their *representations*. Under Calvet's (2006, 57, 137, 7) ecological approach to the study of the interaction of languages among themselves and with their immediate surroundings, languages are not "well-oiled mechanisms" independent of their local ecologies; in fact, being "simply a set of practices and representations" in a given social and historical context, they "exist only in and through" their users and learners, always "reinvented, renewed and transformed" in every act of oral or written communication. On the side of *practices*, we find everyday language users' and learners' actual, repeated, and observable doings involving language and the way they negotiate, accommodate, and adapt these doings to changing affordances in the communicative ecology. Loosely defined, language *representations* refer to the ideas, perceptions, images, and metaphors language users and learners entertain about their own (or other individuals' or group of individuals') language resources and the value they grant to the way they (or others) utilize them. Specifically, language representations are themselves concrete ways of acting, among many others, inseparable from their sociolinguistic realities. In this sense, Calvet (2006, 153) firmly emphasizes the "importance of representations" in influencing patterns of linguistic action and change. As he further observes, language representations "act on practices and are one of the factors of change" in that they "produce in particular *security/*

insecurity" of language form, identity, and status among language users and learners, thereby leading them to adopt and exhibit particular types of "*behavior* that transform practices" (Calvet 2006, 241; emphasis in original) with language and literacy. In a similar vein, second language acquisition (SLA) and foreign language learning (FLL) scholarship that draws on an ecological perspective has brought to our attention the fact that language representations, more accurately dubbed "beliefs"[5] in SLA/FLL, can serve as "*mediational means*", with a considerable "effect on learners—or teachers—and their actions" (Barcelos and Kalaja 2011, 281; emphasis in original; cf. Peng 2011).[6] In this sense, language representational practices, I argue, need to be fully integrated into and taken seriously for a rigorous understanding of and productive intervention in the nature and workings of local language ideologies in the teaching and learning of university-level writing.

Building on such theorizations of the influential role of representations in the way language(s) and inter- and intra-language relations are put into action in literate learning situations, I approach language representations in the present work as telling us something crucial about how language learners and writers in two different geographic and institutional settings make sense of, negotiate, and act in relationship to a complex network of language ideologies in their local academic and nonacademic milieus. More important, I adopt the concept of language representations as socially situated practices themselves, constantly shaping and reshaping subsequent language and literate practice and decision-making, and tag it onto the cluster construct of language ideology itself as one of its ubiquitous manifestations. In doing so, I anchor the operative language ideologies of what I term here dominant monolingualism, alternative multilingualism, and counterhegemonic translingualism in writing and its teaching in actual, observable, and particularly salient practices as opposed to treating them as mystical, amorphous, and elusive forces.

MONOLINGUAL, MULTILINGUAL, AND TRANSLINGUAL LANGUAGE REPRESENTATIONS AND/AS PRACTICES IN TEACHING WRITING

> *My approach is to teach them the standard and not necessarily accept the nonstandard or broken English. We're resistant to tolerating it in writing because that's what they're going to face in the outside business world unless the world changes.*
>
> Kathy, Summer 2012, interview transcript

> It's not that I'm doing it wrong, it [practice of constructing long sentences deemed acceptable in written Spanish] just doesn't fit this language . . . In English, most people won't be okay with it, will find it too confusing or overwhelming or categorize it as bad writing skills. So I tell [students]—it's not that the way you write is wrong, it just doesn't follow the rules of English writing.
>
> Alicia, cited in Leonard 2014, 234

> I tell my students: The [English] language is yours. Bend it, twist it, curse if you must, if doing so will take you to the point of familiarity, of ease, where the written language becomes your vehicle too, your conduit to the expression of your reality. Do it for your own sake. Do it for the world's sake.
>
> Nuñez 2000, 44

Pitted against each other, these perspectives from writing teachers laboring on opposite sides of the globe rest on different representations and views of language and its literate use and therefore demonstrate opposing pedagogical responses to perceived differences between student writers' language practices and the institutionalized practices and conventions of Standard Written English (SWE). Inspired by monolingualist perceptions of the commodification of SWE as the gate to all upwardly mobile trajectories, one of my native English-speaking Anglo-American teacher participants in Beirut echoes a valorization of conformity to standardized English rules and usages. Any difference from what is imagined to constitute static, universal attributes of academic reading and writing is viewed as technical failings and, as described in the first excerpt, "nonstandard" or "broken" language practices in grave need of fixing and correction. On the other hand, challenging such dominant deficit orientations toward what students do with and to language in their writing, the second teacher—one of Rebecca Leonard's (2014) informants, an English as a second language (ESL) migrant teacher in the midwestern United States—demonstrates more acceptance and accommodation of the rich, meaningful experiences with language difference students bring with them into the writing situation. However, despite revealing her multilingual orientation to complex literate negotiations across languages through attuning her own students to the normalcy of language difference in their writing, she still retains monolingualist perceptions of languages (in this specific case, English and Spanish) and language practices as stable, definable, and siloed and their boundaries as secure and impervious. Hence her characterization of students' ways of using language as either successfully "fit[ing]" or "in" one particular language sphere or not.

In contrast, the teacher in the last excerpt shows more advocacy for a translingual ideology, which is radically distinct from the dominant monolingualist orientations echoed in the first excerpt and traditional multilingualist perspectives depicted in the second excerpt in its representations and treatments of language as malleable, negotiable, and changeable. More specifically, in her description of her pedagogical aims, Elizabeth Nuñez (2000) seems to echo a willingness to acknowledge and encourage students' ownership over the language of the academy and their agency in fashioning and refashioning it and tinkering with the putatively impenetrable boundaries shielding its presumed purity and separation from other languages and language practices, with all the challenges this process entails. Seeing and addressing language and language relations from a significantly different angle and perspective than the teachers in the first and second excerpts, Nuñez treats students' actual labor of "bend[ing]," "twist[ing]," and transforming written English in relation to their changing social realities as essential not only for their own personal, intellectual development and growth but also and especially, as she puts it, for increasing opportunities for collaboration, peace, and linguistic and social justice among all literate individuals in the world.

In this section, I elaborate on and further discuss these fundamentally different ideological orientations of monolingualism, multilingualism, and translingualism, implicit in and discoverable from these three language and literacy teachers' framings of actual pedagogical responses to potential moments of language difference in student writing. In my description of the three contending language ideologies that have impinged on the structure and design of writing curricula, pedagogies, and assessments in writing programs and classrooms both within and outside the United States, I identify the key tenets of each ideological orientation and the ways these are tied to and implemented in different approaches to teaching university-level writing amid language difference. Some of the salient principles and features of these three main linguistic-ideological orientations are displayed in table 1.1, which offers a summary of the discussion that will follow.

As table 1.1 indicates, these approaches to teaching writing echo differing conceptions and consequential treatments of language, language relations, and language difference in student texts and vary drastically in the status and value they attribute to standardized usages and conventions, on one hand, and the diverse language and semiotic resources in student writers' repertoires, on another hand. As I'll be arguing against some of these orientations to language and language difference in

Table 1.1. Distinction among mono-, multi-, and translinguality in writing instruction

	MONO-	MULTI-	TRANS-
Language	Stable, discrete, objectifiable, pure and insular entity	Hybrid, heterogeneous; pluralized only numerically as accumulative sum of discrete, static, and impenetrable entities	Emergent, performative, complex, and fluctuating; with porous, blurred, and reworkable boundaries
Language relations	Myth of linguistic purity and homogeneity; Oneness of English	Acknowledgment of language contact; preservation of monocentricity of SWE; unidirectionality of mechanical translation as always into SWE	Complexes of language resources as always and necessarily locally translated and translating; transcentricity and transdirectionality in language relations (see chapter 2)
Language difference in writing	Anomaly, technical failure to be quarantined, obliterated, and overcome	Right to be honored, celebrated, and accommodated only in readings and low-stakes writing	The norm for all language performance(s); resource to be constantly tapped into, rhetorically deployed, and capitalized on
Language standards and conventions	Readymade, objective, abstract, timeless, untouchable, and universal	Pre-constructed, uniform, and finite language forms and usages of the "culture of power"	Negotiated and negotiable; variable and varying; (re)constructed and sedimented through repeated social practice
Expectations for language practice in writing	Evidence of language competence: efficiency, correctness, automaticity, native-like proficiency, uniformity, transparency, and clarity	Valuation of all signs of language competence under dominant monolingualism in finished products; appropriateness of linguistic heterogeneity limited to informal reading and writing	Normalcy and legitimacy of the deployment of full multiplicity of language resources; negotiation, ambiguity, and tension as necessary requirements for unfinished labor of meaning making and translation
Pedagogical goals	Ensuring compliance with language standards and norms; eradicating all signs of erroneous language use and its alleged sources (e.g., negative interference from home languages or language varieties in one's repertoire; literal translation)	Adding more languages when composing drafts and more readings that recognizably mesh and switch between languages and language varieties; "inviting" translation into SWE as complete equivalence and homology; promoting one-way, linear, and smooth flow toward fluent mastery in and attainment of SWE	Maximizing and complicating the "traffic" flow among and across languages and meanings by entering as well as intercepting it; bringing to the fore the complexity and opacity of language negotiations and critical translations (see chapters 2 and 5)

academic reading and writing, I will delineate the nature of the interrelated language representations and practices tied to these language-ideological debates underlying past and more contemporary approaches to teaching writing, as well as the central concepts and concerns that have motivated each. For the purposes of this chapter, however, my description of each approach is by no means a comprehensive survey of the field's politically active intellectual history and vibrant literature on working with language (and by implication culture) and its diversity.

Unidirectional Monolingual Ideology: Utopian Imaginings of Language

What has been dubbed in scholarly conversations and publications in diverse language- and literacy-related fields as a forceful monolingual language ideology is not, as language anthropologist Susan Gal (2006, 14–15) argues, an actual feature of the natural world but rather the quintessential invention of European Enlightenment,[7] which largely continues to survive to our modern times. This relatively recent ideological construction of language has more to it than just designating the quantitative presence of only "one" clearly demarcated language as the norm. As Yildiz (2012, 2) explains, monolingualism refers to a lot more than a simple quantitative European-inflected view of language. In fact, it represents "a key structuring principle that organizes the entire range of modern social life, from the construction of individuals and their proper subjectivities to the formation of disciplines and institutions, as well as of imagined collectives such as cultures and nations" (Yildiz 2012, 2). Operating under an equation of the perfect homology among nation, state, and language, or what has been called the "Herderian triad", a dominant monolingualist ideology equates native-like language usage with "social behavior" and "good citizenship" (Bex and Watts 1999, 7–8) and enforces one language variety, namely, the standardized variety, for use in all communicative situations regardless of medium, context, and purpose.

The controlling metaphor for language under a unidirectional monolingualist ideology is that of a closed, fixed "code" and a transparent "conduit" linking preexistent structures and forms to pre-formulated, intrinsic meanings (Park and Wee 2012, 114). From this utopian view, the ultimate goal of communication in the context of language learning is reduced to the neutral transmission of a putatively fixed, commodified body of grammatical and semantic knowledge without any loss, contamination, or transformation. Language and literacy practices that are not consistent with monolingualist ideology's default sets of representations of language and assumptions about proper language use in literate situations are perceived as threatening the unity of individuals, communities, nations, and their institutions—most prominently, the academy and its well-mapped linguistic and disciplinary boundaries (Gal and Irvine 1995; Yildiz 2012; Horner and Trimbur 2002). Such conceptualizations of language and language use, which have obscured from view the normality of historical and more contemporary language contact and cross-border traffic, are affiliated with what Mary Louise Pratt (1987, 49–50) has described as "linguistic utopias," which operate from the reductive perspective of "a 'linguistics of community'" that imagines languages, language practices, and the language communities producing them "as islands, as discrete and sovereign" entities. Influenced by structuralist views of language initiated in the twentieth century by Saussure and further popularized in more recent times by Chomsky's generativist thinking toward the nature of language and language competence, a monolingualist ideology is essentially concerned with language as a shielded, homogeneous system that remains in a frozen state locked in the universal. Granting sovereignty and agency to the language itself, a monolingual language ideology drives attention away from individuals as agentive language doers, the particularities and complexities of everyday language use, and all aspects of difference that are deeply intertwined with the macro-frame of social, cultural, historical, economic, and political forces.

Despite dating to late eighteenth-century European thought, a dominant monolingual language ideology has had and still has a powerful influence on writing instruction[8] in US institutions of higher education (see Horner and Trimbur 2002; Matsuda 2006; Shuck 2006; Horner et al. 2011), with far-reaching implications for other institutions across the globe as I demonstrate in chapters 3 and 4. A long-held English-only monolingual ideology projects an image of language generally, and the imagined utopian entity of SWE more particularly (also referred to as Edited American English), as a definable, systematic, neutral, and transparent system that can be dealt with in acts of reading and writing separately from the temporalities, contexts, cultures, discourses, bodies, and identities that produce it. In this sense, language and literacy practices are conceived as seemingly "independent of human will or intent" (Gal 2006, 15; cf. Gal and Irvine 1995, 968) or sustained meso-level negotiations of the micro and macro considerations of power and difference in everyday literate experiences.

Historical and continuing manifestations of this forceful monolingualist English-only ideology[9] in academic English writing and its instruction include a heavy focus on the full attainment and blind, automatic reproduction of a fixed system of readymade spellings, pronunciations, lexical items, and grammatical constructions in written texts, a focus that falsely represents both language and literacy as fundamentally divorced from their laborers, their changing material realities, and ecological affordances. A central principle and feature of a dominant monolingualist English-only ideology in university-wide language and literacy education is that of placing a premium on language correctness, native-like fluency, and mastery of standardized language usages and rules, all of which are symbolically constructed as in every student's best interests personally, academically, and professionally (as expressed in the first excerpt introducing this section). Relatedly, writers and language learners under monolingually oriented writing pedagogies are expected to follow fixed, linear stages of development to reach fluent mastery of the "target" language and its writing conventions, which is deemed a necessary and sufficient condition for ostensibly guaranteed upward social and economic mobility.[10] Teaching writing from a monolingual ideological orientation to language eschews alternative language and literacy practices that emerge in the writing classroom as arguably interfering with and hindering a presumably tension-free, unidirectional flow of knowledge and linear progression toward a static, unquestioned endpoint, that is, an ideal state of (near) native-like command of academic English. In the name of false ideals of the homogeneity, universality, and stability of language(s) and language practice(s), any traces of language difference or lack of conformity in student writing are easily reduced to signs of unwitting technical failure or ignorance that mask linguistic (sometimes even cognitive) deficiencies. Under writing pedagogies that take a monolingualist orientation to teaching writing, whatever language and semiotic resources students might be bringing with them into the writing classroom and however they might be utilizing those resources in their constant doings of language in diverse literate situations remain invisible, excluded, and ignored; at best, they are viewed as deficits and problems to be wholly eradicated and erased.

Additive Multilingual Ideology: More Languages-as-Entities Is Better

In response to a unidirectional hegemonic monolingual ideology, which rests on assumptions and ideas about language—specifically English—as ideally uniform, homogeneous, and pure, an alternative multilingual ideology acknowledges the heterogeneous and hybrid character of language. In fact, multilingual-oriented opponents of a monolingual ideology acknowledge that its "surgical removal of language" from the contexts that have brought about its practice offers, at best, an "amputated" view of language and language relations in our contemporary world (Kroskrity 2000, 5). Moving beyond the homogenizing, centrifugal tendencies of a long-standing monolingualist ideology that does not adequately reflect the robust dynamics of relations of language and cultural difference, a multilingual ideological model of language shows greater inclusivity, tolerance, and accommodation of the broad repertoire of languages, language varieties, world Englishes, and ways of writing them that literate individuals constantly carry with them.

Nonetheless, despite rejecting dominant monolingualist representations of language as uniform and singular, a traditional multilingualist ideology still retains some of its tenets. First, as the multiplicity of languages, language varieties, and Englishes at home as well as in educational contexts get recognized, accepted, honored, and legitimated under an ideology of traditional multilingualism, each of these languages, varieties, and hybridized ways of using English is still conceived of as an isolatable, distinct, and self-contained entity closed off from the others with discrete, self-evident, and clearly demarcated boundaries as commonly constructed under a long-standing monolingualist ideology. That is to say that the languages (and, by implication, sociocultural identities associated with them) a multilingual ideology recognizes as plural and hybrid are still seen and treated following dominant monolingual representations and norms as distinctly identifiable "objects that can be 'had'—isolated, named, counted, and fetishized" (Woolard 1998, 16).

Second, such traditional multilingual orientations risk the danger of leading to the territorialization of language(s) more broadly and English(es) more specifically where each code of communication remains separate, isolated, and hierarchized in clearly defined spheres of labor: public, private, academic, personal, professional, and the like. Echoing residual monolingualist representations of language and language use, a traditional multilingual ideology perceives particular languages and Englishes as well as ways of using them as suitable solely for certain communicative spheres and contexts and not others. Bruce Horner's (2011) concept of an "archipelago" best demonstrates the nature and operation of languages, language varieties, and English(es) and the imposed character of relations between them under a traditional multilingual model of language, its uses, and users. Borrowing and further extending Horner's metaphorical framing of the archipelago, I adopt a 3-D graphical representation (figure 1.1) of how a multilingual model imagines multiple codes of communication as essentially discrete, insular, and free-floating islands, free of any "internal difference and external intrusion" (Slevin 2001, 133). In its acknowledgment of the heterogeneity of language, this traditional multilingual ideology posits at the archipelago's center a reified, single core of SWE surrounded by a set of equally discrete "code-islands", namely, technical or professional English (e.g., English for business, law, journalism, engineering), and most distant from this allegedly stable core are separately labeled languages other than and othered by English (e.g., Spanish, Arabic, French, Italian, Mandarin)[11] along with the living Englishes of day-to-day transactions and negotiations at home, on the web, at the market, on the streets, on city walls, and so on (including, for example, African American Vernacular English, Cajun Vernacular English, Singlish, Spanglish, *rojak* English). Under a traditional multilingual ideology that sustains residual monolingualist assumptions about language, language use, and language relations, the task for language users and learners is to select only the codes deemed appropriate for their assigned communicative situations and corresponding goals: SWE for school and at the workplace, legal English for composing legal documents and proceedings, Spanish in Spanish class, Spanglish for face-to-face or online communications with friends and family, switching and meshing codes in hip-hop or graffiti literacies, and so forth. In doing so, language users and learners are expected to automatically leap from one code-island to another while maintaining the discrete, stable, and fortified character of individual code-islands between which no (inter-)flow of traffic is imagined, expected, or accepted. Movement (if at all recognized and encouraged, usually in the form of translation as a mechanical endeavor [see chapter 5]) between various code-islands, as represented in figure 1.1 by unidirectional arrows, is construed as an automatic remote control channel-hopping process.

Third and relatedly, by overlooking drastic changes in the realities of sociolinguistic and educational landscapes with the constant intermingling, interweaving, and interpenetration of languages, Englishes, and language practices, this traditional multilingual[12] orientation does not account for but instead disguises the considerable and ineluctable traffic, overlap, and interaction across boundaries as language and literacy laborers and their resources, practices, texts, and contexts are constantly moving not in isolation but in an intricate web of social significance. More precisely, under a multilingualist model, the inevitable changeability of the code-islands themselves along with the literate individuals producing and burdened by concrete labor within and across these code-islands in relation to the pulls and pressures of spatio-temporal,

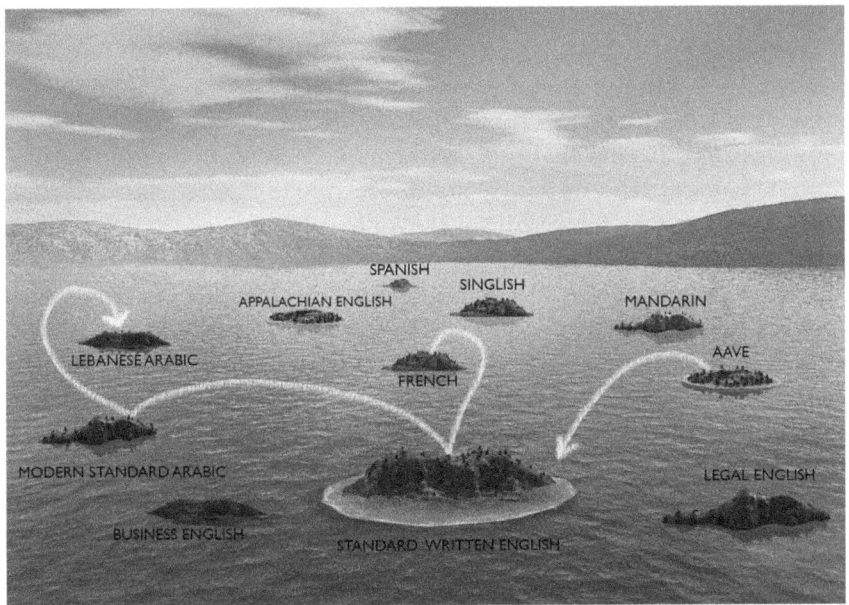

Figure 1.1. Archipelago model of language-in-use and language relations

cultural, sociopolitical, and economic fluctuations are rendered invisible and go unrecognized.

In sum, traditional multilingual orientations to language and language usage do no more than multiply languages and ways of using them and romanticize their plurality based on such putative multiplications, hence their characterization as "additive" models (de Jong 2011, 62–63). Rather than questioning and dismantling hegemonic and blinkered monolingualist views of language that lie at the core of the problem, multilingualist understandings of language and its diversity risk the danger of turning into a mere addition of monolingualisms in language representations and practices, yet in a new guise of linguistic and cultural plurality and variability (see Pennycook 2010; Makoni and Pennycook 2007). This points toward a very disconcerting parallelism between traditional additive multilingualism and dominant monolingualism: while the former foregrounds labor on simply one island with one reified, pure code (namely SWE) and demotes or dismisses all others by virtue of their status as ostensibly impure, secondary, irrelevant, or inappropriate, the latter extends the same reified assumptions to a collection of bounded, self-standing islands to form an archipelago of Pratt's (1987) imagined "linguistic utopias". For instance, alternative types of multilingual/bilingual education curricula to mainstream English-only instruction, which aim to promote academic and linguistic proficiency in English as well as other languages, have been critiqued for creating further linguistic differentiations by scheduling these different languages at different times of the day and dividing them into specific bounded spaces. This imposed "border-making design" between English and other languages, as Samina Hadi-Tabassum (2006, 5) argues in a critical study of a dual immersion program, represents and treats "each language [as] separated and segregated into its own discrete space and time and . . . not allowed to mix with the other" and subsequently influences the development and use(s) of these languages in local ecologies.

When it comes to university-level writing and its teaching, allegiance to an alternative multilingual ideology that recognizes heterogeneity in writing both within English and across languages has contributed to elevating the status of students' language and cultural repertoires from sources of language problems and errors in academic writing to be completely eradicated and discarded—as a dominant monolingualist ideology would have it—into legitimate and sophisticated "home languages or dialects" (Bean et al. 2003), "mother tongues" (Elbow 1999), and language "rights" (CCCC 1974; Delpit 1988) to be affirmed, valued, and celebrated. Such alternative views of the plurality and hybridity of language and language use in writing have opened doors for pedagogic opportunities that acknowledge the entitlement of language learners and writers, particularly in FYW classrooms, to tap into and reflect on the languages, language varieties, and literacies in their repertoires. One of the most common strategies through which proponents of multilingual-oriented writing pedagogies have ensured a place for the rich tapestry of cultures, ethnicities, and Englishes finding its way into US college/university writing classrooms is by presenting students with "invitations" to compose in their often stigmatized "home languages" or language varieties. Such invitations, however, are restricted to early or mid-process drafting stages, that is, low-quality or "informal" phases of writing, as an "exploratory," "free-writing" exercise to experiment with and further develop their own "voice"[13] (see, for instance, Elbow 1999; Bean et al. 2003). These multilingual pedagogical invitations are argued to provide writing students—mainly those marked as the racially and, by extension, linguistically othered in the imaginings of the dominant "culture of power" in both social and educational realms (Delpit 1988, 285)—with an "easier, freer, safer, more intimate and natural fount of language and thinking" (Bean et al. 2003, 31). As such, these romanticized and fetishized representations of "home languages" and varieties as key to achieving "safety," "intimacy," and "comfort" (Bean et al. 2003) in the writing classroom indirectly dismiss and obscure the limitless intellectual and meaning-making possibilities[14] of those languages and varieties even in rigorous, high-stakes academic work (as we shall see more explicitly in chapters 3, 4, and 5).

As these pedagogical models continue to construct student writers' "home languages" and language varieties as "rights" to be honored and accommodated only in low-stakes writing situations, all writings composed using them must automatically be translated into SWE, the institutionalized language of "power and prestige" (Elbow 1999, 358), presumably needed for students' empowerment and full participation in the mainstream social and academic culture (cf. Delpit 1988). The overriding aim of these writing pedagogies of language rights, of tolerance and accommodation of difference, therefore, remains the attainment of accuracy and native-like fluency in reproducing and conforming to standardized practices of language use upon hopping to the more dominantly acceptable and appropriate code of SWE in "finished, revised, copy-edited" (Bean et al. 2003, 37), and successfully polished drafts. Hence, under these island-hopping writing pedagogies, the primary goal is to ultimately inculcate language learners and writers into a single, monolithic, and crystallized entity of SWE, the mastery and possession of which is solely deemed marketable and exchangeable in the global-local linguistic marketplace. Therefore, proponents of such approaches to university-level writing instruction operate under the commonplace view of language learners' and writing students' need to "acquiesce," "give in" (Elbow 1999, 362), and accept the hegemonic, stable character of the language of the academy along with their own diminished to nonexistent agency over its equally stagnant, universal, and neutral standards and conventions.

Another key principle of a dominant monolingualist ideology that these multilingualist pedagogical models retain is that of the indoctrination and transmission of the rules and conventions of SWE. In so doing, multilingualist writing pedagogies not only forge a representation of the stability and distinctness of language categories, including SWE and writing students' "home languages" or language varieties, but also overlook the constant and inescapable mediation and changeability of both language constructs in actual practice. Residual monolingualist assumptions about language relations are manifested through island-hopping writing pedagogies in the following ways: (1) promotion of a routinized unidirectional view of translation as located on a linear trajectory always starting from home languages/varieties and ending in SWE as the predetermined, incontestable target; (2) treatment of the act of translation solely into SWE as a mechanical transposition and transfer of the same message by means of a different code; and finally, (3) erasure and eschewal of what translation scholars Susan Bassnett and Harish Trivedi (1999, 13) describe as the inexorable complex "traffic[king] between [sic] languages", language varieties, and meanings both shaping and taking shape within cultural and socio-historical relations of power. In addition to dismissing the fuzziness and porousness of language boundaries and the impossibility of "neat separation between languages" and language varieties (Auer 2007, 336), a traditional multilingual ideology guiding such pedagogies and curricular designs evades any sense of movement among the languages, language varieties, texts, or contexts involved in the act of translation. Such intellectual slippage becomes clearer, for instance, in Peter Elbow's recommendations to one of his writing students with Puerto Rican–based Spanish in her repertoire to experience the benefits of "put[ting] her Spanish text *completely aside*" (cited in Bean et al. 2003, 35; emphasis added) while "*composing explicitly in [Standard] English*" (emphasis in original). As I have argued elsewhere, such a multilingual-oriented approach to language difference in writing posits students' language resources and practices as discrete possessions to be "picked up or eliminated", left behind, or "completely put aside" (Bou Ayash 2016, 570) as one moves between equally fixed, discrete academic texts and contexts. To borrow Min-Zhan Lu's (2009, 711) characterization, a traditional multilingualist approach to teaching writing represents and treats language resources as easily identifiable, bounded objects to be automatically and effortlessly "switch[ed] on and off" with no effect on the constitution of these resources, their uses, and their users. In this sense, such traditional multilingualist representations of language use in writing bear the imprints of monolingualist assumptions of languages, written texts, and the identities that produce them as internally uniform and completely isolated entities, floating in a vacuum, and divorced from each other and from the real sociocultural, historical, political, and economic forces that shape them.

In an attempt to develop linguistically and culturally relevant and responsive writing pedagogies, another common multilingualist practice increasingly gaining popularity among well-intentioned writing teacher-scholars, especially in FYW programs and classrooms, is that of assigning apparently nonconventional texts that mix different codes, genres, and styles—such as the subversive writings of Gloria Anzaldúa in *Borderlands / La Frontera (1999)*, bell hooks's *Ain't I a Woman (1981)*, Geneva Smitherman in *Talkin and Testifyin (1996)*, Haunani-Kay Trask in *From a Native Daughter (1999)*, among many others—or adopting and implementing composition readers or literary anthologies that center around themes of language and cultural difference—the likes of Dohra Ahmad's *Rotten English (2007)*, Keith Walters and Michal Brody's *What's Language Got to Do with It?* (2005), and Gary Goshgarian's *Exploring Language (2015)*. While such practices are certainly useful for making language matters central and visible in writing classrooms, as Alastair Pennycook (2007, 41) cautions, "it is not enough to assume that more [in a merely additive manner] is better." More precisely, such commitments to making a "safe" and "inviting" place for more languages, more Englishes, more vernaculars, more cross-cultural references and relations, more code-meshed/code-switched texts, more multilingual-affiliated language policies, and so on can still lack critical or altering potentialities if not coupled with epistemological and ideological interventions in dominant language representations and practices and the real damaging effects they have been, are still, and will be causing.[15] In other words, while placing the variability and heterogeneity of linguistic and cultural production at the center of their pedagogical and curricular agenda and assisting in broadening students' conceptualizations of how language works across difference, such multilingual pedagogies can easily take a rather unintended turn by getting ensnared in the same monolingualist assumptions and representations of language, language relations, and language practice they are supposedly designed to challenge and escape in the first place.

Translingual Ideology: Qualitative Reconceptualizations of Language and Language Work

With traditional views on multilingualism inadvertently sustaining particular connections with a dominant unidirectional monolingual agenda and failing to significantly rethink its static, reductive view of language and language relations, a counterhegemonic ideology of translingualism has recently emerged in composition and other related fields as an opposition to the linguistic myopia of monolingualism and a corrective to traditional multilingualism. Contesting widely propagated yet bankrupt representations of the homogeneity, rigidity, and stability of language, a translingual language ideology treats language as a social, embodied act that is not only diverse and hybrid but also in a constant state of flux, mobility, and fluctuation; always an integral element of the dynamic process of the fashioning and refashioning of identities, bodies, texts, cultural relations, and socio-historical contexts.

We have been witnessing the genesis of a substantial body of scholarship in various language- and literacy-related fields[16] questioning the validity of dominant monolingual and residual multilingual representations of languages as definable, value-free entities with rigidly identified boundaries and highlighting the pressing need for a fundamental unthinking and rethinking of the key concept of "language" itself in ways that account for its negotiability, performativity, and contingent constructedness. Aligned with a larger move in contemporary social and language theory toward the notion of practice, which shifts attention away from a false view of language as a fixed, abstract system and purely cognitive category, translingualism looks at and stresses the repeated doings and actions involving language in spatial-temporal contexts. The heart of the matter is that a translingual language ideology problematizes and disrupts the kind of systematicity and internalization embedded in traditional structuralist assumptions about language as an autonomous system preexisting its performance. In this respect, Suresh Canagarajah (2007, 928), for instance, theorizes language generally, and lingua franca English specifically, as a form of "complex social action" in relation to ecological affordances and not "a product located in the mind of the speaker." In a very similar token, Pennycook (2010), building on Theodore Schatzki's (2001, 29) practice theory, develops the view of language as a "local practice" and argues that language is the by-product of "meso-political action", the constant, active mediation between repeated individuated activities of the everyday and larger complex sociocultural, historical, economic, and (geo)political structures. As Pennycook (2010, 9) further argues, a counterhegemonic translingual ideology distances itself from dominant attempts to capture language generally (and SWE specifically) as an "autonomous system that pre-exists its use, and [language] competence as an internal capacity that accounts for language production."

When we think of an emerging translingual ideology in relation to writing and its teaching, this immediately necessitates shifting dominant monolingualist ways of thinking about reading and writing as the unregulated by-products of (usually near native) language competence toward an understanding of the socioculturally embedded and embodied ways of using and reusing language in diverse scenes of reading and writing. In fact, advancing a translingual-oriented approach in teaching writing, Bruce Horner and colleagues (2011) remind writing teacher-scholars who wish to implement translinguality in their work that they can no longer remain preoccupied with the degree to which student writing seemingly conforms to or deviates from the syntactic and notational conventions of SWE. Instead, they need to divert their attention to what student writers "are [actually] doing with language" (Horner et al. 2011, 305) in their reading and writing by drawing on which concrete language and communicative resources and with what consequences to their linguistic and social life and world. Contesting a monolingualist ideology and a traditional multilingual ideology signaled through responses to language differences in writing as, respectively, "problems" and "errors" to be remediated or fully eradicated or as "rights" to be merely honored and tolerated, translingualism in teaching writing sees them as valuable *resources* for active and consequential meaning making to be deployed and developed more effectively and strategically. But more than this, a translingual ideology informing the teaching and assessment of writing insists on the normality (hence unmarkedness) and necessity of "difference as the norm" of all literate exchanges and transactions, "conceived of as acts of translation" within and across languages, language varieties, and ways of using English(es) during deliberate decisions that deviate from as well as iterate standardized usages and meanings (Lu and Horner 2016, 208–9; cf. Lu and Horner 2013). From this translingual perspective, full, perfect, or (near) native-like mastery of pre-constructed language standards and conventions, as traditionally defined under monolingualism, no longer in itself guarantees communicative success and effective language negotiations without the "alertness, creativity, and strategic thinking and action" necessary to "align diverse [language and] semiotic resources" with ever-changing ecological factors (Canagarajah 2013b, 174).

Under a nascent translingual orientation to language, language relations, and language difference, to be asking whether to "invite" students to utilize the full range of their language resources when composing would be to invoke the wrong line of inquiry and unproductive labor. In other words, posing the "invitation" question—the likes of Bean and coauthors' (2003) overarching yes/no question—is actually an indirect implication that these language resources are not always already present, on the move, and operating in the writing classroom, sometimes even "behind the backs" of writing teachers (Canagarajah 2013a, 7). In fact, the language resources writing students necessarily and inevitably bring with them to acts of writing are not countable, identifiable objects like the backpacks they can casually pull on, take off, or "leave . . . at the door" (Jordan 2015, 369) or like their laptops, smartphones, or tablets, which they can simply turn on or off without affecting the way they form and transform language itself, its relation to other languages, their own sense of self, their local ecologies, and their positionality/ies with respect to others around them and the world. Put differently, the real, practical, and mobile resources our writing students have picked up in various formal and informal language and literacy learning trajectories throughout their lives and which they draw on in their academic work cannot be easily discarded, set aside, or kept in place, as they are always performatively realized. In this sense, a translingual view of language, language relations, and language difference in teaching writing acknowledges the need and maximizes the opportunity to traverse traditional (physical, linguistic, and cultural) boundaries through tapping into the full complexity and richness of the various language and discursive resources college/university students constantly bring to their academic reading and writing experiences. From the translingual representations and practices perspective I am advancing in this book, the more pressing question, then, becomes one of how writers' language representations become appropriated, fluctuate, and interact with the local affordances of writing classroom pedagogy and the degree to which these particular contextual influences have the potential to either stifle, constrain, or potentiate writers' abilities to mobilize and put their highly subjective language and semiotic resources to work as translingual.

CONCLUDING REMARKS

The trajectory I have followed in this chapter has taken us from a brief consideration of the general concept of language ideologies into an emphasis on the significance of the interconnected pairing of language representations and practices as strongly necessary for our growing understanding of the nature and operation of local language ideologies in diverse writing situations as mediating links between micro worlds of language-in-use and macro sociocultural, political, and economic conditions. Surely, as I further develop throughout this book, a focus on the conceptual and analytical tool of language representations—as themselves social practices with a profound impact on other ensuing language and discursive practices—is useful in further sensitizing writing teacher-scholars and students alike to matters of local language ideologies and the perpetual tensions encountered throughout their negotiations. I have examined the ways hegemonic monolingual, alternative multilingual, and counterhegemonic translingual ideologies of language are imbricated in writing instruction in terms of their distinctive principles, features, and treatments of language use, language relations, and language difference in writing. I have particularly described how advocates of these three conflicting linguistic ideologies in teaching writing differently theorize, represent, and pedagogically address investments in cross-border work based on differing representations of language and the status and value assigned to SWE and to perceived differences between the norms and conventions of SWE and students' actual language resources and practices.

Composition studies scholarship has played a prominent role in destabilizing dominant monolingualism's flawed assumptions about and continued deprecation of writers for language differences in their writing, and diverse statements and pronouncements[17] by leading professional organizations have set the tone for and articulated the close connections between language policy and writing pedagogy developments in ways that honor and support language diversity. More recently, the vast and increasing number of journal articles, books, and edited collections that contest dominant English-only monolingual ideologies in US composition research and instruction[18] suggests that there is a growing recognition among writing teacher-scholars and program administrators of the need to re-envision the field's ideological, intellectual, political, and pedagogical commitment in relation to the constant and unavoidable complexity, intermingling, and interpenetration of languages, Englishes, and language practices in reading and writing. However, there is still much to be done in terms of correcting the effects of a forceful monolingualist ideology and confronting its continued, sometimes disguised, epistemologies and workings in the design of individual writing courses and of program-wide writing curricula, pedagogies, and assessment tools in most universities in the United States and beyond. As we shall see further in this book, ethnographic accounts from writing program ecologies in both Beirut and Seattle point toward shared challenges in negotiating English-only monolingualism's stranglehold on language and literacy practices and learning experiences.

"Still at the beginning stages" (Horner et al. 2011, 310) of its conception, reworking, and enactment, translingualism in composition, emerging in response to dominant monolingualism and its residual effects on traditional multilingualism, has been relatively (perhaps valuably) slow in influencing language policies and pedagogical and assessment practices in writing programs and courses (for a handful of such developmental efforts, see Horner and Tetreault 2017). Given the influential function of language representations and their intricate relationship with practices involving language, I am arguing that writing teachers-scholars who wish to refine intellectual engagements and labor with translingualism need to resist the urge and popular demand to rush into postulating a specific set of identifiable, unified, and stabilized prescribed teaching practices and activities, ready for "rolling out" in any writing classroom—as a monolingualist ideology would have us desire—at the expense of the much-needed questioning and reworking of the local ways of thinking about and subsequently doing language in writing that lie at the root of the problem. With this in mind, I focus exclusively in chapter 2 on complexifying our understandings of emerging translingual language ideologies as underscoring a very particular way of conceptualizing and representing language guided by deliberative inquiry, intellectual curiosity, dialogue, and openness in the hope that these can conceivably spark critical pedagogical reflections and inventions that require the co-collaboration of all those laboring with and across language and cultural difference, that is, writing scholars, program administrators, and teachers, in concert with students. In more precise terms, I turn next to considering how a translingual approach to writing and its teaching necessitates taking up translingual-affiliated language representations (i.e., new images, metaphors, and theoretical vocabulary) as much as reworking from a different standpoint familiar language-related notions in teaching writing that have become relatively unchallenged, pervasively naturalized, and commonsensical in our contemporary composition discourse and practice.

2
WORKING TRANSLINGUAL LANGUAGE REPRESENTATIONS AND/AS PRACTICES

A broader, differently based notion of the form in which we encounter and use language in the world is . . . needed.

(Hymes 1973, 60)

The invention of a language and consequently the way it is named constitute an intervention in and modify the ecolinguistic niche.

(Calvet 2006, 248)

One of the major aspects to attend to with regard to language and our material work with language and its difference, to borrow Dell Hymes's (1973, 60) characterization[1] more than four decades ago, is our "usual conception of it" in composition studies. We have seen in the previous chapter that a monolingual English-only ideology dominating US college composition propagates the fictitious view of language generally, and Standard Written English (SWE) in particular, as a discrete, singular, internally uniform, and autonomous object, existing in and of itself outside and beyond relations of power and difference. An interrelated concern lies in how a monolingual ideology in its most common guise of traditional multilingualism affirms and often romanticizes writing students' "rights" to their own languages or language varieties, yet as separate, hermetically sealed, and enumerable categories.

Mindful of the forcefulness of a monolingual ideology while also remaining attentive to the disconcerting epistemological continuity between monolingualism and traditional multilingualism, I have strategically positioned the current chapter at our particular juncture in this book. That is to say, I deliberately situate the ideas developed here in between the macro-frame of the language ideologies guiding the teaching of university-level writing discussed in the previous chapter

DOI: 10.7330/9781607329046.c002

and the more micro-level analyses in subsequent chapters of how the multiplicity and potential contention among these language ideologies get played out in distinct geographic, institutional, and social contexts. By doing so, I urge my readers to pause before and throughout their encountering of the empirical data in chapters 3, 4, and 5 and to think more seriously and deliberately in terms of the language representations and practices associated with a translingual paradigm. I am aware of the uneasy relationship many of us, as novice or experienced writing teacher-scholars and writing program administrators, might generally be experiencing with the construct of translingualism itself and its actual enactment in various domains and components of our and our students' literate life and work. For that reason, I briefly articulate in this chapter my own sense to date of some of the translingual language representational practices that can potentially create concrete conditions of possibility for intervening with and rewriting the popularized yet blinkered monolingualist constructions of language, language relations, and language learning at the very core of the problem. More directly, so we can productively engage with the ethnographic accounts I will be presenting later, this chapter serves, in a sense, as a mesopolitical space that intentionally (and perhaps annoyingly) interrupts our normal reading flow (i.e., our predisposed expectations for a more immediate transition into data analysis) and compels us to be cognizant of the conceptual tools and metaphors that have been—and continue to be—taken for granted in our and our students' engagement with language and language difference in writing, its teaching, and its learning in higher education worldwide. In fact, as Louis-Jean Calvet (2006, 152) asserts in the above epigraph, practices of conceptualizing and representing language constitute the "motor of linguistic change." In other words, they can, as I am suggesting here, considerably intervene in the current dynamics and realities of apparent language-ideological tensions in writing and its teaching, which are triggered and escalated by an apparent lack of fit between the invented yet powerful language representations of a dominant monolingualist ideology and its multilingual surrogate, on one hand, and, on another hand, what an emerging translingual ideology emphasizes about the inherent fluidity, malleability, and mobility of language as actually practiced.

Attempting to open up possible ways to escape from the monolinguistic conduit-metaphor thinking and the logic of the alternative multilingualist archipelago model (as presented in chapter 1), which are responsible in the first place for determining the nature of what they invent and claim to describe, I develop in this chapter a more dynamic descriptive and terminological basis for thinking and talking about language, language-in-use, and the whole set of language relations from a translingual perspective. However, I do not adopt the working images, metaphors, and relevant terms I introduce here as possessing an "objective reality out there" (Canagarajah 2013b, 16), as a dominant monolingualist ideology makes us believe, but rather as constantly open and subject to contestation, rethinking, and change. In fact, just like the construct of language they label, portray, and evaluate, these translingual representational practices are necessarily vulnerable to and require sustained and vigilant revision and reconstitution.

The issue, then, is not one of simply disposing of the old and established terms and ideas we've inherited from dominant and residual monolingualist thinking about language and replacing them with new translingual-oriented ones. Instead, the key to moving forward is a realization that the (individual or collective) naming, imagining, describing of language(s), language-in-use, and language relations and narrating them into being in such-and-such a way are already constructions of sociocultural, political, and ideological movements, that is, are in and of themselves acts of languaging that determine ensuing practices, relations to, and engagements with language(s). Reconstructing and reworking our current ways of thinking about and treating the language resources and practices of the writers and writing communities we are meant to serve through our scholarship, teaching, and administration is therefore an important first step in dismantling the continuing pressure of dominant monolingualism and its residual effects in traditional multilingualism and in avoiding the tendency to get ensnared in the straitjacket of its language descriptions and conceptions. To pursue this further, I now turn to a discussion of an alternative set of metaphors and corresponding vocabulary that more effectively captures the complexity and dynamics of language, language use, and language relations actually and continuously occurring in literate transactions and situations. Following this articulation of some possible translingual descriptive and analytical practices, I briefly consider what such reconceptualizations of language necessarily mean for several fundamental concepts pertaining to university-level writing instruction and assessment and underlying many of my student participants' literate learning experiences and complex language negotiations—concepts such as language competence, language standards, language errors in writing, writerly agency, and reader accountability amid sticky literate engagements.

TAKING UP "TRANSLINGUAL" DESCRIPTIVE AND EXPLANATORY PRACTICES

Critical approaches to language(s) and literacy/ies have contributed a new language of description and more nuanced representation that calls attention to the degrees of "unpredictability" (Canagarajah 2013b, 26), "complexity" (Blommaert 2013, 6, 8, 10, 14), "mobility" (Blommaert 2010, 3), "messiness" (Ramanathan 2006, 223; Ivanič et al. 2009, 176), "*opacité*" (Bernabé, Chamoiseau, and Confiant 1989, 52), "movement" (Pennycook 2010, 14), and "fluidity" and "flow" (Pennycook 2007; Pennycook and Otsuji 2015, 87) involved in the negotiation and (re)fashioning of language(s), subjectivity(ies), identity(ies), and meaning(s) amid the changing materiality of localities and social relations. Rather than continuing to adopt "purity", "boundedness", "transparency", and "fixity" as the starting assumptions about language and language work in literate situations, the intricately tied phenomena and processes listed above are becoming central concerns in the study and enactment of translingualism. Therefore, to help shift dependency away from the established constructions and images of language, which appear to have "exhaust[ed] the limits of their explanatory and descriptive powers" (Blommaert 2013, 8) in the face of exceptionally complex language contact and difference, there is an exigency for "a new vocabulary" (Blommaert 2010, 1) and set of "metaphors of movement" (Pennycook 2010, 141), more reflective of the true character of language and its workings across time and space. With that in mind, I present below in broad terms three models of the rhizomatic banyan, the urban traffic flow, and the messy entanglements in electric cables, which can serve as starting points for the way we might potentially view, treat, and do language(s) translingually in our own work and in evaluative judgments of the work of literate others in our local ecologies.

The Banyan Tree Model

Bilingual education specialist Ofelia García (2007), building on Sinfree Makoni and Pedzisai Mashiri (2007), adopts the botanical image of the banyan tree—with an intricate history in many South Asian cultures—which grows horizontally, vertically, and laterally all at the same time. As the ancient banyan tree grows, it ramifies and sends down a multiplicity of branches, which in turn eventually take root all around the tree and end up enveloping it. The mesh of branches with special aerial roots expands over time and across space and gives rise to newer trunks. As this natural cycle keeps repeating itself over and over again, all the trunks form an intertwined and entangled web of banyan vines. Unlike most common "normative" trees in North American or European landscape, like red maples, oaks, pines, aspens, or firs where it is possible to identify the different parts of the tree (i.e., the trunk, nodes, branches, twigs, and roots), the banyan's juxtaposed branch-root system is coextensive with the tree itself as it expands outward and across. In other words, the sprawling banyan defies boundedness in space and time, and it becomes almost impossible to tell the main "mother" trunk, or the supposedly "authentic" and "original" trunk, apart from newly formed ones supporting its expanding canopy.

This confusion and nullification of endings and beginnings in the banyan's close-knit foliage, but in unique alliance with each other, hints at the character of our and our students' language and meaning-making practices, the iterative performances and movements within and across languages, language practices, literacies, cultures, ideologies, texts, and meanings "up, out, and down at the same time" (García 2007, xi). More specifically, the typology of the banyan's structure of intricacy and interconnectedness inspires a dynamic understanding of the practices of languaging, reading, and writing as simultaneously "rhizomatic" (Deleuze and Guattari 1987), emergent, and always in a state of becoming, that is, as renderings and translations but with the "symbiotic intermingling" (Bassnett and Trivedi 1999, 10) of the originals with the translation,[2] a central point that is emphasized in critical translation studies and that I will come back to and further develop with concrete examples in chapter 5. Approaching practices of languaging, reading, and writing as involved in complex relations of rhizomatic translation opens up diverse levels of difference and sociocultural meanings that are commonly erased, obscured, muted, glossed over, or left out by politics, histories, dominant economies, and grand ideologies (again, see chapter 5 for more on this).

The Moving Traffic Model

Because the notion of fixity, fortification, and relative immobility might be implicated in the image of trees with their root systems burrowed into identifiable spots and with the extra baggage of filiation tied to them,[3] a useful alternative that opens up productive ways for reflecting on the fluidity and movement of language and its (re)working is Probal Dasgubta's (2005) global road traffic analogy. One can visualize the high volume of traffic in superdiverse urban landscapes, resulting from the to and fro passing of vehicles and people who in the midst of their busy days are preoccupied with commuting, doing business, talking, languaging, and making meaning on the go. In relation to the superdiverse urban contexts I detail in this project, this image particularly comes to life during the iconic annual Seattle Seafair festivities with thousands of spectators standing on a nearby bridge or lakeshores with good viewpoints and a fleet of sailboats, powerboats, big yachts, kayaks, rafts, and tubes crowding the area as the US Navy's Blue Angels take their aerial acrobatics to the sky.

The chaos and perpetual motion embodied in the city's traffic metaphor helps capture the powerful de-territorialized, indeterminate flow of languages, literacies, ideas, meanings, texts, and their translations that both the city's dwellers and its visitors carry around with them on a daily basis. Just like the ongoing movement in traffic with the endless coming and going of vehicles, motorcycles, trains, buses, taxis, bikes, pedestrians, passengers, ferries, boats, airplanes, and so on, language users and learners are constantly part of the powerful trafficking of languages, language varieties, accents, styles, registers, texts, meanings, and worldviews (see Pratt 2002; Kramsch 2006). This is not to suggest, however, that the traffic as a whole is always moving, running smoothly, and unobstructed. In fact, everyday talk about experiences of immobility through and around the metropolis amid acute traffic problems and ongoing construction projects is exactly what unites twentieth-century urbanites in both developing and developed nations across the globe. In most cases, the overall desire to keep the traffic moving and actually get somewhere at a particular time necessitates navigating and working around various nonhuman actants, the gatekeeping practices of members of traffic law enforcement, and sometimes even non-rule-following traffic mates who knowingly or unknowingly impede the traffic flow. For instance, in present-day Beirut, densely populated with various remnants of conflict and war, the widespread practice of intensifying "security by the state for 'the few'" by installing security checkpoints and erecting concrete and barbed wire barricades—which close off not just street blocks leading to the residences of class and political (hence kinetic) elites but entire neighborhoods—has resulted in channeling, regulating, and constraining the potential for movement in various parts of the city (see Monroe 2016, 10). In this sense, new mobilities studies in the social sciences have disrupted the illusion of continuous, "unfettered mobility" and free-flows (Hannam, Sheller, and Urry 2006, 7) as the pulse of modern city life and instead emphasized how asymmetrical relations of power and difference structure the politics of mobility, thereby contingently producing occasioned "intermittent movement" (Sheller and Urry 2006, 213), varied time-space "immobilities," "fixities[,] or moorings" (Hannam, Sheller, and Urry 2006, 3). With such "regimes of flow" moving at variable and shifting intensities, "speeds, scales, and viscosities" (Sheller and Urry 2006, 213), the traffic in meaning and language that we and our students are necessarily and inevitably part of is equally "contingent, precarious, [and] governed by idiosyncratic habits, subjective histories, [local-global hierarchies,] and other negotiable material" (Dasgupta 2005, 47).

The analogy of the flow of traffic reminds us—and we may still need reminding—that our and our students' current labor within the confines of the language of the academy, that is, SWE, makes only *one* kind of contribution to the global traffic of academic knowledge construction, consumption, and evaluation. Given the complexity of the communicative patterns and networks of the twenty-first century, language users and learners as well as their language and semiotic resources are in a constant and unavoidable state of transition, motion, and transformation and are never firmly located in one specific homogeneous linguistic and communicative domain, space, or time, as monolingualism would traditionally have it. In fact, they are constantly part of a much broader and more complex traffic in language and meaning. In other words, there is much more to their meaning-making practices and shifting relationships with language than the kind of unidirectional, narrow "sub-traffic" (Dasgupta 2005, 42) a monolingual bias in academia demands, recognizes, legitimates, and fosters. As Claire Kramsch (2006, 102) argues, a dominant monolingualist English-only ideology is "the name not only for a linguistic handicap, but [also] for a dangerously monolithic traffic in meaning," generally imposed, managed, and steered by those in power. As I will further demonstrate in chapter 5, it is broadening and diversifying precisely this contingent and shifting traffic flow in language and meaning that is the goal of the translingual perspective on language and language relations I am advancing in this book.

Chaotic Arrangement of Overhead Electricity Cables Model
Another image that comes to mind, especially for those of us who've experienced urban life outside developed nations, is that of the tangled mess of unauthorized electricity connections (sometimes even for telephone, internet, and cable TV), designed and redesigned by ordinary city residents or unlicensed businesses. Figure 2.1 shows aboveground utility poles at a highly populated, poor residential area in Beirut strung with jumbles of electric power lines as too many wires running in every

Figure 2.1. Wire madness in cityscapes (author photo)

direction are unofficially hooked or curled up for power theft. This has become a common sight in densely populated urban areas throughout the world. In spite of efforts to remove such illegal cables hanging from every street lamp and electric pole and to control and penalize this practice, residents continue risking their lives and those of others around them and simply string these cables up again within the hour.

In the midst of this entangled web of illegal subsidiary wires around the "main" cables, streams of moving and highly volatile electric charges pass through and flow continuously. However, this flow of energy in the metaphor I am proposing here is no longer predictable, unidirectional, and linear starting from point A (i.e., power plants and main energy suppliers) to point B (i.e., households of paying customers), as it is now intercepted by (compulsory) supply to hundreds of bad-paying or unbilled city dwellers who constantly find silent and insidious ways to tamper with dominant electricity networks. Despite being an eyesore and, more important, a safety hazard, the chaotic, messy features of these unequal, unstable, and heterogeneous linkages and interconnections create new arrangements of sociocultural engagement, power, and difference.

In view of all of this, the descriptive and analytic models I've explored above—despite their limitations[4]—help capture the polydirectionality, or should I say *trans*directionality, of literate individuals' complex communicative and linguistic practices, which are interlocked and "build on each other in multiple ways and directions—up, out, down, across"—while remaining "rooted in the terrain and realities from which they emerge" (García 2009, 8). The result is a tremendously complex web of various levels of interactions and interpenetrations that extend horizontally, vertically, but also sideways in often unpredictable ways to the extent that the ideological boundaries demarcating these networks are increasingly blurred and fluid. Armed with such insights about complex understandings of networked language practices and language relations, this book takes *transdirectionality*—and not simple one-sidedness as imposed by monolingualism—as well as *transcentricity*—and not the centrality and dominance of a single language-as-entity—as the norm for a highly congested traffic and flow of languages, language practices, literacies, translations, and meanings in the writing classroom, as I discuss further in chapter 5.

We have seen in chapter 1 how monocentric approaches to teaching writing aligned with a dominant monolingual ideology promote a unidirectional progression solely toward a static, universally applicable, and tightly knit core (in this case, English or more accurately SWE) deemed necessary and sufficient for upward socioeconomic mobility. We have also seen how those aligned with a traditional multilingual ideology pluralize languages arithmetically while qualitatively maintaining their very existence and describability as stable, enumerable entities, as well as their discreteness and segregation from their ecologies and each other—just like the dominant monolingualist approaches they allegedly distance themselves from. In this sense, one of the main problems with such multilingualist approaches to teaching writing, as I described in chapter 1, lies in their primary focus on what Michael Halliday has termed "glossodiversity" (cited in Pennycook 2010, 97), that is, the numerical multiplicity or *diversité* of codes or languages,[5] at the expense of "semiodiversity" (Pennycook 2010, 97) or the concept of *diversalité* introduced by Caribbean literary writers Jean Bernabé, Patrick Chamoiseau, and Raphaël Confiant (1989, 52), that is, "la diversité des significations," or the diversity, breadth, and movement of meaning(s) within languages.

A translingual approach to writing and its teaching, by contrast, does not simply validate and quantitatively increase the number of language entities involved in reading and writing situations but rather qualitatively engages and diversifies the networks of sociocultural and historical meanings and interpretative possibilities, or what I am calling here *transversality*. As a result, translingualism in teaching writing intensifies deliberations over how the potential ramifications of meanings get "muffle[d], absorb[ed], appropriate[d], transpose[d], conceal[ed]" (Pratt 2002, 33) in the writing and interpretation of texts and at what expense. My felt need to create the term *transversality*, given the absence of the English equivalent of creolists Bernabé and colleagues' notion of *diversalité*, is further illustration of the necessity to break from monolingualist ideology's representations of language and language practices and what it deems to be possible in language and practices with language, as well as of the inherent difficulty in doing so. The concept of transversality I propose here (and further explicate in chapter 5)—that is, a more dynamic, qualitative understanding of language relations as the transdirectional and transcentric flow of multiple, uneven, and often colliding meanings, practices, resources, and worldviews—helps open up a much-needed space for reconfiguring language difference in writing as outside the oddity, exceptionalism, and exoticization that are set as typical monolingualist and multilingualist responses in writing instruction. The translingual character of English as in complex, opaque relations of difference, entanglement, and translation—much like the ever-spreading banyan, the powerful flow of city traffic, and the messy cable connections in third world nations explored above—is and should always be seen as "the norm across the world" (Pennycook 2008, 42) for all language and literacy laborers, both those representing mainstream social identities and those who are culturally, economically, and hence linguistically marginalized. Under this translingual take on English and its practice in teaching writing that I am advancing here, coming up with entirely new and exciting pedagogical designs and assessment tools is beside the point. Instead, at the heart of the matter, as I have been arguing all along, is an exigency for reintroducing into existing writing curricula, pedagogies, and assessments English in its full complexity and depth and for constantly putting it in the service of transversality in reading and writing.

"TRANSLINGUAL" RECONCEPTUALIZATIONS IN WRITING INSTRUCTION

Such a shift from looking at and treating English as an identifiable entity with a fixed, abstract structure and clearly delineable boundaries and focusing instead on its actual dynamic doings and re-doings in changing spatio-temporal contexts should also be an occasion for a reconsideration of many of the core concepts pertaining to its learning and the identity of its learners. In other words, for well-grounded interventions in writing programs and classrooms rooted in and operating out of a translingual way of thinking about language and its (re)workings, it is essential to revisit and reconfigure again and again the traffic of widely used concepts in the English language and literacy teaching enterprise broadly conceived and in the teaching of college/university-level writing in particular. Let us now turn to some of these key language- and literacy-related concepts, which have become highly suspect under a translingual framework in that they are premised on monolingualist understandings of English as a discrete, unitary entity with a single prescribed core (grammar and lexicon). My re-examination of these common concepts, however, is in the interest of a critical engagement with and unsettling of their wider, often neglected linguistic-ideological associations and not so much a comprehensive summary of serious divisions and contestations surrounding their definitions and the prioritization of those definitions in the literature.

Language Competence in Writing as Performative
Dominant theorizations of evaluative constructs like competence, fluency, and proficiency in language and literacy learning and development are founded on problematic monolingualist representations of the native English speaker (NES) as putatively the yardstick or "gold standard" (Trimbur 2008, 149) for measuring all users'/learners' linguistic and literate performances. According to John Trimbur (2008, 157), "The very naturalness of birth that territorializes languages by identifying them with nativity and nationhood . . . invests in the native [English] speaker a kind of linguistic priority—and consequently, a linguistic sovereignty." This same monolingualist line of reasoning also marks the language learning-in-action of those identified and treated by the dominant culture and its ideology as falling outside the NES norm as restricted, incomplete, and, in the words of Trimbur (2008, 157), "secondary, artificial, and derivative." Therefore, in mainstream language and literacy education, unidirectional English-only monolingualist ideology has resulted in the "conflation" of the "optimum" degree of academic English competence and proficiency with (near) native-like English (Jenkins 2014, 104, 132; Cook 1999).

Contrary to what such monolingualist assumptions about language learning and evaluative judgments about language competence would lead us to focus on, translingualism starts from an entirely different premise. In essence, a translingual language ideology in writing and its teaching problematizes and dismantles the mystique invested in inadequate, "limited[,] and unfair" NES standards and norms (Canagarajah 2007, 927) and the specter of the native speaker's unrealistic "ownership" of English,[6] which confines English-language proficiency in writing to an imagined capacity to reproduce and work *within* its abstracted, uniform set of standardized structures and usages. In early work, Suresh Canagarajah (2007, 932; emphasis added) perceptively observed that a performance-based conceptualization of language competence needs to take into account the "versatility and agility" of language learners in negotiating various types of texts, literacy traditions, discourses, language practices, and contexts and "*not* mastery and control" over a definable set of pre-given language conventions and forms. Taking a similar translingual-oriented position, Bruce Horner (2016, 101, 119; emphasis in original) argues that from a translingual perspective, learners of language and academic writing actively and collaboratively engage in the ongoing reworking and rewriting "*of* language" itself, which is prone to and "in need of such (re)writing" and transformation, but always and only "in concert and negotiation with others." Operating from the principle of transversality, which carries the torch for translingualism in writing and its teaching in this book, language competence in written communication would thus be assessed as the strategic participation in but also disturbance and disruption of the traffic of meanings. In more precise terms, fluency and proficiency in written communication correspond to the "ability to translate, transpose and critically reflect on social, cultural and historical meanings conveyed by the grammar and lexicon" (Kramsch 2006, 103) while participating fully and effectively in tension-fraught negotiations with potential readers and their particularized identities, social positionings, and linguistic affiliations.

Second language acquisition (SLA) scholars Alan Firth and Johannes Wagner (1998, 91) have noted that language competence is not a product stored in an individual's head and entirely retrieved without any reference to the material context of communication as traditionally conceived but is rather fundamentally interactional, contingent, "transitional, situational, and dynamic." In fact, Firth and Wagner (1998, 91) point out that language users—whether those who claim native ownership over English or those who claim it as their additional, second, or foreign language in their repertoire—"will always be 'learners' . . . in some respects" for the sole reason that "new or partly known registers, styles, language-related tasks, lexical items, terminologies, and structures routinely confront language users, calling for the contingent adaptation and transformation of existing knowledge and competence, and the acquisition of new knowledge." More recently, Jan Blommaert (2010, 103; emphasis in original) argues emphatically in his critical sociolinguistics framework of mobile language resources in the age of globalization that "no one knows *all* of a language," and this assertion not only includes the additional and foreign languages one knows or is attempting to know but also, and above all, one's so-called native/mother tongue. In this regard, as a corrective to an inadequate view of perfect, full, and optimum competence based on the degree of attainment of standardized language usages and meaning productions, Blommaert (2010) observes that we need to think in terms of the "truncated" (9, 103, 180)—very "fragmented" (9), "chequered" (133), imperfect, "'incomplete'" (9), and often "'unfinished'" (196)—character of the complex language and literate resources and practices *all* literate individuals deploy for a wide range of rhetorical effects and communicative functions (cf. Blommaert and Backus 2013).

From this standpoint, all language and literacy laborers (ourselves included) are always far from perfect users, writers, and rewriters of the language, but their perpetual meaning-making practices are either successfully accomplished or not through the concrete, collaborative labor of combining the differentially developed language and literate resources and competencies of all parties involved in the communicative act at a particular time and place. Gradual transformations and interventions in dominant monolingualist assumptions about language use and language competence therefore start with us, as writing teacher-scholars and program administrators, developing the humility to recognize and the curiosity to further explore the potentialities of our additional role as lifelong translingual "learners", designers, rewriters, and translators of English together with our colleagues, students, and local communities.

Language Standards and Conventions as Regulated, Sedimented Practices

Underlying the ideology of monolingualism is a particular view of not only language as an abstract, closed system but also its grammar and lexicon as consisting of structural/lexical units arrayed in specific patterns determined by truly uniform rules and standards that are deemed to hold the linguistic system together and guarantee its continuity. From such a perspective, language standards and rules of usage are seen as rigid, static, and timeless, existing and enclosed at an abstract level in the writers' mind prior to any actual use in situated literate interactions.

This particular view presupposes the neutrality, transparency, and universality of language standards and conventions; in addition, it treats conformity to them as in and of itself producing, guaranteeing, and maintaining shared meaning and comprehensibility, especially in educational and professional landscapes.

Such monolingualist representations of language as a stable system with equally static, a-temporal, and indisputable standards and rules are basically inconceivable under a counterhegemonic translingual project in composition. Building on Anthony Giddens's theorization of structuration and Paul Hopper's (1998, 157) understanding of the emergent, sedimented nature of language and its grammar, a translingual orientation takes seriously a conceptualization of standardized structures and rules of written English as "always provisional, always negotiable, and in fact as epiphenomenal," that is, as outcomes and by-products of routinized usage and frequency and not *the* sources of mutual intelligibility and effective communication (whether in oral or written linguistic production). Giddens (1979) argues that linguistic rules and conventions cannot be exhaustively described or examined apart from time-space intersections, as they are recursively implicated in socially and culturally situated practices. For Giddens (1979, 65; emphasis in original), language rules and practices are closely connected and co-constitutive, as they can "*only exist in conjunction with one another.*" In this sense, linguistic and social structures are in a constant relation of reciprocal structuring and restructuring, as simultaneously the "medium" as well as the achieved "outcome" of regularized social practices (Giddens 1979, 69). Hopper's notion of "emergent grammar" and particularly his views on "sedimentation" tie in interestingly here. For Hopper (1998, 157), "there is no natural fixed structure to language." In fact, language systematicity or regularity, in his view, is "an illusion produced by the partial settling or *sedimentation* of frequently used forms into temporary subsystems" (Hopper 1998, 157–58; emphasis in original). In other words, the apparent fixity and structural regularities of language standards and conventions that writing teachers and their students have come to expect and accept as sole signs of correctness and high-quality language usage in reading and writing are institutionally and ideologically propagated myths (Hopper 1998).

Specifically connecting these considerations to the teaching and learning of writing, Horner and Trimbur stated as early as 2002 that taking a translingual orientation toward language—which they referred to at the time as an actively "multilingual ideal"—does not in any way suggest the sidestepping or "abolition of standards" and conventions of writing or even the denial of the necessity for teaching them. Instead, translingualism necessitates stripping these language standards and conventions of their monolingualist mystique as ostensibly transparent and static givens and recognizing their actual and long-lost character as "contingent, local, and negotiable" (Horner and Trimbur 2002, 620–21). Conceiving of and treating the rules and conventions of standardized language usage in writing as the kind of situational, constructed, sedimented, and historically contingent institutionalized practices that they actually are can help writing students develop a greater sense of agency and responsibility in making informed decisions about their written language and their particular language choices and practices in relation to the exigencies and local materiality of their literate act(s) (for more on this, see chapter 5). Of central importance here, then, is that the focus should not be on the degree of adherence to or deviation from a fixed set of abstract language standards and conventional forms in student writing as much as on the rhetorical, material character of their practices, chosen meanings, and complex decisions while negotiating, like all the rest of us, varied affordances and constraints in local writing ecologies. In this sense, the goal of teaching and assessing writing from a translingual stance toward language and its difference is no longer a question of acquiring and producing grammatically correct structure and proper, idiomatic usage but of "*expanding a repertoire of communicative contexts*" (Hopper 1998, 171; emphasis in original) and occasions for the dynamic negotiation and creation of rhetorical meanings in written texts across relations of power and difference.

The Logic of Language Errors in Writing as Collaborative Social Achievement

The same set of reified monolingual and multilingual assumptions about language, language abilities, language standards, and the sociocultural identities of language learners as fixed, identifiable, and bounded has largely impeded theoretical understandings and subsequently institutional treatments of and responses to matters of language "error" in academic writing. With a view of standards and conventions for English writing in academic contexts as a "fait accompli," "history in the sense of something [stabilized, settled] in the past about which there is little now to be done" (Horner 1999, 139), dominant monolingual and residual multilingual approaches to language and language difference and, by extension, "error" in English writing have isolated errors as "frozen, instantiated object[s]" (Williams 1981, 159) divorced from the social constitution of written texts and the language and literate practices that produce them. Under these simplistic representations of errors, the production of odd language forms or meanings in writing is generally attributed to an individual writer's clumsiness, lack of cognitive or linguistic development, or imperfect perception regarding the existence or degree of seriousness of the error or even its expected correction.

Challenging pre-formulated monolingualist conceptions and treatments of written "errors" in student texts as apparent, indefensible deviations from the putatively fixed, uniform conventions of grammar and mechanics, a translingual approach to language and language difference in teaching writing foregrounds the locatedness of errors at the intersection of complex issues like power, status, authority, structure, and agency. With a complex practice-based view of language as well as its standards and conventions of usage, a translingual approach to teaching writing treats what are ostensibly assigned to the realm of "errors" in student writing—that is, signs of lack of conformity to some honored rule to be underscored, condemned, and ultimately amended—as exercises of agency and active negotiations of language differences with an eye toward the possible kinds of stylistic, rhetorical, discursive, and communicative effects they *might* and *do* produce in written texts. Accordingly, a translingual model recognizes that what are deemed successful or flawed in language and writing practices are in actuality matters of shifting, contingent, and collaborative sociocultural relationships between both writers *and* their readers as they jointly labor and belabor to construct and derive textual meaning in light of variable, often conflicting, political, epistemological, and ideological considerations.

Pertinent to this discussion is an example from my personal experiences as a writer while pursuing my graduate studies that I would like to examine more closely here. Upon receiving written comments on an initial draft of a seminar paper, I noticed that my professor was inquisitive about my decision to violate what seemed to be an elementary technical rule for working properly with quoted materials and to adopt instead a British style of placing periods and commas at the end of a quote outside rather than inside close quotation marks. In my mind, the North American rule and convention that all periods and commas "ALWAYS go inside" single and double quotation marks (Straus 2015; emphasis in original; cf. Blakesley and Hoogeveen 2012) seemed contradictory to investments in academic integrity and responsible intellectual work, especially when those punctuation marks were not directly part of the quoted material in the original source. Apparently, while I initially attributed my practice of not conforming closely to the rules of punctuation in Edited American English (EAE) to my non-mainstream sociocultural identity and my schooling both inside and outside the United States, it turned out that I shared this notation practice with one of my Anglo-American cohorts who was only schooled in US institutions.

My professor continued to view this practice with suspicion while simultaneously showing efforts in written feedback and one-on-one conversations to make sense of it and its intended function. At first, I left those individual "errors" of punctuation untouched in ensuing revisions, as I perceived them as less serious or urgent in comparison with higher-order concerns. However, as my professor persistently commented on this specific non-standard punctuation practice in subsequent years, particularly in more high-stakes texts like my dissertation chapters, I decided to address the ambiguity this practice was creating for my reader (and possibly others) while still preserving my sense of its substantial rhetorical function. As a result, I chose to put all periods and commas inside quotation marks, following the punctuation rules of EAE, but when the commas and periods were not used in the original quotations I was integrating into my own text, I placed them outside to maintain the integrity of the original writing. As a result, my writing incorporated a mélange of both American and British practices, thereby creating further confusion for my professor who advised for more consistency in following rules of mechanics. Upon further inspection, this practice was also adopted in written texts produced by—what Min-Zhan Lu (2004, 27) calls "Master Designers" in particular fields of interest—renowned English as a lingua franca (ELF) scholar Jennifer Jenkins (2014), scholarly work of high caliber appearing in a reputable international publishing house like Routledge. Surprised—and perhaps instructed—my professor wrote back to me with the following revelation:

> You'll see from her [Jenkins's]/Routledge's practice (and this has been confirmed for me by other publications) that the practice you and [X] have been following, and I've been correcting, of putting periods and commas "outside" double quotation marks is now becoming the norm. So congratulate yourself on being part of the cutting edge of notational practice, and enjoy my chagrin for having tried to "correct" this practice for all these years. Perhaps you can use this as an illustration of some of your arguments? I promise never to "correct" your ", or ". again. Sounds like you and [X] have always been just more au courant than me. (personal communication, 2013)

In opposition to the prevalent tendency among academics to "condemn error and enforce a rule" (Williams 1981, 165), with them serving as final arbiters, this professor enacted favorable dispositions of deliberative inquiry and intellectual curiosity in understanding the logic and meso-politics of my "errors"[7] in writing, thereby demonstrating eagerness but also humility to learn *from* and *with* a mentee. The tug-and-push dynamics of our negotiations, which spanned over several years, over a socially sanctioned notational practice have immersed us both in a process of joint learning-in-negotiation, self-revision, and transformation. My professor had to learn anew the rhetorical function and growing normativity of this nonconventional notational practice. I, for one, as I will demonstrate in chapter 5, have become determined to make a more deliberate effort to carve out in the design of my own undergraduate writing courses various opportunities for optimizing the kind of resolutely dialectical thinking and doing of language, writing, and learning that such back-and-forth negotiations have afforded me. It is these moments of productive tension, which served as catalysts for profound self-reflection and personal growth as a writer and thinker, that I have been (and intend to continue) re-creating for my own writing students. This notational practice of placing punctuation marks that are not originally part of cited material outside quotations remains a trend I deliberately keep up, and not a technical editorial oversight, in composing the manuscript you are now reading.

Taking up a translingual understanding of written errors and language differences in teaching writing does not necessarily mean that student writers need to undertake the challenging task of convincing us of the acceptability of their usages but is rather a matter of positioning them materially as agentive negotiators who are fully responsible for their meaning-making practices at all stages of the writing process. Rather than reading student writing with an eye for errors in them and for what they don't but should do with language, we need to resist the temptation to continue to represent ourselves (hence our disciplinary labor) as invested with an institutional responsibility to rescue the language of the academy from all the assaults it is being and has been subjected to. Instead, it is our professional responsibility to participate in helping current and future generations of college/university writing students recognize and experience the fact that their actual labor of putting language into active use in writing is "always taking place translingually" or that, as Trimbur (2016, 226) further explains, "we are all—students, teachers, literary writers—constantly negotiating [with varying degrees of effectiveness] multiple languages, conventions of writing, and linguistic loyalties."

Writerly Agency and Reader Engagement as Dynamic Co-Writer-Reader-ship

Challenging the narrow confines of monolingualist thought that privileges linguistic structure over human agency, translingualism aligns in its particularized conceptualization of agency with the work of Giddens (1979, 69; emphasis in original), which accentuates the "*mutual dependence of structure and agency.*" From this perspective, what particularly warrants our critical attention are the individuality and meso-politics of emergent language performances that make meaning construction and its negotiation possible and not the putative internalization or automatization of invariant, systematic, and rigidly stable structures and conventions of use. Hence, taking a translingual stance necessitates speaking and thinking in terms of enactments of "agency *in* language" performances and not the "agency *of* language" (Duranti 2004, 451; emphasis in original), which has a long tradition within dominant monolingualism of the reification of language as a self-standing agent with its own agenda, goals, and intentions independent from the subjectivities and the physical and social ecologies that make variations in its production possible in the first place. A translingual framework grants power and agency to writers who, in their accomplishment of transversality, mobilize their diverse language and semiotic resources by making either apparently grand, irregular, and unauthorized or seemingly "small, ordinarily unrecognized, often unintended shifts in meaning, function, and context" in their writing (Lu and Horner 2013, 595). When it comes to matters of language use in writing and its learning, Horner and Trimbur (2002, 620; emphasis in original) have argued that writing "students like the rest of us writers, do participate in *re*-inventing—not simply reproducing but potentially altering—the language of the university in each act of writing," reading, and hence learning.

These in situ practices of writing and rewriting language generally, and English in particular, with every occasion of communication are performed and actualized always in a context of adjustment to other literate individuals or groups of individuals. In other words, they are subject to (and themselves taking place in) the presence or absence of uptake in time and space, or what Hopper (1998, 161) calls collective "reinforcement" or its nonexistence among all parties involved in a literate transaction. From this perspective, held accountable for their language and writing practices, translingually oriented writers exercise and enact their agency in and through the way they intentionally provide for the availability and utility of rhetorical cues and language or semiotic resources that would allow for successful negotiations and renegotiations of relations of power, authority, and difference in their own texts. In this sense, effective negotiation and construction of meaning in written texts is not an individual, one-sided activity consisting of private thoughts and intentions. Instead, it demands practical and attitudinal transformations on the part of readers who are equally accountable and need to strive for "a new kind of reading" (Trimbur 2016, 220), a translingual reading practice characterized by versatility, inquisitiveness about and openness toward the normalcy of ambiguity, unpredictability, opacity, and murkiness of language and meaning-making practices in writing, thereby resisting dominant valuations of efficiency, clarity, transparency, definiteness, and determinacy. In fact, meaning derived while reading (rereading, writing, rewriting, and translating) across difference needs to be seen as resolutely dialectical, social, and performative.[8] As Canagarajah (2007, 928) argues, "There is no meaning for form, grammar, or language ability outside the realm of practice." Along the same lines, Firth and Wagner (1997, 290) observe that "meaning is ineluctably negotiated" and negotiable, as both agentive writers and intellectually invested readers alike are obliged in any textual transaction to put forth ceaseless interpretation, translation, and negotiation labor.

A newly emerging ideology of translingualism, then, puts center stage a collective rather than an individual sense of intentionality, responsibility, and reflexive monitoring (Horner, NeCamp, and Donahue 2011, 288; cf. Agnihotri 2007, 80; Canagarajah 2013b, 130). Full translingual engagement in language and literate acts is the product of perseverance, mutual support, and finely tuned cognizance on the part of *both* writers and readers of key principles of "*synergy* (i.e. putting forth one's own efforts) and *serendipity* (i.e. accepting the other on his/her own terms, being open to unexpectedness)" (Khubchandani 1998, 21; emphasis in original). The success of a translingually sensitive and affiliated literate and textual transaction, therefore, involves and requires "a series of co-'s":[9] cooperation, collaboration, co-contribution, and co-participation in the resourceful and reciprocal negotiation, co-construction, and rewriting of English. *Co-writer-reader-ship* is a potentially relevant identity property for agentive writers and their equally invested readers who are conjointly responsible for doing translingual English work within, on, and across differences (of language, culture, identity, context, genre, modality, discipline, and the like), overcoming probable hurdles and breakdowns together to establish meaningful and consequential literate transactions.

CONCLUDING REMARKS

Moving forward, Lu and Horner (2016, 216), in their introduction to the *College English* special themed issue on "Translingual Work in Rhetoric and Composition," stressed the exigency for writing teacher-scholars and their students to take up the "labor and responsibility", with all the excitements and anxieties that might invoke, of "reworking . . . translinguality", since the new term itself functions "neither as recipe, nor ingredient to a recipe, for redressing our dominant [representations and] practices in mediating language and language relations. Rather, it is at most, and at its best, an occasion and invitation for us [all] to work to do so." As I have already suggested, how we are to precisely take up such calls—that is, without perpetuating, albeit unintentionally, the very language ideologies and epistemologies we wish to defeat—in our own communities, institutions, writing programs, and classrooms depends to a large extent on how we understand and represent languages, the relationships among them, and our students' differential engagements in reworking them and these relationships.

What I have argued in this chapter is that if we really no longer posit languages as observable, neatly segregated entities existing outside human interactions and relations, as monolingualism and monolingual multilingualism would have it, we should remain wary of the ideological underpinnings of the conceptual tools and metaphors we use in describing and evaluating language and particular ways of orienting toward and doing language. As a corrective to the blinkered language on language and language difference we've regrettably inherited from a pervasive ideology of monolingualism, I have discussed a range of relevant metaphors that are imbued with a sense of flow, movement, intricacy, messiness, and change in time and space, with notions such as transdirectionality and transcentricity at their very core. In a similar vein, many of the classical terms driving dominant monolingualist and residual multilingualist thinking and practices in mainstream language and literacy education (from competence, standards, errors, agency to the labor of readers and writers) need to be radically revised and reconstituted in ways that attend to the actuality of language as a socially defined and oriented practice. As I have pointed out in this chapter and throughout this book, English, its ongoing learning (and hence rewriting), its standards and rules, and the agency and responsibility of its (re)workers in reading and writing are always a translingual work in progress. As we continue to reflect on the implications of such evolving translingual language representations and subsequent practices on our current and future composition work, what is ever more pressing is escalating our, our students', and colleagues' awareness of and engagement with inevitable, constant translation and the cross-border traffic of languages, cultures, meanings, and functions in the production, interpretation, and evaluation of academic written texts. Placing translation in pursuit of transversality in writing at the center of a translingual way of thinking about language and cross-language relations in teaching writing is an issue I briefly touched on in this chapter and will pick up again and further extend in chapter 5.

A translingual stance turns the table on established ways of seeing and treating written English as an a priori object of mastery with an essentially stable inner core (of constant structure, lexicon, and meanings)—with diversity and difference, if acknowledged, occurring only on the edges and posing a problem to be quarantined and kept under control. These fundamental ideas about language and language difference have been promoted, legitimated, preserved in the discourse surrounding language and language difference in higher education in the United States and elsewhere, and subsequently institutionalized in particular domains of relational praxis—for example, language and language education policies, translation, pedagogy, and decisions about assessment. How seemingly irreconcilable language representations (as/and practices with language) under monolingualism, traditional multilingualism, and emerging translingualism in these different domains operate, coexist, and clash locally in superdiverse cityscapes like Beirut and Seattle will be the topic of chapters 3 and 4, respectively. Rooted firmly in critical ethnographic explorations, the following chapters take a step toward expanding our ongoing understandings—in dynamic, complex ways up, down, and sideways, much like the banyan, the urban traffic flow, and messy electric wirings—and reworkings of the contemporary material implications of tension-fraught negotiations of local language representations and practices in university-level writing, its teaching, and its learning. As we will witness in both writing program ecologies in Beirut and Seattle this book is devoted to exploring, while the "language entities" around which local language policies and writing curricula and pedagogies are designed and pursued are sociocultural, ideological inventions, the effects they have on the literate lives, experiences, and labor of actual language learners and writers (as well as their teachers) are quite serious and sometimes even damaging.

3

UNPACKING LOCAL LANGUAGE REPRESENTATIONS AND/AS PRACTICES
Portraits of Postmonolingual Tensions from Beirut

Part of a long line of French-educated family members from the heart of Ashrafieh—one of the oldest Christian cities of East Beirut—and a graduate of a prestigious French lycées in Lebanon, Lucas expressed a strong attachment and affiliation to "the language of Racine, Rousseau, Montesquieu, et Voltaire." Taking pride in being a "Francophile," he further explained: "I define myself by French. I write in French. I compose plays in French. I read in French. I think in French. I live in French. I don't know how to be honest but in French. I am sad and happy in French." In reference to centuries of French cultural and linguistic influence in Lebanon that peaked during the 1920 to 1943 mandate era, Lucas lamented the fact that a hegemonic monolingualist English-only ideology governing academic knowledge production at his current university distorted historical and existing language relations and propagated forgetfulness about the country's specific socio-historical and linguistic realities within colonialism, post-colonialism, and late modernity: "We tend to forget that English in Lebanon came AFTER French. I despise the fact that we're trying to eliminate this part of our national identity and I BLAME it on English. We have three main languages in one small country. It's a force. But we are forgetting it."

Despite Lucas's favorable dispositions toward the advanced French language and literate practices he brought with him to writing at the university, English-only demands impinged on his individual language choices and practices in writing. He described the challenges of sustaining literacies in both English and French amid English-dominated ideological structures in his American-style institution. As a pre-medical sociology student who dreamed of pursuing his medical studies in the United States one day, Lucas viewed composing in English while demonstrating fluent mastery in its standardized rules and conventions in his coursework as "hardly a choice at all" but rather "*the* obvious choice,"

DOI: 10.7330/9781607329046.c003

especially when "thinking of academic and professional opportunities in the future," though that meant "sacrificing [his] own comfort" and "giving up" his French linguistic expertise and affiliations.

Similar experiences of difficulties in upholding strong identifications with and commitments to French language and literate resources in an English-dominated playing field were described by another Christian Lebanese student, Nathalie (insisting on a French pronunciation /ˈnaˈtalē/ of her pseudonym), who was pursuing a degree in computer communications engineering and two minor degrees in math and business. This is evident in Nathalie's tension-filled negotiations of her English writing teacher's unequivocal marking of the phrase "penchant for" as an instance of language error in Nathalie's writing and of the accompanying suggestion to replace it with the more acceptable phrase "partial to" in the following sentence: "Personally, I find myself penchant for Landers's side."

I prompted Nathalie to explore her own sense of the significance she attributed to this particular choice in her reading response essay. "It's not that I structured it in French in my mind and then translated it into English" were the first words she uttered to justify her violation of proper English grammar and usage in her writing, as if attempting to dispel any associations I might make with literal translation, the strategy of non-native English speakers (NNES) who allegedly don't know any better. As she considered possible revision options based on her teacher's suggestion, Nathalie found herself, as she described, "trapped" at the crossroads of either preserving her sense of a linguistic, professional self or meeting an obligation for "correctness" in language use and leaving "a good impression on [her] academic readers." Affirming her sense of affiliation with French, she expressed a desire to cling to her original choice of the term *penchant* (which she repetitively used with a French pronunciation /pɑ̃ʃɑ̃/), as it "preserve[d] the Frenchness in [her] in [her] English writing." Tracing the etymology of the term *penchant* in the Merriam-Webster online dictionary, Nathalie pointed out to me that its origin is "French, from the present participle of *pencher* 'to incline'" and "Latin *pendere* 'to weigh.'" She explained that while "penchant" referred to a propensity resulting from an intellectual act of "careful weighing" and deliberation, the notion of "partiality" her teacher recommended induced a degree of prejudice resulting from what the dictionary definition described as "a personal and sometimes unreasoned judgment." In addition to preserving her linguistic alignments with French, her choice of the term penchant was strongly tied to her professional identity as a prospective computer engineer whose strategic decisions, as she explained, needed to be seen as based on "sound reasoning" and as countering an image of mere bias and temperament she felt her teacher's suggestion for correction projected. Despite this detailed articulation of the rhetorical goals behind her language practice, Nathalie still chose to succumb in her revised draft to the norms of formal correctness and accuracy implicit in her teacher's error correction.

Dominant segregationist representations and treatments of the language of the academy as a disembodied, preformed entity that preexists its use in various literate situations have created for Nathalie as well as Lucas a false yet classic dilemma of striking a balance between having to produce successful writing through conformity to putatively predetermined, value-free language forms and meanings, on one hand, and, on another hand, a strong desire to produce language deemed more "authentic" and "true" to one's sense of personal, academic, and professional self. Countless student writers like Lucas and Nathalie are walking into university writing classrooms every day with a wealth of dynamic language and literate resources in their repertoire, that is, the "concrete accents, language varieties, registers, genres, modalities," styles, and lexis (Blommaert 2010, 102) they deploy for performing a range of literate tasks and subject positions. However, as we shall see in the rest of this chapter, drawing on and tapping into these complexes of mobile resources in productive, agentive ways remains fraught with tensions, since such attempts get refracted through a powerful monolingual structuring principle and regulated by the deeply ingrained monolingual representations and practices of various academic gatekeepers. The persistence of such difficulties among these and other writers with different language and sociocultural profiles I introduce in this chapter demonstrates the strong grip monolingualist representations of language have over their language resources and practices in localized negotiations and constructions of meaning across difference in academic writing. As I pointed out in chapter 1, Louis-Jean Calvet (2006) argues that existing alongside these resources and "practices" with language and academic literacies are language "representations" understood as practices themselves or *in vivo, in situ* ways of thinking and acting on situations involving language, its learning, and its use(s). In addition, Calvet (2006, 241; emphasis in original) perceptively stresses the importance and significance of such rationalizations and representational practices surrounding language and its perceived structure and ongoing practice, in that they "produce in particular *security/insecurity* and this leads to types of *behavior* that transform practices" and considerably modify them in their local ecology. Sinfree Makoni and Alastair Pennycook (2007, 20, 22) make a similar point when they call for increased "local knowledge" and complex understandings of the interrelationships among what language users and learners believe about their own (and other individuals') language resources and practices, the real and situated ways they access and mobilize these resources for meaning making, and "the material effects—social, economic, and environmental—of such views and uses."

With this frame in mind, the present chapter examines *what* representations of language and language learning Beirut's young writers carry with them into their academic literacies work, *how* these representations fluctuate and interact with changing actions, identities, contexts, and ecological affordances, and *with what consequences* to their linguistic and literate life and work. In more precise terms, the current chapter highlights how multiple and often conflicting local ways of thinking about and ultimately doing English get negotiated and renegotiated in interactions with the diverse ecological contingencies of the cultural and sociolinguistic realities of the society these young writers take part in, nationwide language policies and language-in-education policies of the academic institution they attend, and curricular and pedagogical designs in the writing program or classroom space in which they operate. Before unpacking some of the complexities and contradictions encompassing my participants' language and literate learning experiences and realities from the angle of language representations intertwined with practices, it will be useful to understand the particularity of their local ecologies, which impact and in turn are impacted by the relationships among the various complexes of language resources available to them and the different ways these resources are often marshaled and mobilized for different social, rhetorical, and meaning effects or denigrated as an aberrance from a universally accepted English-only norm. I start by briefly sketching some of the contemporary language relations emerging in the streets of present-day Beirut and then move to offering an account of some of the value-laden understandings of language and language difference projected through nation-state and institutional language policy and acted upon or against in my participants' respective writing program and classrooms. As in the next chapter that presents data from Seattle, my purpose behind this broad-brush approach is by no means to offer an exhaustive description of the macro- and micro-political contexts of learning and teaching English-language and academic literacies but rather to give a general sense of some of the battling orientations toward language and its teaching, learning, and use that might have given rise to the kind of ideological tensions and contradictions my student participants had to come to terms with as they traversed various literate and social contexts.

LANGUAGE REPRESENTATIONS AND PRACTICES IN BEIRUT'S SOCIOLINGUISTIC LANDSCAPES

> The "national language" of the Lebanese people is their humanistic cosmopolitan multilingualism[1]–that is, the Lebanese are natural polyglots by definition, heredity, cultural accretions, and geographical necessity.
>
> (Salameh 2010, 46)

Emerging as a result of colonialism, emigration, and trade, language heterogeneity in a port city like Beirut[2] is perceived in the public imaginary as a source of cultural pride in that the notorious agility of Lebanese people in working within and across multiple language resources in daily functions is believed to ensure various privileges and valued cultural openness both locally and globally. Practices of shuttling between and mixing local language resources of Arabic, English, and French in ways that often mesh them all together are widely accepted as the norm rather than the exception and are viewed as a symbol of the nation's resilience and creative adaptability in an increasingly volatile and politically charged region. The country's iconic greeting of *Hi, Kifak? Ça va?* (for "Hi, how are you doing? Are you well?")—which combines the English "Hi", the Lebanese Arabic first-person singular masculine *Kifak* (or singular feminine *Kifek* or plural *Kifkon*), and the French *Ça va*—is a clear indication of what Beirut city dwellers are doing with and to their language resources and, most important, how they view and treat them not so much as discrete entities easy to pin down but rather as fluid and mobile, with porous boundaries. I have argued elsewhere (Bou Ayash 2013, 98) that this code-meshed greeting enabled Lebanese youth to actively "perform a modern, hybrid identity more aligned with the transcultural and translingual flows in the cosmopolitan Beiruti culture" and move beyond the "singular, fixed, and compartmentalized identities" that each of the English-only, Arabic-only, or French-only greetings imparted. As I moved around in one of the city's superdiverse neighborhoods, Ras Beirut,[3] where my research site is situated, it was hard to miss how the interpenetration and intermingling of various linguistic, discursive, and semiotic resources that make up Beirut's complex sociolinguistic landscapes—that is, urban Lebanese Arabic vernacular, Modern Standard Arabic[4] (written using either Arabic or Latin script), French, English, and numbers[5] to replace Arabic phonemes not

Figure 3.1. Translingual practice in Lebanese license plates

available in Latin script (see Bou Ayash 2013, 99)—appeared on various bumper stickers, greeting cards, T-shirts, and commercial license plates sold as Lebanese souvenirs and symbols of the local culture's practice-based cosmopolitanism, openness, and fluidity in cross-border connections (figure 3.1).[6]

A particularly vivid illustration of the active use of language resources and practices amid the restlessness of Beirut's street life is manifested in what Busi Makoni and Sinfree Makoni (2010, 269) refer to as the local "taxi-lingua culture."[7] City dwellers and tourists can attest to the fact that Lebanese taxicabs—the most commonly used and affordable forms of public transportation in Beirut and locally known as the shared *service* taxi (with a French pronunciation /sɛrvēs/)—are productive, mobile spaces for the most dynamic and flexible moments of language and cultural contact in everyday exchanges in the city or, say, for translingual language practices "on wheels." As they move through and around the city, local cabdrivers actively take any linguistic and communicative resources in their possession and strategically weave them together into complex linguistic and semiotic forms while negotiating meaning back and forth with passengers who've summoned them. Interestingly, drivers in the city have initiated the local language practice of attaching the Arabic dual number suffix –*ein* (the transliterated version of بين) to English or French greetings—as in Hi-*ein* (two Hi's), Hello-*ein* (two Hellos), *Bonjour-ein* (two *bonjours*), and *Bonsour-ein* (two *bounsours*)—where tourists or out-of-city visitors are greeted with not one but two salutations in keeping with the local tradition of generosity and hospitality. This translingual practice, its meaning, and its social negotiation are depicted in the following exchange, taken from a YouTube video,[8] between a Lebanese taxi driver and a curious French tourist inquiring about the driver's idiosyncratic structure of *Bonjourein*, which sounded unfamiliar to the French national's ears:

TOURIST: Taxi? Sassine?

(*Taxi stops for passenger to get in.*)

TOURIST: Bonjour.

DRIVER: Bonjour***EEEIIIN***.

TOURIST: ça veut dire quoi "Bonjourein"?

[What does "Bonjourein" mean?]

DRIVER: yi'ni deux fois marteyn. Bonjourik, Bonjourak, Bonjourkon. Deux fois Bonjourein.

[This means that you greet a female individual, a male, or a group of individuals not once but twice.]

TOURIST: Mais c'est du Libanais ou du Français?

[But is it Lebanese or French?]

DRIVER: C'est la France bas au Liban.

[It is the language of France but as practiced in Lebanon.]

(*Taxi stops at destination and passenger pays the fare as she gets off.*)

TOURIST: Alors, au revoir***EIN***.

[So, two goodbyes to you.]

DRIVER: Au revoir.

(Author transcription and translation,
La France au Liban "Taxi," Laser Films 2010)

Conveyed through a high-rising intonation with a distinctive elongated final syllable indicating a welcoming gesture, this local language creation does not simply pluralize greetings in numerical terms (one bonjour + one bonjour = two bonjours) but rather diversifies their meaning potential for intervening in the inequalities of economic transactions between willing sellers and potential buyers of labor services in a fast capitalist market. In addition to being an indication of a welcoming, courteous reception to people riding in the back of the cab, this local practice embodies an agentive shift in relations of power and labor between the driver and his customers who now operate under the new, altered dynamics of a more intimate host-guest relationship. In this sense, empowered by this localized language design, Lebanese cabdrivers rarely allow the luxury of a moment's silence or settle for mere lighthearted small talk but rather tend to continue their tradition of hospitality to the lucky "guests" who have chosen their services to get around by generously sharing their intriguing stories and life experiences with them. In the above exchange, in response to the tourist's inquiry about whether such a local language practice is "in" one language or another as conventionally defined, the Lebanese driver deliberately subverts the native French speaker's idealistic notions of language purity and authenticity and her futile search for origins. More specifically, he represents this translingual practice as involving the strategic borrowing of specific bits of French and Lebanese Arabic language resources in one's repertoire and placing them together in new collocations that produce a new set of culturally and socially specific meanings and values. As the shabby gray-haired driver speaks in terms of the re-localization of practices with language, the tourist nods enthusiastically, indicating that she is able to attribute meaning to it as a competent listener and communicator. These collaborative negotiations end with a humorous twist when the French foreigner, upon reaching her destination, shows positive uptake and creatively adopts the same translingual language practice herself as she steps out of the cab by bidding the local driver farewell with her own re-localized expression *au revoir-ein* (two byes) instead of the conventional *au revoir*.

In light of this vibrant local language situation, with the diversity of language use both a statistical and lived sociocultural reality, the translingual nature of language relations on the ground with the constant interaction and flow between and among language resources and practices came quite naturally to many of my student participants. In fact, at the onset of my fieldwork in Beirut, I often found myself responding to some students' questions about language choice and practice when participating in semi-structured interviews: "Does this have to be only in English?" "Is it all going to be in English?" "Is it okay to respond using the 'Lebanese' way, you know, like mix English with French and Arabic?"

To further illustrate the specific language practice they preferred in conducting this research, they often made direct references to the re-localized *Hi, Kifak? Ça va?* greeting, which best sums up the nature of local language relations, or what Steven Seidman (2012, 5) has eloquently described as "the making of difference and otherness" through language in Beirut.

LANGUAGE REPRESENTATIONS IN LANGUAGE AND LANGUAGE-IN-EDUCATION POLICIES

National ideological and political transformations throughout the country's history—from continuing patterns of missionary contact to French rule, independence, and an extended civil war period, followed by postwar reconstruction and economic rehabilitation—have added to the complexity of the local language and language-in-education situation, which to a certain degree continued to reverberate through many of my student participants' language representations. One of the major landmarks of language diversity in Lebanon is the introduction of French and English as foreign languages into Lebanese society through the arrival of missionaries, which started in the first half of the nineteenth century and persists to the present. Various missionaries—most prominently, the French Jesuits and the American Evangelical Protestants—introduced Western influences into the Lebanese educational system by establishing bilingual schools, which taught either French or English alongside Arabic, and various institutions of higher education throughout the country, one of which is the institution I focus on in this study.

Following the dissolution of the Turkish Ottoman Empire in the middle of the twentieth century, French colonialists strategically foregrounded their political, military, and economic presence in Lebanon with cultural and linguistic pollination (see Calvet 1998) through imposing French educational systems and a strict language policy chiefly promoting the use of French alongside Arabic as official languages, with the far-reaching dominance of the former. Though the English-medium missionary schools were far more influential upon their establishment than the French-medium ones, the status and role of the English language in Lebanon altered drastically amid the consequent French rule (Shaaban 2005, 104). After the country's independence from France followed by years of civil war, decisions about language policy in primary and secondary education were fraught with friction in a post-conflict society still torn between Arabic and Western ideological and political orientations. Language and literacy education, as Kassim Shaaban and

Ghazi Ghaith describe, became inextricably linked to religious and political affiliations, with Lebanese Christians favoring the language of their so-called protector France, most Muslims focusing on Arabic as the symbol of the country's national Arab identity and allegiance, and minority groups (like the Druzes and Greek Orthodox) who had strong ties with American Protestants preferring English as the medium of instruction (cited in Diab 2000, 178).

Aimed at promoting social cohesion in a war-affected ecology, reformed Lebanese educational policies affirmed the nation's Arab identity and harmonious relations with neighboring Arabic-speaking nations by declaring Arabic the only official language. Equal emphasis was placed on the development of literacy in French and English as foreign[9] languages in the national curricula as an attempt to simultaneously preserve strong historical ties with the ex-colonizer France and participate in the globalized economy in which English dominated. Treating all three languages as equally crucial for sociocultural engagement and economic and geopolitical openness and advancement, Lebanon's contemporary language and educational policies have shifted from (English-Arabic or French-Arabic) bilingualism to Arabic-French-English trilingualism. However, English in twenty-first-century Lebanon, as echoed in teacher and student participants' accounts below, is endowed with greater power and capital in the minds of its users/learners, though French, as Lucas pointed out earlier in this chapter, has become deeply rooted in Lebanese culture and its educational system and has historical priority over English as a legacy of colonial rule.

Not surprisingly, though the streets of the city and the particular neighborhood the American-style university, Beirut University (BU), under study here is located in are chiefly about the flow of services, bodies, ideas, language, and cultural resources as a statistical, cultural reality, the actual translingual nature of local language relations has remained largely invisible in BU's educational landscapes. BU models its educational goals, curricula, standards, and practices after American higher education systems that are dominantly shaped by a tacit language policy of English-only monolingualism. Aside from a single sentence on the homepage of the university's website that declares English as the sole language of instruction except for courses in Arabic and foreign languages, BU, like most modern Anglophone universities across the globe (see Jenkins 2014), has no official language policy that it explicitly integrates as part of its mission statement or educational philosophy or that recognizes the wealth of languages used alongside English on and beyond its campus grounds.

BU's past and contemporary institutional language policies have not been immune to the messiness and complexity of language politics at a national level. When BU was first established, for instance, Arabic was the sole language of instruction, and English and French were taught as foreign languages. This official shift in the language of instruction at BU from Arabic-only[10] to English-only occurred gradually over the ten-year period 1873–83. As one of its presidents back then stated in an annual report, the importance of this radical transformation in light of "the demands of the times" lay in exposing students to English as a critical tool for "direct access to the wealth of literary, scientific and philosophical works" (cited in Jeha 2004, 112–13). However, in order not to run the risk of linking the value of intellectual work at BU to English-only knowledge production, this university president showed in his reflection on this new English-only language policy a high degree of commitment to acknowledging and valuing the specificity and distinctiveness of Lebanese sociolinguistic landscapes: "But we do not forget that we are within the borders of the great Arabic-speaking world . . . our higher standing is not obtained at the expense of the Arabic, but *the two* [languages] *are advancing together*" (Burns 1963; emphasis added).

Particularly noteworthy is how these representations of language relations in pre-colonial Lebanese society were apparent in the president's own writing practices of mixing both languages, as demonstrated in one of his personal correspondences in 1873: "By taking two or three goatskins—such as they carry *samni* [cooking fat] in and inflating them one can go with perfect safety . . . We were intending to go up to the Quarry where we are getting out *blat* [stone paving-blocks] . . . After lunch I returned to Beirut, went to the *warshy* [construction site] and found all going well" (cited in Rugh, Rugh, and Howell 1994, 66 author translation in square brackets).

More than a century after the president's report, though both languages continue to be "advancing together" at BU, they do so in separate trajectories in educational landscapes, with the exception of courses on the theory and practice of translation offered by the English Department and the Department of Arabic and Near Eastern Languages (see chapter 5 for more on such translation instruction). While official national-level language polices show sensitivity toward local sociolinguistic realities, position English in relation to existing language resources, and aim to expand the linguistic repertoire of members of Lebanese society, my student participants' perspectives about language relations and language use in writing that I describe in this chapter point to dominant institutional and programmatic efforts toward the containment of language difference. Particularly, the overwhelming majority of my student participants were anxious about BU's "correct use of language" policy statement in the 2011–12 undergraduate academic catalog, which represented "clear, correct, and responsible use" of English as a "basic requirement for graduation" and cautioned against "substandard written or oral expression." "Your bad English can make you fail a course," one biology pre-medicine student explained to me. Terms like "clear," "correct," and "responsible" used in reference to the *kind* of English deemed appropriate for academic engagement on campus are not (perhaps ironically) clearly defined, and students are left to draw their own conclusions about what such contested qualifiers might mean, most likely in association with a native-like English benchmark. When it came to the preferred form of academic English work faculty members had in mind, there was usually little ambiguity. One of my writing teacher participants, for instance, explicitly described an alignment between her individual characterizations of "good" and "effective" student writing and those of the larger institution she worked for as "something that a native English speaker [NES] can fully understand and make sense of." Lurking behind this institutional policy statement are monolingualist representations that propagate among students and faculty a normalized view of "correct," "good" forms of language use following NES norms as self-evidently desirable and of significant forms of language difference in writing (or "substandard" English) as anomalies or signs of unwitting technical failure to be obliterated and overcome.

LANGUAGE REPRESENTATIONS AND PRACTICES IN THE FIRST-YEAR WRITING PROGRAM

Though the label of "American-style" in reference to institutional and writing program ecologies inherently carries with it a "baggage of linguistic and cultural imperialism" (Schaub 2003, 89), writing instruction at BU has to some extent managed to cater to the particularity of the local educational and sociolinguistic context by generally moving away from uncritical exportations of Anglo-American textbooks and writing handbooks.[11] BU's first-year writing (FYW) program adopts a custom-published composition reader as a collaborative project between teachers and students whose diverse voices are in conversation with the texts. Various editions of this reader have incorporated reading materials on topics of local relevance to contemporary Arab youth or reading selections characterized by their inclusion of a meshing of languages, language varieties, and writing genres, such as Judith Ortiz Cofer's "Volar" or "May He Be Bilingual" and Luc Sante's "Lingua Franca." Much like the institution it is situated in and serves, the writing program, however, lacks explicit, straightforward statements on language, its effective use, and its learning both on its official website and in instructional materials. Despite efforts toward embracing and accommodating the uniqueness of local language and cultural diversity at the level of textbook development and design, still circulating within this writing program culture were perceptions about the centrality, fixity, and oneness of English in academic written discourse and general monolingual tendencies to obscure, pathologize, background, and curtail alternative language usages and meanings.

Most of the writing teachers at BU were Lebanese nationals with graduate degrees in English language or literature or in education, many of which were earned at this institution or abroad, with more Anglo-American teachers hired in recent years. During my fieldwork at BU, it was obvious that a large number of the writing teachers I interviewed were frustrated by the natural presence and use of students' toolkit of language resources in their written texts. As the following complaints illustrate, most of these teachers expressed annoyance with what they diagnosed to be traces of translation from Arabic, French, and Englishes into academic English writings:

> The translation [in student writing] kills me. You could hear the French and Arabic throughout.
> They [students] don't write in English but in Anglicized Arabic or French or if they do write in English, it is usually internet slang English.

With translation and cross-language relations in writing generally perceived as "*the* number-one enemy" in university-level language and literacy learning, in the words of one teacher, the majority of the writing teachers I interviewed prohibited any traces of non-English-language practices in English syntax, semantics, or lexicon and were uncompromising in their demand that students maintain the status quo by conforming to putatively fixed Standard Written English (SWE) rules and conventions. Viewing SWE as an impenetrable monolith and "immune," as another teacher declared, to language contact and change, these writing teachers showed strong pedagogical allegiance to indoctrinating a static, uniform set of standardized writing conventions and practices. "This is not how we write in English," "Think in English," "Stop thinking in Arabic or French" were among some of the responses they reported adopting to safeguard against the proliferation of non-standard discursive and linguistic practices, which are vibrant in sociolinguistic landscapes, into student writing. These "wakeup calls" for writing development, one teacher claimed, helped "expunge" the use of written English in the context of other languages and language practices in a linguistically and culturally diverse classroom. Such monolingualist pedagogical orientations, as echoed in the above suggestions to students, posit a stable core to English, as if it were a hermetically sealed entity on its own to be fully mastered and fluently learned in the writing classroom only in its own presence, divorced from the sociocultural ecologies and identities that bring it about and give it meaning. As far as students' chances of joining the global traffic of language resources and consequential meanings and sociocultural relations (as described in chapter 2) through English in their written work, the highway is blocked solid.

From a different point of view but still striking a similar chord, a handful of writing teachers demonstrated more sensitivity and tolerance toward the emergence of language difference in student writing, which one teacher perceived as "pointless to resist." Confronted by ideological conditions and linguistic hierarchies largely not of their own making and for which they often felt unprepared, these teachers reported adopting the common FYW pedagogical practice of engaging only in oral discussions with the fluid, hybrid character of English usage evident in assigned readings from the course reader, but they had reservations against allowing their students to demonstrate similar agentive deployments of diverse language resources in their own writings. Fairly aware of the dynamic flow of language and semiotic resources in students' sociolinguistic realities and experiences, one of these teachers echoed concerns that local translingual practices did not carry sufficient symbolic power in the academy and among its gatekeepers to be legitimized in student work: "I don't know to what extent that is accepted by the language police like grammarians, textbook authors. I don't feel I have the authority." In the name of what another teacher described as faithfulness to a fixed "community of minds" with equally fixed, identifiable, and definable practices, these teachers relentlessly tended to bracket away the constant and necessary mediation and traffic among various language resources in actual practice in favor of the illusion of SWE as stable, neutral, and separate from those resources and the identities that refashion them in the doing. As I've pointed out previously, such multilingualist approaches to teaching writing remain shallow in their commitment to language heterogeneity and hybridity and residually maintain a monolingualist English-only mind-set. In fact, they only quantitatively validate and represent languages—which are reduced to discrete, bounded, and quantifiable entities in textual materials—without giving the responsibility and perpetual need for qualitatively countering such dominant representations of languages, which contribute to immobilizing their continuous practice and difference in the first place, the attention they deserve and require.

POSTMONOLINGUAL TENSIONS IN STUDENT WRITERS' TESTIMONIES

Within this institutional and programmatic setting, the majority of my student participants had a strong desire to mobilize the dynamic flow of the language resources and ways of using English they viewed as essential to their literate sense-making in and beyond the FYW classroom context, a desire authorized by the translingual nature of language relations in sociolinguistic landscapes and national language policy. At the same time, they expressed shared concerns that their abilities to uphold such a desire got complicated, even stifled, by institutionalized representations of proper language usage in academic written English work as relatively fixed and insular. In unpacking how they differently reconciled these conflicting understandings of and workings with language and language use, I particularly emphasize the considerable impact of what I am referring to here as a range of *language ideology brokers*[12] in local ecologies—namely, parents, family and community members, peers, language policymakers, teachers, and so on—in either impeding or fostering these students' abilities to move with ease and confidence within and across language and semiotic resources in literate situations.

As will be clear in the analysis below, some students explicitly identified parental beliefs and language socialization practices—consciously and otherwise (sometimes predetermined by economic or [geo]political forces beyond parents' control)—as having potentially significant effects on how they oriented to what languages or forms of language they drew on and produced in various literacy learning situations. University teachers' involvement in shaping the extent to which students' engagement with their toolkit of language resources in their repertoires would ebb and flow was also acknowledged. Some students' accounts pointed toward stark contrasts between the understandings about language, language use, and language relations associated with their disciplinary work at the university and projected futures, on one hand, and what they routinely experienced in their FYW courses, on another hand. For instance, while they believed to be locked into an apparently single, universal style and form of written language usage in FYW, they spoke of various disciplinary orientations and interventions directly impacting their perceptions of the importance of working with language as fluid and malleable for effectively producing and communicating disciplinary-specific knowledge (namely, in civil engineering, graphic design, nursing, sociology, and psychology) in various composing tasks. Other students seemed to succeed in finding ways to work nimbly between the cracks of imposed English-only imperatives guiding FYW instruction and quietly destabilize them. Reconfiguring dominant language relations in English writing classroom and turning them to their own advantage, these students reported that code-meshing and incorporating non-Anglophone academic sources (namely, Arabic, Spanish, French, or Italian) were essential meaning-making practices in their academic literacies work.

In the sections below, I present the experiences of Nathalie, Naser, Lucas, Diva, and KAPPA as they moved between fluid and fixed understandings and uses of language generally and written English particularly in their ever-dynamic writing lives and work. Highlighting some of the struggles and successes they experienced while navigating the postmonolingual tensions of learning academic reading and writing, I demonstrate how the cluster of ideas and images about the nature of language and what constituted competent language use in writing that they accumulated over time and brought with them into their various literate encounters appeared to be heterogeneous and highly contingent on social and pedagogical affordances. More specifically, the abilities of some of these student writers to utilize and expand their available resources were constrained by dominant and residual monolingualist representations underlying family experiences, institutional policies, and FYW teaching practices—representations of English as a discrete, autonomous entity that masked their actual experience of the flexibility and permeability of language. In contrast, the fact that such established views were countered by the translingual representations of other student writers and influential language ideology brokers in their surrounds seemed to facilitate these writers' engagement with the full multiplicity of their language resources and with cross-language relations in writing. The analysis this section offers therefore underscores the need for continuous work toward the development of complex translingual repertoires among FYW students by primarily targeting the side of language representations that affects both our own professional practices and students' concomitant engagements with intra- and inter-language difference in academic writing, hence the potential for considerable change and transformation in the way(s) language relations are imagined and put into action in local writing program and classroom ecologies.

English as Flawless and Flow-less

Every time Nathalie had to wake up in the early hours of dawn to make the several-hour bus ride from her northeastern town to her university campus through one of the country's most massive traffic jams on the Zouk-Centre Ville highway when a prestigious, more affordable French-medium university was in the near vicinity of her residence, her father's words rang in her ears: "English is the language of technology, science, and business. The whole future is in English." Like Lucas, to whom continuing his postsecondary studies in the French educational system was "useless" for his academic and career prospects and the need to "master English" was unavoidable, Nathalie had strong hopes that those treks, with all the physical and financial trouble she endured to get to BU, would be symbolically and materially rewarded in the long run. Joining the well-documented struggles of countless English language and literacy learners from various walks of life in other geographic locations with globally driven economies (see Prendergast 2008; Pedersen 2010; Kapp 2012; Lu 2010; Gentil 2005; Ivanič 1998), Nathalie articulated a familiar sense of ambivalence, frustration, and insecurity in learning English amid complex meso-political language negotiations.

Constant pressures from her father have led Nathalie to perceive English as a "commoditised, containerized" entity (Luke 1996, 322) with cultural and political neutrality and a universally high exchange value under the logic of capital conversion within and across various linguistic and educational markets (cf. Rubdy and Tan 2008). By gaining access to the "right" language and "right" way of using that language at a university adopting the "right" linguistic medium of instruction, despite its inconvenient location and costly tuition, Nathalie had a strong desire to "move up very quickly" (Prendergast 2008, 94) and "buy . . . her way into" (Luke 1996, 327) highly mobile social and professional networks. The putatively durable ontology of the right "brand of English" (Prendergast 2008, 8), in this case EAE, and its unquestioned hegemony in Nathalie's imagination ultimately made it the very and perhaps sole "lubricant," as Prendergast (2008, 127) convincingly puts it, for aspired transnational mobilities and connections. But because of the central importance Nathalie attached to "perfection" in English-language usages and forms, she had great fears and insecurities that she did not possess a sufficient level of proficiency to secure such promised mobility: "I love to go abroad for new engineering projects and meet new people in my field. I want to attend conferences and discuss my ideas in the United States and Canada and be a link with my Arabic world. And I don't want my language to be the barrier." In fact, she recalled how during her first year in the engineering program, one of her esteemed professors was a target for collective ridicule from the so-called English-educated engineering students in her cohort for his non-standard English pronunciation and usage in both his lectures and final project prompt. In Nathalie's words: "I don't want to become like him. I feel ashamed when I make language mistakes when speaking and writing in English. I won't be satisfied with myself. I'm always concerned about sounding correct. Correctness in my opinion is the ONLY way to get my ideas delivered the way I want them to. At [BU] and in the future, if your language pronunciation is weak, people won't take you seriously. *El Anglais bta3ti wahra w byi7termooni aktar* [Correct English grants its users (Nathalie among them) the veneration and respect of others]."[13] As Nathalie described, it was a shocking experience for her to witness how even a senior engineering professor who possessed high cultural and economic capital was forced to deal with the consequences of utilizing devalued language and literate practices in the context of local-global linguistic mobility. Confirming her father's representations of the primacy of native-like English both inside and outside the local national context, this incident reminded Nathalie of the prestige, "image, respect, and everything else" that full or advanced competence (if even achievable) in English-language and literate communication might potentially confer in social, academic, and professional circles. Her near-automatic conflation of English-language and literate competence with native-like correctness, accuracy, and fluent mastery in the reproduction of standardized usages and conventions clearly emerged from the above quotation.

In addition to the impact her peers' reaction to her professor's pronunciation and spelling mistakes had on the high premium she placed on automaticity and proficiency in her literacy learning and development, Nathalie's convictions were perhaps also stemming from the value accorded to such skills in her English teacher's written feedback and assessments. For one of our prolonged conversations about her academic written work, for instance, Nathalie brought a pile of essays and short reading response assignments from her English classes, asking for my advice on how to best address all the markings and written comments her teacher had provided. Most of them seemed to point to Nathalie's ways of using English in writing: "Please visit the writing center at [BU]. It will help you a lot"; "Avoid language mistakes"; "Revise language use"; "Needs more revision for awkward wording." As she attempted to make sense of these suggestions, Nathalie was helplessly searching for some magical solution, which in her mind would be "fast enough for [her] language to improve" in ways that would be perceived by her teacher and peers as grammatically, lexically, or stylistically correct and appropriate.

Nathalie, who after a French-medium primary and secondary education was thrown rather dramatically into an American English-only educational system and academic culture with which she was unfamiliar, seemed to be experiencing what Roz Ivanič (1998, 7) has described as "crises of confidence." The set of corporeal metaphors of "hitting a wall," feeling "trapped," and "swallow[ing]" and almost choking on "a rock" that she adopted best crystallized her lived experiences with academic English language and literacy learning in compliance with monolingual English-only demands at her university: "**I always feel I'm hitting a wall** when I have an idea and I can't write it in a good way that is satisfying to my English teacher . . . **I feel trapped** because I don't know what to do." Nathalie was clearly influenced by monolingualist representations of English as a single, discrete, stable, and uniform set of practices to be fully mastered, implicit in her teacher's comments on her writing and her father's insistence on the promise of native-like English for improved academic and career prospects. As a result, she viewed moments of language difference in her academic written texts as serious indications of a lack of conformity, hence personal failings and severe deficiencies in her language and literate competence. Holding on to a reductive view of English as a hermetically sealed individual possession with a fixed set of rules and conventions she needed to blindly honor and reproduce for her own academic and professional success, Nathalie placed so much emphasis on her degree of competence in academic reading and writing as an individualized capacity and a matter of getting standardized linguistic and notational practices either right or wrong.

Recalling her initial excitement to be joining her current American-centric university, Nathalie was surprised to find that the institution's goal of socializing its student population into an English-dominated intellectual environment clashed with her expectations for a greater presence of other vibrant local language resources. Nathalie tried hard to make sense of this clear disconnect between the primacy of translingual language relations both in the popular imaginary and in day-to-day experiences in Lebanese society and the current monolingual state of language relations in the overall design of her institution's curricula: "I'm starting to forget the French language at [BU]. I'm trying to **recover what I've lost and maintain my proficiency level** by reading more French books . . . I thought I would be **gaining another language**. But now, I am losing one to another. French keeps getting far. I've realized recently that I'm **losing this connection with French**. But I don't want to lose it. It represents my childhood, a phase in my life when I was at school." It is clear from Nathalie's articulated concerns that a reductive yet prominent ideology of subtractive multilingualism retained a powerful hold on her literacy learning, with the primacy of English at her university curtailing, in her view, the development of her existing French language and literate resources.

As she complained about the absence of institutional and instructional resources for developing her advanced French academic literacies, which tied together her present and past literate experiences, Nathalie spoke in terms of maintenance and loss as if her language resources were discrete entities to be locked away and accessed again at different times, places, and spaces of her literate life. She seemed to conceive of the English- and French-language resources in her repertoire and her competencies in using them "as separate containers, side by side, that are more or less full or empty" (Prinsloo 2012, 28). More specifically, learning English, in Nathalie's view, seemed to be at best a numerical addition to her knowledge of French. The only alternative she could imagine to the demanded English-only academic labor at her university was a traditional multilingual model whereby her French academic literacies would develop alongside English, yet with both advancing in disparate, insular academic spheres and non-intersecting trajectories. The possibility of actively reworking English itself as well as her current and emerging engagements with English in light of her strong, continual relations with French was never acknowledged or legitimized in FYW pedagogy and curriculum design at her institution and thereby in Nathalie's own imagination. Overall, her father's explicit representations of English and her peers' reaction to language errors in oral and written communication, combined with her teacher's covert representations in writing assessment and feedback, reinforced Nathalie's monolingualist view of language where neither English nor French was imagined as constantly changing, internally diverse, and flowing into and out of one another.

(Im)Mobile Languages-in-Use: Disciplinary versus First-Year Academic Literacies
Naser from Haret-Hreik, a predominantly Shi'ite town in the southern suburbs of Beirut, had a lifelong passion for visual design and Arabic calligraphy. Exposing him to the intricacies of the Arabic language on a day-to-day basis, Naser's father, an Arabic language and literature professor, was an active agent in informally socializing Naser into the language of his Islamic faith and the marker of Arab unity and identity through

engagement in various language-mediated activities at home, such as the voracious reading of scripture and poetry and sometimes even direct instruction in Modern Standard Arabic syntax and stylistics. Naser explicitly expressed his linguistic and literate attachment to Arabic and viewed it as a means for developing and maintaining meaningful and authentic aspects of his relations to the self, others, and the world: "I define myself by Arabic. I write in Arabic. I read literature in Arabic. I think, live in Arabic."

Given his close connection to the Arabic language, which reaffirmed both his religious and national identity, Naser spoke with enthusiasm about the meaningfulness and relevance of his everyday disciplinary labor, which allowed him to strike a balance between a curiosity to learn the practices and principles of modern design and his expertise in Arabic academic literacies. As a first-year graphic design student, Naser was fond of several projects he was working on, particularly because the professor in one of his major courses created spaces for all participating students to mobilize their expertise in various languages and modalities distinct from the language of instruction and dominant mono-modal composition practices at the university while demonstrating their understanding of design-related concepts, principles, and techniques. For one of his projects, for instance, Naser described creating a typographic illustration of the various meanings of Arabic words of his choice while experimenting with different design decisions—such as typeface, type size, color, contrast, scale, orientation, placement on the page, and so on—to produce particular communicative and aesthetic effects (figure 3.2). For another project, he composed a travel narrative of his movements and interactions in the cityscapes of Beirut. In one of his accounts of social encounters in Beirut's metropolitan life, as depicted in figure 3.3, his strategic choice of handwritten Arabic text and hand-drawn watercolors with specific details intentionally excluded from the sketch, as Naser argued, added a sense of fluidity, vagueness, crudeness, and un-finishedness to his artwork and designs.

At the time, Naser was also working on an autobiography about his individual experiences studying at the department of architecture and design in which he juxtaposed Arabic text with computer-generated minimalist black-and-white images in the basic narrative frame (portions of which are represented in figure 3.4). Using simple, impressionistic illustrations with a two-color palette, Naser represented himself in the first panel in relation to other graphic design students in his cohort as part of a collection of undistinguished, faceless miniature black figurines amid the expanse of white space—like mere copies of one another in

Figure 3.2. Experimenting with design practices and functions

their vast field of study. "I am just another communication arts student in this program; there's nothing special about me or the space I occupy," he wrote (my translation). However, after a series of panels documenting his experiences of growth and self-actualization as a young graphic designer who possessed alternative linguistic and semiotic resources at an Anglophone university where the hegemony and centrality of English could not be ignored, Naser's visual representation of his academic and professional identity in the concluding panel transformed into a white radiant figurine positioned at the corner of the contrasting black space he occupied, as if ready to break free from seeming conformity and similarity in relation to his surroundings.

Graphic design professors in Naser's discipline showed an appreciation for and awareness of the meaning-making potential of his language, cultural, and semiotic crossings and how they could benefit his designs, his sense of agency and versatility as a young contemporary designer,

Figure 3.3. A memoir of urban explorations

Figure 3.4. Graphic narrative for major course project

and his aspirations for a future career at a local or regional marketing and branding agency. Presented with pedagogical affordances and opportunities to imagine and experience the mobility and fluidity of language and semiotic resources in academic disciplinary literacies, Naser was able to treat language (and modality) as dynamic and malleable, involving and requiring design and redesign for functional and aesthetic effects; thereby he enacted the situated practice of meshing the full multiplicity of his meaning-making resources to his own advantage. However, as he transitioned from this supportive literate learning environment into his afternoon English writing classes, Naser had to automatically adjust to the reallocation of value to the advanced Arabic language and literate resources and graphic competencies he brought with him into his academic English work, as they appeared to have restrictive mobility in that particular space. The undergraduate writing and languaging tasks Naser engaged in in specialized disciplinary courses in ways that were productively networked across his home, university, and future work life contrasted sharply with a dominant approach to language and literacy in his English writing courses as discrete from learners, their changing local ecologies, and diverse meaning-making resources. While his undergraduate program's translingual orientations to language, language relations, and language use in the communication arts influenced his perceptions and mobilizations of the wealth of resources at his disposal as accessible and valuable for deepening his disciplinary knowledge, Naser's sense of the non-negotiable, unchangeable nature of English in FYW limited his view of what he might be able to do with his developing English-language resources and what his working relation with such doings might be.

Influenced by a dominant monolingual valuation of native-like correctness and efficiency in the reproduction of standardized usages and conventions in the FYW classroom, Naser explained that, in his view, effective English language and literate practices required that he fully "separate and isolate" his personal linguistic and cultural affiliations. As Naser asserted, "Through English, [he] can't go back to [his] definition of writing [in Arabic] as autobiography, reflection, creativity, and authenticity." With his individual writerly voice or "the capacity for semiotic mobility" (Blommaert 2005, 69) constrained, Naser stated that he felt compelled—much like Nathalie—to uncritically follow "the few right things" from a clearly defined, fixed "set of skills [he had] to learn," master, and "choose from them as they are." In essence, Naser's monolingualist view of English as a monolithic, well-fortified entity prevented him from seeing any opportunities to rework his developing knowledge of written English as itself necessitating and undergoing constant design and redesign.

Naser's difficulties in navigating these conflicting representations of language and language relations and subsequent demands over the nature of language use associated with academic and disciplinary literacies led him to speak out in a plea for writing teachers not to "detach us [him and his classmates] from our native language like this in the English writing course when we're daily exploring the world through Arabic . . . Arabic provides a larger context I can work with even in graphic design and not like English where **I have really narrow spaces**." Naser seemed to experience and exercise Arabic with his father at home as well as in his graphic design work and English in academic literacies at school as unproblematically compartmentalized, autonomized, and self-standing entities never fluid in relation to each other. As such, he talked about a conventional multilingualist view of language relations as the sole answer to his current problem in FYW, that is, a numerically pluralized approach that simply accommodated both English and Arabic, but with both occupying segregated spaces with well-defined impermeable boundaries.

Felt tensions when negotiating discontinuities between the translingual nature of language use associated with specialized disciplinary discourses and literacies and deeply entrenched monolingualist assumptions about language fixity and rigidity in university-wide FYW courses also played out in Lucas's accounts of his academic literacy learning and development. Lucas described making a conscious decision to only enroll in FYW course sections taught by native-speaking American instructors who in his mind were guaranteed to demonstrate and model "perfection in accent and fluency." With producing anything but impeccable language and literate usage viewed as a sign of "personal failure" in Lucas's eyes, he expressed a great deal of anger and disappointment that his English writing teacher constantly "correct[ed his] English grammar" and usage. Lucas was utterly shocked that his English language and literate resources and practices did not move well across boundaries of academic disciplines and programs at his Anglophone university. In fact, the language and literate resources and practices he had previously learned and picked up through reading scholarly texts by disciplinary specialists were refracted through, regulated, and re-valued by yet another educational marketplace of academic textual production and reception in FYW program ecologies under which the same material or symbolic value and significance of his language practices did not necessarily "make the journey" (Leonard 2013, 31). As he complained,

[English teacher's name] would go on and on about saying that I should not have long sentences whereas in sociology, for example, if you read Weber who is infamous for his extremely long and complicated sentences, that's all you read. He speaks gold. He's one of the fathers of sociology. He is the worst of the worst when it comes to that and it's not incorrect; it's style ... I've been really angry about this for months ... For [this teacher] to tell me that my sentences need to be short, so short to the extent that I can't be stylistically eloquent, is **academic genocide** if you want.

With extensive reference in the above excerpt to the writing practices of German sociologist Max Weber, whose scholarly work has profoundly influenced Lucas's sense of his own relation to social theory and research writing, Lucas seemed to allude to the fact that different underlying disciplinary values were embodied in such stylistic and rhetorical variation, value systems he felt writing pedagogies and assessments in his FYW class did not attend to. Such compartmentalization of literate performances and knowledges along curricular and programmatic lines further foregrounded how the dominant valuation of efficiency, concision, and transparency as putatively universal attributes of written communication that seemed to inform his writing teacher's expectations clashed starkly with a more local discipline-related economy of writing in which the practice of adopting long, wordy, and dense English sentences could pass as good, intellectually hefty, and sophisticated expository prose.

As both Naser and Lucas moved among courses within the same institutional ecology, the act of mobilizing the wealth of language resources and practices in their repertoire, which received relatively quick uptake in their disciplinary discourses and work, became sticky and tension-ridden in the FYW classroom. Experiencing such language-ideological disjunctures and contradictions firsthand, they each realized that the translingual and transmodal practices fully credentialed in their respective specialized disciplines (either through responsive pedagogical orientations and approaches or leading scholarly work) were no longer valued meaning-making resources they could potentially capitalize on but rather a liability in their academic English written work.

Thinking and Writing (in) English as Translation
In constructing and enacting their language and literate identities, Nathalie, Naser, and Lucas found it challenging to negotiate between dominant representations of the fixity and boundedness of English in the FYW classroom and alternative representations in their society or specific disciplines. In contrast, my next two participants were much more successful in asserting their agency and making a conscious

decision, though at their own personal risk, to treat and rework English in relation to their other language resources as fundamentally hybrid, mobile, and open to translation in their written texts. Armed with a translingual view of English that their family experiences of heightened geographic and linguistic mobility afforded them, both Diva and KAPPA managed to deliberately shift and intervene with English-only norms of language usage in FYW through demonstrating an active search for productive sites for engaging in translingual practice in their academic written work.

Diva lived most of her life in Greece and had recently moved to her father's home country, Lebanon, to pursue her postsecondary education. As she was part of a linguistically and culturally complex household in which the nature of language relations and language usage was neither stable nor predictable, handling complex language and communicative negotiations with a Greek non-Arabic-speaking mother and a Lebanese non-Greek-speaking father came naturally to Diva. Describing how she grew up seeing and practicing English as a link language across family members with diverse language resources, worldviews, and identities, she stated that "there are these two sides in [her], Arabic and Greek, and English is in the middle; and it's just what keeps [her] and [her] family together." Diva's parents encouraged her to develop proficiency in English, which contributed to "bind[ing] . . . and bring[ing] everyone closer"; in Greek, which gave her a sense of "uniqueness" and "privacy" in an English-dominated world where "almost everyone nowadays knows English"; and in Arabic, which represented "the Arab in [her]." Describing her constant engagement with the total complex of her concrete language resources in everyday language and literate practices, Diva explained that "I cannot communicate in English only. Nor can I communicate in Greek and Arabic alone. My sentences don't make sense to me at least. Right now, **I live, think, and write in all: Greek, Arabic, and English**." Diva further reaffirmed that it was really "important" for her to "write in this style," which meshed *all* the language resources accessible to her, because "it is only this way of using English that keeps [her] together." Given how much this fluidity and heterogeneity of her language usage mattered to her sense of self even in local educational landscapes, Diva complained that a tacit policy of English-only dominating academic writing pedagogies and practices in her English writing class was clearly at odds with the naturalness and meaningfulness of such cross-language relations in her and her classmates' sociolinguistic realities and lived experiences: "We shouldn't be limited by what we should say and how we should say it. We're in an

American university but it's all based in Lebanon. *Yi3ni* [in fact] we've based our knowledge in different languages. This is how we live: in English AND other languages."

Diva's representation of the full multiplicity of her language resources as intermingling and co-dependent for literate meaning making in both sociolinguistic and educational landscapes influenced her sense of ownership over her resources and the way she put these resources into work in her English literacy practices. In composing a short reading response paper for her FYW course, for example, she showed a strong commitment toward tapping into the full spectrum of rhetorical and linguistic resources and sociocultural meanings available to her: "What goes in my mind is a mixture of words, *kalimet*—words that make me think in a certain way so that I'm able to express myself *les kai*—as if it is all some universal language. What goes on in my head when thinking or when I'm speaking to someone is just a list of words. Three languages, one meaning—what they mean to me. I could feel detached, *ma ile jledit hada, kai den thelo na kano tipota*. For I don't want to do anything."

In her opening paragraph, Diva used the term *words* followed by its Lebanese Arabic translation *kalimet* and the Greek phrase *les kai* with its English translation "as if." Considered in relation to SWE conventions, Diva's use of "words, *kalimet*" in the above quotation would be marked out as needlessly redundant and inefficient. However, read as emergent from the context of Diva's idiosyncratic writerly voice and the sociocultural particularity of her local ecologies, the term *words* and its colloquial Lebanese Arabic equivalent, as Diva explained, were no longer interchangeable in her own writing. In fact, the Romanized Lebanese Arabic *kalimet* acquired new meanings and dimensions and moved beyond what the English term *words* in its vicinity could express. As Diva further explained the kind of transversality she was hoping to produce in her writing, she argued that "the English term *words* is so plain; it's just words. But when I think of the Arabic *kalimet*, I think of the authentic Lebanese *jaw* [atmosphere] with its defiantly frivolous ambiance even during the worst of times. The Arabic *kalimet*, is so *m3ajja2a* [crowded with meanings], you can feel the life inside of it." In this sense, Diva's alternative interpretation of *kalimet*, which diverged from its more normative meaning, echoed what she described as the defiant cosmopolitan outlook of Lebanese culture, which she saw as constantly grappling with open local and regional political tensions yet demonstrating an unusual joie de vivre. What is particularly worthy of our attention here is that Diva did not simply multiply the number of languages in her writing, as a traditional multilingualist ideology would have it, but was more concerned about emphasizing the "crowdedness" and traffic of meanings or transversality such translingual work and engagement with her language resources allowed her to achieve. In more precise terms, Diva took the qualitative difference in meanings and sociocultural relations in her language use as seriously as the numerical plurality of her languages-in-use.

As she introduced non-English resources into the rest of her text without providing direct English translations for them, Diva deliberately utilized indirect rhetorical cues in her writing to assist her non-Arabic- and non-Greek-speaking readers. Showing signs of actively accommodating her readers and aiding their co-construction of meaning, Diva made sure her English phrase "For I don't want to do anything" at the end of her opening paragraph served as a loose translation of the transliterated Lebanese Arabic phrase *ma ile jledit hada* (ما الي جلادة حدا) 'I'm not in the mood for anything' and the transliterated Greek phrase *kai den thelo na kano tipota* (και δεν θελω να κανω τιποτα) 'I don't want to do anything' (based on Diva's translation and interpretation here). In response to my question about how she maneuvered and navigated such translingual practices in her essay in a considerably narrow space of academic uptake under imposed English-only imperatives, Diva asserted that she knew "it's a big risk writing like this in an English class, but you just have to do it sometimes" as a highly meaningful and embodied performance of the hybridity of ones' personal and academic identity.

Despite holding strong convictions about her felt need to treat English as dynamic and constantly changing and changeable in her own writing, Diva was aware of the lack of favorable conditions for a desired uptake in relation to her translingual language representations and practices. In fact, she remained attuned to the complex dynamics of power and the global economies of academic textual production and reception that forcibly permeated her own linguistic and semiotic mobilities. Diva was cognizant that the translingual language representations and practices she developed in contact zones outside the confines of the FYW classroom were in tension with dominant monolingualist representations and the preferred academic literacy practices they dictated, representations that neglected the fluid, hybrid character of English and the agency of writers like herself in constantly putting it to work as such. As Diva negotiated this constellation of contradictory representations and practices, the significance and value she originally attributed to cross-language relations and the emerging forms of language usage in her writing had to be recalibrated in the high-stakes "game" of academic writing for success at her university. Coming to the realization that "there's no [more] room for taking risks" with her "own way of using English" in academic written work, Diva felt the need to "play it safe" in her final research paper on anti-domestic violence laws in Lebanon and meet her instructor's dominant expectations in order to pass the course, maintain her grade-point average, and move on with her academic career. Carefully weighing the risks and rewards of maintaining her preferred ways of making meaning in the writing classroom, Diva made a conscious decision to perform language and identity in her writing in ways that steered clear of any recognizable signs of difference or the blending of her multiple language and cultural resources. In Diva's complex negotiations of the affordances and constraints of her local writing ecologies, this process of give and take was a crucial part of navigating her diverse language and cultural resources under competing representations of language, language usage, and language relations.

I now turn to the experiences of KAPPA, who, much like Diva, moved between and across a wealth of vibrant language resources in his everyday language and literate experiences. I met KAPPA through a teacher contact who put me in touch with him. He was majoring in landscape design at the time and later informed me that he had transferred into the graphic design program. KAPPA grew up reading and writing Latin, Italian, and French texts at home and at school in his hometown of Trieste in northeastern Italy before briefly moving to Lebanon to live with his aunt while attending the university. KAPPA's Lebanese mother and grandparents piqued his interest in the works of Lebanese writers, like Amin Maalouf in French and Gibran Khalil Gibran in English, while his Italian father exposed him to Italian literary masterpieces by Dante and Sicilian novelist Leonardo Sciascia.

Born into a family of globe-trotting diplomats and intellectuals who shuttled back and forth among Italy, France, and Lebanon, KAPPA was socialized into appreciating his diverse language resources and investing his time and energy in further advancing his academic literacies in English, French, Italian, and Latin. KAPPA described seeing his English academic work in the FYW classroom as always in relation to the rich tapestry of the vibrant language and literate resources in his repertoire, which he has come to call his "*modo di dire*," or his unique "way of saying and communicating things." In Kappa's own words, "This *modo di dire* makes me smile. **I feel my English is enclosed in rigid structures** and sometimes **it's nice to break the structure through this *modo di dire*.** I'm not always able to say what I want exactly in English, so I use this *modo di dire* and I sometimes translate directly from it. It's more me than formal English sometimes."

Representing his *modo di dire* as critical not only to his identity and socio-cultural conditions but also to his intellectual advancement, KAPPA rejected common monolingualist assumptions that drawing on his valuable language resources in academic writing can be a hindrance to successful language and literacy learning and development: "I can't accuse this *moda di dire* of being a problem in my writing. I cannot blame it." In fact, Kappa actively mobilized his specialized language resources—which he picked up and enhanced throughout his family's travelings across multiple and distant places—in his academic English writings by incorporating scholarly work published in languages other than English. For an argumentative essay on the Mafia and its culture of Omertà he wrote for his FYW course, for instance, he used one Italian book, an English translation of another, and an Italian documentary film. Before doing so, however, he made sure to get his English teacher's permission to use non-English sources because he was aware that his own representations of the meaningfulness and necessity of cross-language writing practice might not be shared by his teacher, since in an English writing classroom dominated by a tacit English-only policy it's a given, as he put it, that "all sources have to be in English." When I inquired about Kappa's motivation for burdening himself with the challenging and time-consuming labor of translation, he explained that pursuing cross-language relations in acts of reading and writing "enriche[d]" the complexity of his arguments and conveyed a sense of locality and authenticity: "I feel original and authentic when I make connections to Italian and Italian scholarly sources; it **enriches my writing** . . . An Italian source helps you **get the inside eye of the problem**. You're getting opinions from the locals and not from Americans about how ordinary people actually think. No other source in any other language can **give a better inside view**."

Though working with primary and secondary Italian sources added desired intellectual depth to KAPPA's writing, he voiced several concerns pertaining to the lack of training and preparation in effectively working with non-English texts in his FYW classroom. Uncovering some of the uncertainties and messiness involved in strategically selecting, reading, interpreting, and translating passages and selections from foreign sources for his research paper and many of his other writing assignments and projects, KAPPA still felt constrained by the lack of exposure in FYW to the necessary tools and resources for locating, incorporating, and citing foreign language sources. He explicitly expressed his disappointment in such dominant monolingualist treatments of language and language relations in the FYW classroom, which rendered his tension-filled negotiations of valued translingual work with dominant monolingual research writing and citation practices invisible: "I'm not sure how I should cite an Italian source. I am not sure if it's okay to include sentences or titles in Italian in my English writing, as my teacher and the students in class don't speak Italian. How do I work with these sources properly? They don't talk about my problem. It's strange that they don't do that here when most students know more than one language." Speaking against the limitations monolingualist representations imposed on his own academic literacy practices and those of others, KAPPA represented the ordinariness of crossing and moving among fluid language boundaries in local writing ecologies as requiring much more attention and open engagement in FYW pedagogy. KAPPA felt unguided and under-prepared to pursue his dynamic and evolving engagement with cross-language relations in his academic literacies work and believed he couldn't do so confidently and comfortably. This demonstrates the degree to which a global monolingualist valuation of an English-only, presumably translation-free written product has placed powerful constraints on his sustained relation with English as always dependent on translation for the dynamic construction of meaning in his academic written texts.

While I lost touch with most of my participants after they graduated from BU, KAPPA was among the very few I was able to reconnect with. Three years after our initial prolonged conversations, KAPPA informed me in email correspondences that he was finishing his last year in the graphic design program and preparing for his final senior project. He was particularly excited to share with me that he had just gotten back from a summer trip to Italy "with a lot of books (in Italian) that could eventually feed into" his high-stakes senior project, which "will though have to be written in English" and assessed formally and thoroughly, so once more he "will have to do a meticulous work in order to move back to English." As he continued to maneuver the complexity of this back-and-forth literate movement in his attempts at translation, KAPPA was overzealous about letting me and my readers know about his insistence on laboring and belaboring to reap the personal and intellectual rewards of an intense investment in cross-language relations throughout his future academic and professional career: "The way I deal with English academic writing has not changed [since our last interview] and will probably not change a lot. I will always try to enrich my texts with sources written in Italian or French, sometimes even Latin."

(RE)WRITING LANGUAGE REPRESENTATIONS AND/AS PRACTICES IN FYW

In light of what Christiane Donahue (2009, 233) has characterized as a dominant "import/export model" of internationalizing writing instruction, we see in this chapter clear manifestations of how academic writing pedagogies shaped by US English-only monolingualist understandings of and practices with language are purely transmitted to and adopted in one of Beirut's American-style postsecondary institutions while remaining stripped of their local significance and largely severed from ever-dynamic sociolinguistic realities on the assumption that they have transparent, friction-free, and universal applicability. This specific urban Lebanese context of postsecondary language and literacy education is particularly unique in bringing out the complex postmonolingual complications that arise from student writers' efforts to come to grips with the consequences of English-only monolingualism that dominates their educational landscapes, locating and keeping the de facto language of instruction firmly outside the open, translingual flow of other language resources that are vibrant in their local sociolinguistic landscapes but also legitimated at the level of national language policy. The profiles of Nathalie, Naser, Lucas, Diva, and KAPPA detailed in this chapter indicate that their attempts to disentangle these inconsistencies and contradictions surrounding language, language relations, and language difference in their local writing ecologies, with varying degrees of success, are fundamentally a matter of representations and how these representations are locally bound up with and profoundly shape and reshape their literate workings and doings of language(s) in various writing situations.

In Beirut's American-affiliated educational landscapes, with a stranglehold of English-only monolingualism and, at best, its traditional multilingual surrogate, English as conventionally defined is by no means the only player for the transnationally mobile student writer (the likes of Diva and KAPPA) or even for the local Lebanese student writer (like Nathalie, Naser, and Lucas) who still meets the challenges of complex language negotiations on campus grounds or in public arenas. With all student writers from Beirut profiled in this chapter, we witness the importance of preserving and capitalizing on the complexity of language relations and expertise to their personal, social, academic, professional, and intellectual development. However, their abilities to openly and actively mobilize the diverse linguistic and semiotic resources at their disposal were constantly negotiated against the contradictory language representations circulating in their local surrounds and the preferred practices associated with those representations. For instance, holding passionate beliefs about the value and significance of the wide range of language and semiotic resources in their expanding repertoires, Nathalie and Lucas were hoping for a greater engagement with French academic literacies at the university and Naser with advanced Arabic and transmodal literacies. To Diva, her idiosyncratic way of using English in writing with all her fluid language resources enmeshed together closely connected different parts of her life-worlds. Clearly, Kappa's use of non-English-medium academic sources advanced his and his readers' intellectual grasp of research.

While Nathalie, Naser, and Lucas struggled to mediate between dominant representations of the primacy and fixity of English in the FYW classroom and alternative representations they encountered daily in their lived realities and academic disciplines, Diva and KAPPA handled these points of friction differently through deliberately challenging and intervening with English-only monolingualist representations and practices, thereby putting their own academic success at risk. In their tedious path toward academic English literacies, Nathalie, Naser, and Lucas were guided by a skewed perception of their diverse language resources as discrete, reified, and fixed entities appropriate for distinct social domains and a false assumption that effective language use in academic writing amounted to fluent mastery of and native-like command over ostensibly static, universal SWE rules and conventions. As a result, they positioned themselves as possessing abstracted, "multiple, discrete language competences to be used in mutually exclusive contexts" (Kilfoil 2015, 439)—as in sociolinguistic versus educational landscapes, home versus school, or disciplinary versus university-wide FYW courses—and, in this sense, developing their English language and writing practices ultimately became a dreaded academic task. Contrastingly, by virtue of living transnationally mobile literate lives and being informally involved in effective language-ideological brokering practices, which offered them early exposure to the normalcy of translingual language relations and usages, student writers like Diva and KAPPA took up more agentive roles and demonstrated a greater sense of control and negotiation over their language resources and practices in producing their academic written texts. With a view of English as dynamic with fuzzy boundaries, Diva's English writing practices in low-stakes writing genres took on different sets of meanings and social relations beyond the confines of what English-only monolingualism represents as an essential inner core with constant pre-given meanings. With a similar understanding of English as fluid, negotiable, and open to translation, KAPPA undertook the laborious task of drawing on his Italian literate resources in his academic written English work.

This is not to suggest, however, that Diva's and KAPPA's paths toward desired translingual academic literacies proceeded entirely without tension. In fact, Diva practiced restraint and self-control over her translingual language practices, as she was self-conscious of the English-only expectations of the academy and of the potential risks of continuing to practice language as such in high-stakes writing situations. As for KAPPA, he complained that there was no proper support and careful scaffolding for his translingual literate work in place in the design of his FYW course curriculum. His representation of his translation labor—which has become a sustained meaning-making practice in his writing across the university—as unguided, unacknowledged, and unrewarded is suggestive of the powerful stranglehold monolingualist language ideologies and representations have over what constituted worthy knowledge and intellectual engagement in the production of academic written texts. Monolingualist representations of the language of the academy as uniform, insular, sedentary, and devoid of difference have prohibited writers like Nathalie, Naser, and Lucas from entertaining the possibility of consciously reworking and modifying English and their other language resources to meet their changing goals. The same established language representations have also constrained writers like Diva and KAPPA from fully and confidently pursuing what seem to be accepted and expected ways of working with English in a location like Lebanon, conducive to translingualism in its national language policy and local sociocultural imaginary.

The language representations these first-year student writers openly, clandestinely, or inadvertently brought with them to how, when, where, and why they put English into work in the academic writing classroom are not simple, abstracted, stabilized, and decontextualized ideas about language and its literate learning residing in their minds. In fact, their multiple and competing representations of language and language practice were constantly triggered, deepened, resisted, complicated, and reworked in dynamic engagements and collaborations with a range of language ideology brokering interventions. For example, most notably for Nathalie, her father's deep commodification of English as inherently holding the promise of global material and social power has led her to chase an unattainable NES norm in her English language and literacy learning, and this has been an ongoing source of anxiety and insecurity for her. Naser's experiences learning Arabic at home with his father in its own presence influenced his allegiance to a traditional multilingualist view of his Arabic language resources as independent of rather than interdependent and intermingling with his developing knowledge of English academic literacies at school. Deeply familiar with and part of the constant movement of people and their language and literate resources, Diva's and KAPPA's families brokered them into the possibilities of understanding and putting English into literate work "as a language always in translation" and transformation, "a language of translingual use" and meaning-construction (Pennycook 2008, 34).

While we cannot control such informal sociocultural influences on students' specific language representations, facilitating and further developing translingual language representational practices is still to a great extent within our reach. The experiences recounted by my participants have revealed that classroom language policies and pedagogical and assessment practices can offer either significant pulls or pushes for the construction and cultivation of translingual understandings and treatments of language and language usage in academic literacies work. Naser, for instance, appeared to treat and ultimately utilize his advanced Arabic literacy and graphic resources as translingual and transmodal in his discipline-based writing thanks to his graphic design professors who provided effective classroom affordances for fostering informed disciplinary language and literate perceptions and practices among students. Regrettably, the pressure of producing what constituted acceptable language forms and usages in compliance with monolingual English-only demands appeared to interfere with how the same alternative representations he was exposed to in graphic design gained uptake in his academic work in FYW. We have also seen, especially with student writers like Naser and Lucas, that the persistence of curricular and departmental divisions on the nature of language, particularly English, and the precise form it must take in academic written texts have created problematic pressures and constraints on their literacy learning and development and their experiences of them, thereby preventing them from seeing much value in learning academic English literacies in FYW to their ongoing "development of disciplinary or work-related writing skills" (Bergmann and Zepernick 2007, 132).

Equally deserving our special attention are the metaphorical conceptualizations of English shaping the embodied learning and writing experiences[14] of many struggling writers like Nathalie, Naser, and Lucas—familiar conceptualizations that cluster around physical and emotional duress and tension, such as "hitting a wall," swallowing a "rock," confining one's possibilities to "really narrow spaces," or even undergoing linguistic and "academic genocide." Such representations display these writers' language-ideological compliance to English-only monolingualism by accepting, even partially, the negative images of themselves as language learners, images that are propagated and maintained in the academic imaginary and its myriad collaborative institutions. Upon continuing to speak in terms of "linguistic injury" and their "vulnerability to language," as Judith Butler (1997, 1) warns, our writing students indirectly "ascribe an agency to language, a power to injure, and position [themselves] as the objects of its injurious trajectory." It is dominant representations of their language practices (e.g., "broken", "bad", "fractured", "butchered", or "substandard"), derided as deviant or potentially threatening to the oneness and purity of SWE, that lead to such frustrations and insecurities about "one's language practices, and traditions of such practices, deleterious to [translingual] engagement with these" (Horner 2016, 64–65). As we embark on the challenging task of continually and more systematically developing translingual-oriented language of description and representation for language, language use, and language difference in writing, we need to take very seriously the need to refrain from describing what it is we strive to teach our students, that is, academic English writing or the English language itself, as this tangible invincible, durable 'object' that miraculously "does and does not do things to and for people" (Pennycook 2007, 73) who in reality are solely responsible for its coming into being and for its "living" character in the first place. We cannot continue—however intentionally or unintentionally—to generate, support, and promote deep-seated representations and treatments in the writing classroom of language generally and SWE particularly as an autonomous entity, existing in a galactic void and "leading a life of its own outside and beyond" (Yngve 1996, 29) the subjectivities, bodies, movements, and performances of the literate individuals who are constantly actualizing its repetitive and recurrent doing. Instead, we need to bring to the fore of our students' consciousness and awareness the multiplicity and sometimes contention and contestation in the specific ideas, desires, investments, commitments, language affiliations, and allegiances we bring along with them into everyday literate doings within and across English and other language resources.

The academic frictions chronicled in accounts from Lebanon are in part the result of a successfully ingrained and naturalized emphasis in the popular and academic imaginary on "locat[ing] language and competence in the mind of an individual" language learner or writer (Canagarajah 2013b, 32; cf. Horner, NeCamp, and Donahue 2011, 287–88; Lillis and Curry 2010, 62–63). The kind of rethinking and rewriting of the construct "language" itself, as I have indicated in chapter 2, necessitates radically shifting our and our students' sense of languages as individualized belongings and instead seeing them in their very essence as already products of socially situated and networked practices, requiring the shared, collaborative labor of literate others for successful communication and meaning. As Daniel Moore and Laurent Gajo (2009, 150, 143, 144) argue, such counterhegemonic understandings of language and its learning instigate more "open and flexible conceptions of language [and literate] competence" as the "situated mobilization[s]" of highly individualized complexes of language and semiotic resources while working within and across various social networks and, as such, as "always subject to evolution and change."

These undergraduate writers' accounts and lived experiences of "immobility within movement" (Prendergast 2008, 147) in Lebanon indicate that they "object to, and are intimidated by, the subjugation of their linguistic lives[, abilities,] and habits to academic languages and discourses" (Johns 2005). To preclude translingual imaginings and doings of language in acts of academic reading and writing for many of these young writers is to hinder important opportunities for knowledge making and intellectual advancement. Rather than continuing to view and treat language as a fixed, self-contained entity "ontologically distinct from mobility, which could be tagged and labeled, and its trajectories tracked, blocked, or modified across boundaries and borders" (Stroud and Prinsloo 2015, xi), we can and should renew and enliven our students' attention to the naturalized not natural, the performed not preformed, the variable not unvarying nature of English—an attention that often comes more seamlessly to them in other spheres and domains of their literate life (e.g., in everyday sociolinguistic realities, academic disciplinary work, digital communication, online composing spaces) but that a dominant blinkered monolingualist ideology in the teaching of FYW has sought to eschew, sideline, and cover up. As Lucas firmly reminds us, and we might indeed need frequent reminding, "we [writing teachers and students alike] are living this relationship between languages every day, so why not talk about it, discuss it, take advantage of it, incorporate it."

CONCLUDING REMARKS

Driven by a shared sense of the exigency for working against a dominant and residual monolingual English-only ideology and defying its gravity in writing and its teaching, US compositionists are still gradually developing local understandings of and engagements with translingualism, which is "itself vulnerable to and in need of constant reworking" (Lu and Horner 2016, 216), and translation in local institutional and writing program ecologies. In fact, Kate Mangelsdorf (2017, 199; emphasis in original) has productively brought to our attention the fact that "*translingual [writing] programs and pedagogies* are still in search of their own practices" and, I would add, their own unified, coherent system of linguistic representations, the qualitatively descriptive and explanatory practices that also constitute an active intervention in dominant language politics in composition and that could potentially determine and guarantee the effectiveness and sustainability of such translingual programmatic and pedagogical practices-in-the-making in the first place. To assist in our deliberations over what we could potentially do individually and programmatically in regard to the ongoing challenge of developing more translingually oriented understandings and subsequent doings of language in the teaching and learning of university-level writing in the United States, it is necessary to initiate and sustain cross-disciplinary dialogue with teachers of writing in modern languages other than English and writing across the curriculum (WAC) and writing in the disciplines (WID) professionals. Such collaborations can provide a more nuanced understanding of the complex interaction between the language representations and practices endorsed and fostered in FYW ecologies and those in language, disciplinary, or professional socialization ecologies that students are constantly trying to make sense of as they move among university faculty, courses, instructional programs, academic departments, and other organized sites of knowledge (cf. Hall 2009; Thaiss and Zawacki 2006; Harwood and Hadley 2004). Foregrounding the potentiality for creating mutually transformative relationships between composition scholarship on translingualism and work on writing-related knowledge transfer, Rebecca Lorimer Leonard and Rebecca Nowacek (2016, 260) prompt us to investigate how more informed "teacherly values and beliefs" surrounding language, language difference, and language relations in FYW can play a fundamental role in influencing "a writer's sense of options and actual choices in subsequent classes" in the disciplines, across the university, and beyond and a writer's awareness of the potential consequences of such options and choices for one's linguistic and social life.

In sum, cultivating translingual language representations as themselves performatives that have considerable effects on ensuing practices with language and literacy must become an ongoing long-term project in the teaching and learning of university-level writing, something that will definitely be challenging, labor-intensive, and fraught with frictions but must continually evolve as translingual written English itself does even as I write this passage. Joining a multiplicity of voices that foreground the centrality of local knowledges (Canagarajah 2005; Dor 2004; Makoni and Pennycook 2007; Tardy 2011) for effective intervention in dominant English-only monolingual ideologies, I argue for more systematic and sustained explorations of the nature of our students' local understandings—whether explicitly articulated or implicitly imbricated and embodied in actual practice—about language and its difference, how such understandings mediate between their language and semiotic resources and their changing sociocultural worlds, and the material effects of these mediations on their ever-dynamic language and literate practices and learning experiences. These young Lebanese writers' complex meso-political negotiations of the situated *fawda*, or "chaos of being [linguistically] mobile" (Monroe 2016, 115, 120), in a superdiverse city like Beirut amid ideological, historical, and sociocultural forces of power and control have brought to our attention how "order and disorder commingle," forms of security and insecurity intersect, and moments of fixity and fluidity in understandings of language and literacy and their learning are in a constant push-pull dynamic.[15] The kind of locally driven explorations that I am calling for here and that I undertake in this chapter and the rest of the book can afford us deeper understandings of the dynamics of these side-by-side coexistences and simultaneous absence and presence of dominant monolinguality, traditional multilinguality, and counterhegemonic translinguality in language relations and subsequent language practice in writing. Making an explicit focus of our local interventions the postmonolingual language representations and practices that are constantly flowing in our classes, programs, communities, and on campus grounds and that all our students—whether self-, socially, or institutionally identified as mainstream or minority, native, first, second, or foreign speakers/learners of English—are contending with in the changing contexts of their academic, professional, and civic lives and work can be a powerful way to enact desired change along translingual lines. Chapter 4 will take this inquiry further at a different geographical and sociolinguistic context.

4
UNPACKING LOCAL LANGUAGE REPRESENTATIONS AND/AS PRACTICES CONTINUED
Postmonolingualism in Seattle

As will become clear in this chapter, the language ideological tensions and their material ramifications that are the central concern of this book and that have characterized my fieldwork in Beirut also unfold in my explorations at a global research university in Seattle. Despite profound differences in the historical, cultural, geopolitical, and sociolinguistic realities that have shaped the complex local politics and ideologies of English and its teaching in university-level writing, the perspectives of first-year writing (FYW) students in Seattle suggest that their articulated representations of and practices with English, much like those of their counterparts in Beirut, are continually legitimated, regulated, and often transformed based on their experiences of moving across and between everyday networks of language ideology brokers. A fuller exploration of the ideas they hold about the nature of the language itself and the values and meanings they attach to particular language practices within the physical and social spaces where they live, study, and work offers insights into the postmonolingual dimension of these representations, in that they are neither fully monolingual or multilingual nor truly translingual but replete with variability, complexity, and sometimes even contradiction. In the subsequent sections, the same tripartite lens I adopted in chapter 3 affords us a closer composite look into the interrelationship between local language representations and practices in Seattle's sociolinguistic landscapes, in federal, state-level, and institutional language policies, and in programmatic and pedagogical orientations. As we shall see, these macro-level sites of language ideological brokering, which student writers encounter and manage on a daily basis, are themselves imbricated with mixed and apparently conflicting ways of abstracting language and strong stances for and against particular concrete practices with language.

DOI: 10.7330/9781607329046.c004

LANGUAGE REPRESENTATIONS AND
PRACTICES IN SEATTLE'S CITYSCAPES

Given its place as "the jewel of the Pacific Northwest," Seattle has known high migration[1] rates throughout the years (Putman 2008, 27). Today, 18.9 percent of Seattleites, who have chosen the area for its work and education opportunities, report home and community use of languages and language varieties besides English (Statistical Abstract of the United States 2011). With a simple tour in and around the city's streets, marketplaces, cafés, and restaurants, one is bound to encounter the actual deployment of messy, "mobile [language] resources" but not pure, ordered, and "immobile languages" (Blommaert 2010, 102). Playfully named ethnic eateries and small coffee shops like "Hardwok café" or dishes on restaurant menus like "Whatever you Called?" "boilded fish", and "stair fried beef" on a busy commercial street in the neighborhood that is home to my research site are all examples of language creations that contribute to the unofficial authoring of Seattle's language landscapes. Min-Zhan Lu (2004, 22) argues against interpreting such usages solely in terms of the dictates of standardized US English grammar as "linguistic imperfections to be 'rooted out'" and reminds us of the regulated, "meticulous work" ordinary language users on the streets are doing to "keep English alive," that is, imbued with difference and recontextualized through the changing language resources, beliefs, and expectations they've picked up through a wide variety of formal and informal language and literate learning trajectories.

On one of my linguistic excursions into the city and its various neighborhoods, I was particularly drawn to the choices made and kinds of perceptions motivating them in a specialty bakery's signage, "Ma Boulangerie", written in stylized yellow letters accompanied with the explanatory words in smaller white font "bakery, patisserie, café", which assist non-French-speaking customers. Knowing that the phrase *ma boulangerie* in what we conventionally call and perceive as French literally translates into "my bakery", passers-by and customers like myself who know enough French would initially and rightly wonder why an establishment that specializes in producing a line of gluten-free products would bear the redundant name "My bakery, bakery". However, upon thinking in relation to the symbolic market value of the language resources at play here, it becomes clearer that *ma boulangerie* has a complex of associative meanings attached to it. Interestingly, tapping into both the cultural and culinary capital of French, the Frenchness of *ma boulangerie* functions symbolically here rather than linguistically. It is highly possible that the choice of French-language resources in this shop front sign is guided by strong beliefs in their emblematic success as indexicals of distinctive French sophistication in artisan bread and pastry making.

On the walls of one of Seattle's breakfast locations known for its twelve-egg omelets, the decorative collection of illustrations and accompanying textual descriptions patrons have playfully designed while waiting for their food as they mix languages, Englishes, language varieties, and visualization elements (from drawings, colors, font sizes, shading, letter shapes, geometric shapes, and others) portrays the city's signature blending and bending of resources and practices. The flow of customers as they come and go, enter and exit that particular space has significantly expanded this canvas all the way to the restaurant's entrance where the front door is now covered with graphic and textual creations. Bringing southern barbeque and brew to Seattle's hip Ballard neighborhood, a counter-service joint in a former barbeque wasteland is known not only for its smoky, fall-off-the-bone-style ribs but also for the availability of writable chalkboard walls in its restrooms, with customers mobilizing meaning and language resources as they move in and out. At another jam-packed restaurant large enough to only accommodate ten tables, its whiteboard side wall is an open invitation to its primarily Spanish-speaking clientele usually on a one- to two-hour wait to grab black markers, search for blank surfaces, write, and draw on that fluid canvas (figure 4.1). Covered with dry-erase paint, the interior walls of this Mexican steakhouse are adorned with Spanish, English, and Spanglish used in an interwoven mix to depict local experiences of and connections with the transnational migration of the culinary gene pool of the northwestern Sinaloa region across the US-Mexican border all the way to the Pacific Northwest region.

All these examples of the active textual and visual production of meaning on toilet and interior walls are akin to the out-of-control practice of smearing technicolor wads of chewed-up gum on the city's landmark the Gum Wall, a colorful tourist attraction canonized in most guidebooks, in a brick alleyway wall just below the bustling Pike Place Market. These various forms of transmodal and translingual expression are not mere scribblings, doodles, or crowd-sourced artistic and linguistic creations that cover up static, concrete city walls but are rather an essential part of the mobile expression of how the city's designers, makers, and writers are thinking, doing, and redoing language (and modality) to give meaning to its public spaces. Within this cultural, linguistic, gastronomic, and artistic métissage, it is orientations toward a translingual norm where the whole package of available language and semiotic resources can and must be used to achieve various communicative and social goals that

Figure 4.1. Translingual practice on restaurant walls in Seattle

play a crucial role in how these resources are getting deployed, taken up, and renewed in Seattle's hybrid cityscapes (cf. Arnaut et al. 2016; Pennycook and Otsuji 2015).

LANGUAGE AND LANGUAGE-IN-EDUCATION POLICY TRENDS

In a country like the United States, which lacks a unified, centrally directed policy with regard to the function and status of English or other vibrant languages in its sociolinguisitic landscapes, US language politics has been and remains complex and difficult to disentangle (Ricento 2006; Wible 2013). Despite the absence of a coherent language policy at the federal level, the continuing power of a dominant monolingual ideology in US policyscapes lies in its "subtler workings," strongly influencing the history and current trajectory of ideas and basic assumptions about English—particularly its standardized variety—as the only conceivable American way for desirable civic, economic, and political participation to the exclusion of almost all other language resources (Schiffman 1996, 211; cf. Spolsky 2004; Hornberger and Johnson 2007).[2] While a tacit English-only variant of a monolingual ideology privileges English domestically and trends toward linguistic assimilation and homogeneity, foreign or internationally oriented US language policy initiatives are geared toward ensuring polyglot American citizenry through foregrounding the learning of a strategically selected set of languages designated as "critical" not for the sake of promoting language diversity and foreign language education in their own right but rather for national security and global economic interests (Wible 2009; Sonntag 2015). According to Ofelia García (2009, 198; emphasis in original), contemporary US language and language-in-education policy can be characterized as one of "*tolerance* toward languages other than English at best, most implicitly, and outward *restriction* during some historical periods."

Under such restrictive federal language policy critiqued for suppressing opportunities for schools and districts to develop bilingual education programs,[3] Washington state language policies—unlike top-down educational policy in other western states like Arizona and California, with a heavy-handed push for English-only monolingualism[4]—appear to have increased spaces for such programs.[5] The state's primary language policy, the Transitional Bilingual Instruction Program (TBIP), has played a significant role in providing the "ideological and implementational space" needed for developing and actively promoting academic bilingual education and biliteracy (Johnson and Johnson 2015, 100–101).[6] Washington state ranks tenth in language and cultural diversity in the United States and is among twelve states with the highest L2 writing student enrollment.[7] In addition to endorsing "English Plus" resolutions, the state's underlying culturally and linguistically sensitive philosophy is mainly reflected in its official state-level policy mission statement that recognizes the uniquely situated store of "language and cultural assets" elementary- and secondary-level L2 writing students carry with them into their varied literate engagements and experiences as "*valuable resources to learning*" (Malagon and Chacon 2009, 1; emphasis added). While such clear languages-as-resources orientations are aspects to be praised, David Cassels Johnson (2013, 109; cf. English and Varghese 2010; Stephens and Johnson 2015) argues that as a result of "local language ideologies, idiosyncratic beliefs about language education research, or a focus on test scores, some educators and community members actively promote English-only monolingual approaches, even in school districts that already incorporate bilingual education pedagogy."

Except for a foreign language requirement policy for some of its programs and an additional English-language proficiency requirement policy for international students, my second research site, the University of Seattle (UOS), like most four-year US universities, is typical in lacking explicitly stated language policies that position English in relation to the wealth of language resources of the resident and international student populations increasingly defining it. UOS shifted in 2008 from a quick-fix "remedial" model where any student not demonstrating a particular level of English-language competence, as conventionally defined, upon entry was required to enroll in the appropriate English as a second language (ESL) course series until demonstrating "mastery" of learning outcomes through passing final proficiency exams. Aiming to connect its primary mission of the "advancement and dissemination of knowledge" to the diverse needs of its changing student demographics, UOS transitioned into a "support" model under which students for whom English is not the primary or only language have diverse support options available to them should they be deemed necessary for strengthening their literate abilities. Embracing and championing the ethnic and cultural heterogeneity among its domestic and international students, faculty, staff, and surrounding communities, a large public urban university like UOS represents the rather vague notion of diversity in higher education on its official homepage as something to "value and honor" and as "integral" to its aspirations for "global engagement and connectedness." In addition to international student/faculty recruitment and exchange activity, UOS has a long history of incorporating international dimensions into various areas of university life (teaching, research, service, and outreach activities) through a strong commitment to encouraging its faculty and students to pursue research and education partnerships overseas.[8] In this sense, UOS fits into Nick Foskett's (2010, 45) category of "internationally engaged" modern universities, which drive a globalist perspective and an "internationalization agenda 'at home.'"

Within this dominant discourse of diversity and internationalization, however, the slightest mention of the themes of language, linguistic pluralism, and their role in university academic literacies and knowledge construction is largely invisible, especially on the university homepage and that of its diversity-affiliated divisions[9] and in its 2017–21 university-wide blueprint, which lays out best practices for developing a "truly inclusive and equitable" campus. Aside from descriptions of various types of institutional language and learning support on offer outside of the mainstream structure to its "special" population of "non-native" or "international" students, who are all lumped under and spoken of in terms of a supposedly all-encompassing, homogeneous category, the workings and complexities of language and the potentialities of cross-linguistic engagement in their academic studies seem to be sidelined. As Taina Saarinen and Tarja Nikula (2013, 133) point out in their study of the role of language in internationalization policies and practices in higher education, it is crucial to remain "observant" to the meaningful invisibility of explicit "references to language use" in learning situations, as that can be "indexical" of particular language "ideologies." Perhaps not surprisingly, a dominant belief that "native English = standard English = international intelligibility" (also reigning in the Anglophone campus examined in Beirut), where students are required to conform to and reproduce putatively fixed and standardized native English speaker (NES)[10] norms and criteria of correctness in their academic studies, continues to hold sway (Jenkins 2014, 122).

The institution's native English–oriented language entry requirements (standardized tests, such as TOEFL and IELTS) for international students and the increasing amount of English-language support made available for those who fail to match set language qualifications further perpetuate this dominant monolingualist ideology and make more explicit the taken-for-granted assumptions that NES students representing the unmarked norm automatically possess academic English competence by virtue of their nativeness and that a large number of their non-native English speaker (NNES) counterparts lack the linguistic suitability for academic study. When it comes to the way the university and its bureaucracies orient to English and English-language usage, there is certainly no indication of accepting and valuing the potential contributions—intricately shaped by natural processes of language contact and change—of both international and domestic students' diverse *modi de dire* in their consumption and production of knowledge both on and off campus grounds. Jennifer Jenkins (2014) made a similar observation in her investigations of webspace data from various institutions of higher education, especially Anglophone ones and their branches across the globe. With clear connections to dominant English-only monolingualism, the degree to which the FYW program has espoused, resisted, and reformulated these representations of language and language relations in larger institutional ecologies in its (re)localized thinking about written English and its effective teaching amid pronounced language difference is what I will attend to next.

SNAPSHOTS OF THE FYW PROGRAM'S LANGUAGE ECOLOGY

As part of the broader institutional priorities of advancing a support-oriented model, the FYW program at UOS has moved away from dominant views of its linguistically and culturally diverse students as in grave need of remedial instruction. Instead, it projects valuable dispositions of acceptance and appreciation through representing these students in its 2013–14 instructor's manual as a welcome and "vibrant addition," contributing not only to campus and program diversity but also to the cultural and intellectual enrichment of all students. This positive stance toward the diverse language and cultural backgrounds of student writers—viewed as "a resource" to be "embrace[d]" and "*not an obstacle*" to be "overcome" (emphasis added)—was also evident through a willingness to revisit the program's terms of choice to refer to L2 writers and describe the various type of courses or additional support systems designed to assist in improving their academic English skills while completing their coursework. In line with recommendations in SLW scholarship (e.g., Ortmeier-Hooper 2008; Matsuda et al. 2011; Jerskey 2013) and the CCCC Statement on Second-Language Writing and Writers (2001), institutionalized language identity labels of "English as a Second Language (ESL)" and "English Language Learners (ELL)", primarily adopted by Washington state educational policymakers, have been replaced with the imperfect yet less contended term *multilingual.* In keeping with an understanding that not every language and literacy learning context is necessarily effective for all its "multilingual"[11] student writers, the writing program offers diverse placement and curricular options ranging from "mainstream" FYW courses, specifically designated "multilingual" sections[12] of the regular FYW course and of service-learning or multimodal-oriented composition courses, to FYW course sections directly linked to courses in the university's intensive English program. Two-credit writing studios have also been designed for students who, as indicated on the program website, prefer "additional English language support" while taking any of the aforementioned writing courses.

The writing program's attention to issues of language difference in its customized textbook and graduate-level teacher training has helped establish among the writing teachers I interviewed an overall environment of respect and appreciation of "language variation as *the* norm in any classroom," as described in the 2016–17 instructor's manual (emphasis added). Like the case of Beirut's FYW program briefly profiled in chapter 3, the current program adopts its own custom published textbook, which provides a wide range of pedagogical resources and materials to complement the course outcomes. In its reader section, this textbook caters to language diversity and difference either as a special, creative practice (generally tied to equally special sociocultural identities) manifest in a particular set of high-stakes examples that visibly cross language and cultural boundaries (e.g., Gloria Anzaldúa's widely anthologized essay "How to Tame a Wild Tongue" and a locally developed FYW syllabus that mixes English with Hawai'ian Creole English) or as an explicit theme to critically discuss and write about (e.g., in texts revolving around the linguistic and cultural world of hip-hop, national debates surrounding the legitimacy of Ebonics and its instructional worth in mainstream US education, and so on).

In a program that is the primary user of graduate student labor in teaching its courses, its graduate teaching assistants (GTAs) are exposed through an intensive one-week early fall orientation and the graduate program's quarter-long composition practicum course to a wealth of theoretical and pedagogical perspectives that contest a dominant monolingual English-only ideology persistently shaping US college composition, its study, and its teaching. Conversations about the importance of attending to the rich discursive resources—for example, prior genre knowledge, multimodal and linguistic literacies, cultural experiences and values—FYW students might value and make use of in their literate learning experiences and the role and function of such recognition in shaping various aspects of composition instruction (from assignment sequencing and design to principles of rhetorical grammar) have a strong presence in the program's GTA training and professionalization.

The overwhelming majority of the current program's GTAs were much more inclined to push against a dominant monolingualist English-only paradigm and the conceptions of language and language use attached to it than were the more experienced writing teachers I interviewed in Beirut. It was encouraging that most of the international and domestic GTAs I interacted with attributed the substantial changes in their perceptions about language difference as a resource for meaning making from the way they themselves were taught how to write following a difference-as-deficit model to the kind of training they've received in their current graduate program. As revealed through interviews and individual course materials some GTAs enthusiastically shared with me, my overall impression was that GTAs in the Seattle writing program were accepting and perceptive of the many language and cultural resources present in their program ecologies and no longer saw them as an impediment to successful academic literacy learning and development. Only a very few GTAs did not consider issues of language and cultural difference systematically and comprehensively when planning and preparing their writing courses.

On designing individual FYW courses in ways that occasionally provided opportunities to engage the strengths brought by students from their various local communities, one GTA, for instance, described encouraging students to incorporate language and cultural influences into their writing through asking them to free-write in prose or verse two different versions, one wholly in English and another "all in their home language" (personal interview, May 9, 2016), and then compare and contrast their performance of emotions, personality traits, and identities as they compose "in each language" (assignment prompt). Other GTAs spoke of adopting what has become typical practice in FYW pedagogy of inviting students to "translate" (with the term used quite loosely) their written work to broader reading publics than just academic ones, using all available communicative resources, while others reported giving students the liberty to select non-English popular or academic sources for their research-based writing tasks. Such accommodative pedagogical spaces for language difference are certainly commendable for demonstrating dispositions opposed to English-only ideology. However, as we have seen earlier in chapter 1, there is a kind of paradox inherent in these popular multilingualist invitations, which don't go far enough in destabilizing the dominant monolingualist ideas many FYW students already entertain about the separateness of English, their home language(s), and other language resources in their possession and about the alleged fact that clear, fixed borders actually exist between them, can be readily traced with certainty, and, above all, need to be constantly guarded from the contaminating influences of translation and cross-pollination. In addition, the fact that these well-meaning options are generally presented to students associated with specific national, ethnic, or social identities and collectivities propagates among students an already established belief that "FYW business" is to proceed as usual with the production of a given set of standard conventions and language practices that English-only monolingualism constructs as normative in academic literacies. I will return to this particular point later in the chapter when I consider students' perspectives in detail.

My conversations with the program's GTAs, both experienced and novice, international and domestic, revealed some inconsistencies between the perceptions they held and asserted at the beginning of their courses and those that actually ended up shaping their written response and assessment practices as they were forced to operate within larger institutional and programmatic structures they felt they had no control over. Though they described espousing alternative beliefs of language and the rules and standards governing its use in writing, in the words of one GTA, as "somewhat fluid, [able to] be negotiated," and contingent in their relevance and significance, they also spoke of "pushing harder for them [students] to conform to" the North American ways of doing academic written English, as if those ways were universal, indisputable, and fixed in time and space. Overburdened by meeting program-sanctioned outcomes in a ten- to eleven-week quarter and fulfilling the institutional expectations laid on them, the majority of GTAs reported that they still haven't taken it as their aim to engage students with the dynamics of revision as complex, intentional meso-level language (re)negotiation of students' diverse communicative purposes, ideological positions, aspired social relations, and linguistic affiliations. When it came to writing assessment, several GTAs, through no fault of theirs, described falling back into the pattern of "This is wrong. It has to be fixed," "This is not how I [as a NES] would say this, so I'm not accepting it," "I'm trying to make your English perfect," "This wasn't repaired," or "No, change this to . . . We don't use . . . in academic English writing" in their written feedback.

One of the program's few language-related policies, articulated in the 2013–14 instructor's manual and titled "Statement on Assessment of and Feedback on Grammar Correctness", recommends that its incoming and current GTAs adopt in their response to language errors in student writing one of several pathways, which differ in the timing and nature of cueing students to the presence of errors in their writing in the hopes that this would lead to students independently "catch[ing] grammatical or technical errors," self-editing, and proofreading for correctness in the traditional sense. This program policy seems to only encourage, as one GTA put it, "either a delayed or [an] early approach to errors" pertaining to lower-order writing concerns without explicitly problematizing what in student writing is ostensibly assigned to the realm of errors of language practices in writing, that is, apparent signs of lack of conformity to dominant linguistic rules and notational conventions. Despite a nuanced programmatic approach to the broad and diverse repertoire of its students' linguistic resources and to basic conventions of formal "grammar, punctuation, and mechanics," which are astutely presented to students in the 2014 version of the FYW textbook (476; emphasis added) "not in terms of 'rules' to be memorized and mastered but as *choices* based on 'what is appropriate' given a particular relationship between author and audience", there was little evidence among the GTAs and student participants I interviewed of an understanding and treatment of language difference in student writing as legitimate, rhetorical "choices" rather than error-ridden prose.

While the central role of language and its heterogeneity in the FYW program's curricular and ideological planning and design and in its GTAs' drive and commitment to address matters of language and language difference is certainly admirable, the language representations of the GTAs I interacted with combined with those of their writing students I present below are an indication that the program's current philosophy and orientation is one of celebration and accommodation of language difference along traditional multilingual lines but not yet explicit and active promotion of translingual language representations, work, and relations. And it is to these admittedly selective voices of the program's FYW students that I turn next.

MAKING SENSE OF POSTMONOLINGUALISM IN ACADEMIC LITERACY LEARNING

Constructed and reconstructed within the wider contexts of using, learning, and teaching language and literacy I have described earlier, the language representations echoed by the FYW students I interviewed on the Seattle campus seemed to be variable and dynamic in nature, constantly appropriated and negotiated in interaction with the expectations, actions, and positionalities of other literate individuals whom they perceived as influential and more knowledgeable in their own local ecologies. The analysis in this chapter reveals how these writers' apparently multiple language representations actively engage the push-pull dynamic between language fixity and fluidity, boundedness and flow, discreteness and interconnectedness as they strategically signal their equally multiple and evolving identities, desires, and (local, transnational, and ethnolinguistic) networks of affiliation.

When compared with my participants in Beirut, whose perceptions of and commitment to the value of their rich language and semiotic resources in their academic literacies were pronounced and made very explicit, the FYW student participants in Seattle were much more conflicted about the conferred status and use of their multiple languages and language practices as resources to their literacy learning, as legitimated by Washington state language policy and envisioned in the writing program mission. My participants in Seattle, mainly international students, children of immigrants/refugees, as well as ethnolinguistic minorities, described possessing either advanced academic literacies in languages other than English or working knowledge of "bits and pieces" (Blommaert 2010, 102) of one or several languages or language varieties. However, they didn't automatically see the relevance, meaningfulness, or legitimacy of their concrete language resources in academic literate situations unless such representations were explicitly triggered by contextual affordances. Perhaps not surprisingly, in a superdiverse nation like the United States, operating under what Paul Kei Matsuda (2006) has called a long-standing "myth of linguistic homogeneity" both seen and experienced as the sociocultural reality, the perceptions of the majority of my participants toward their language resources seemed to be closely intertwined with dominant representations of those in the US public or institutional imaginary as inconsequential to their academic knowledge making and exchange across contexts, communities, and individuals.

In the FYW classrooms that explicitly encouraged students either through written prompts or informal oral announcements to make use of their relevant language and cultural resources, those who responded to such invitations found themselves in a somewhat paradoxical situation in that they still had to reconcile the specific role and place of such resources with dominant English-only demands on and appraisals of the quality of their written texts. For instance, in addition to Li Ming whose perspectives I elaborate on below, two other Chinese students, one Russian, and an Eritrean reported that such unguided invitations, which generally lacked careful planning and scaffolding, presented them with a series of material and rhetorical challenges they were left to tackle on their own. As one student put it, such accommodative invitations were "a lot different from anything [they]'ve ever done" or experienced in academic literate situations before or "at least in high school," where they "never had the chance to do anything close to" tapping into their diverse language resources or crossing linguistic borders, as traditionally perceived. As we shall see in the rest of this chapter, the fruits and demands of attempts at such intense translingual labor remained subordinate to what a monolingualist ideology would dispose one to recognize, value, and reward in academic work. That is to say, the complexity of pursuing translingual relations in their writings through translation practice remained hidden and tied to the structuring of monolingualist ideals into writing instruction and assessment practices, which mainly championed a finite set of fixed and relatively settled academic writing conventions and propagated the myth of the transparency and weightlessness of their translation labor. While those students showed a great deal of appreciation for their FYW teachers' accommodative dispositions and attendant pedagogical practices, they still spoke of a noticeable lack of explicit attention to what really mattered to them and to their sustained relationship to translingual work, that is, the behind-the-scenes tedious labor, time, and spatial constraints and the extraordinary messiness inherent in such literate engagements. The sections below introduce the experiences of Nur, Malika, and Li Ming as they attempted to make productive sense of these inherently multiple and colliding representations of language, language use, and language difference in their own literate lives.

"Where you gonna eat, mamak lah?"

Nur, a Muslim international student from Malaysia, proudly gave a lengthy rendition of her nuanced and evolving understandings of language as emerging from its contexts of varied use. After completing a two-year International Baccalaureate (IB) Program, Nur was sponsored by her government and strongly encouraged by her parents, both of whom held advanced degrees from US universities, to pursue a US undergraduate degree. With the abundance and diversity of marine life in the Puget Sound region of Washington state positioned at the nexus of vibrant research, Nur's decision to join the UOS's School of Oceanography became much easier. Showing great intellectual ambition paired with rootedness in her local Malaysian community, Nur described a strong desire to study ocean sciences as a way to "revolutionize" dominant marine environmental politics in Malaysia. Her growing interest in issues of sustainability, "social justice for the environment," and public awareness and her realization of the importance of water resources to her home country's economy owing to its key position on maritime trade routes have emerged as a result of the sobering fact that the rich histories and traditional practices of her Malay ancestors in the fishing trade, as well as the traditional formal language variety of *bahasa baku* closely linked to them, were increasingly "eroded" and "seen as underprivileged and impoverished" by newer generations.

As a result of labor migration waves through the centuries, Nur's homeland brought together a tapestry of languages and language varieties used vibrantly in its sociolinguistic landscapes by the indigenous

Malays, migrant Chinese and Indian merchants and workers, and other ethnic minorities. Apart from English, Nur claimed affiliations to vernacular Malay (the language of her Malay race, the largest ethnic group of Malaysia), *bahasa Melayu*, or formal Malay, that she learned at school, and bits and chunks of the Mandarin and Tamil she picked up from ordering takeaway food and from local inter-ethnic communications. Intriguingly, Nur showed a keen awareness of the actual nature of the language resources within her repertoire as fluid, dynamic, and changing over situations, time periods, and registers. For instance, drawing on examples of early modern Shakespearean English and the use of Malay in local literary works of Samad Said and Keris Mas to support her view, she explained that "there were a lot of [linguistic] changes being done; just as much as English changed over time, Malay changed as well." Growing up and having experienced the fruits and real labor of day-to-day cross-cultural and cross-linguistic negotiations her whole life in a superdiverse nation like Malaysia, Nur reported that her alternative view and treatment of language and its use as "changing all the time" and "really show[ing] diversity" but which she always "took for granted" back home became much more visible thanks to her transnational mobility. More specifically, upon her arrival in the United States, only when the "way we [Malaysians] use English" was put into contact with the way "the local people" in Seattle do English "as their first language" and when some instances of lack of comprehensibility emerged in cross-cultural exchanges was Nur able to realize, to her surprise, how much English has "evolved in Malaysia" and "mixed with the diversity of languages" in local sociolinguistic landscapes.

Clearly struggling to find appropriate descriptors to best capture this fluidity and heterogeneity of language work in Malaysian socioscapes when I asked her to further explain what she meant by saying that "when it comes to language it's really fluid," Nur chose to mobilize her STEM education, particularly her knowledge of the fundamentals of aqueous chemical solutions and the movement of matter. In fact, she astutely invoked the image of solute particles flowing and becoming completely dispersed in a stream of solvent with like intermolecular forces, an image akin to that of the banyan tree I explored in chapter 2 in its reference to confused and overlapping origins and endpoints. According to Nur, the complex linguistic features making up her language usage can no longer be unambiguously allocated to particular languages-as-entities in the traditional sense, as these are imperceptibly merged with other features from different sources, thereby making the task of "tracing" these features to stable and static points of origin very challenging, even futile:

"I don't know, it's hard to trace which one is fluid and which, because like we just **take one word from here, one word from there,** and one word from there so we don't really know like which one is, it's **as though there's a solvent and solute and you don't know which language is the solute and which one is the solvent** . . . I can't trace that. I don't really know how to trace it like specifically . . . **It's just so easy to mix and match the languages.**" The hybridity and heterogeneity of the Malaysian(-ized) vernacular English, or what she insisted on calling Malaysia's "slum language," has become, as Nur explained, a defining, almost unmarked, unremarked practice of Malaysian urban youth subcultures. Based on what I gathered from our conversations, her understanding of the notion of "slum" to describe her language practices and those of local others was not in its simplest, traditional sense, as degeneration and lack of material and symbolic mobility in urban settings. On the contrary, she seemed to refer to the complex appropriation and renewal of language by resourceful urban dwellers like herself getting their own local stuff done, partaking in specific language practices, taking up certain linguistic styles, leaving out others, moving between registers and discourses, combining and deploying fractional features (e.g., lexical items, their cultural semantics, accents, pronunciations) from a variety of language resources available while bringing all of those into a strategic fit with the requirements of the communicative context.

These local translingual language practices are commonly called *rojak* English or *bahasa rojak* (*bahasa* is "language" and *rojak* is "mixture or local salad-like dish" in Malay) in reference to the eclectic mélange of language resources (see Saraceni 2010, 120; Pennycook 2007, 108). As a demonstration of this dynamic *rojak*[13] nature of language in Malaysian lived realities, Nur used an example from one of the most common features of local engagement in urban life: food and drink. As Nur explained, her local language usage, exemplified in this subsection's heading, took a form of English flavored with local references to Chinese, Bangladeshi, or Indian food stalls through the Indian slang "mamak" and adding the pragmatic Malay particle "lah" for assertion and enticing solidarity. Though her earlier biochemical metaphor of fluid language relations revealed that it was hard to trace and maintain the monolingualist language divide between language usages as located "in" one language-as-entity or another, Nur found it necessary here to dissect her practices into separate components only to aid my sense making as an outsider. Dislodged from their conventional origins, Nur's "mix[ed] and match[ed]" language resources with their intermingling of boundaries and social identities reflected, as she observed, a desire for establishing "unity," "building connections", and "appreciat[ing] each others' unique cultural language." She added that such dynamic fashioning and refashioning of language and her sense of self and community was made possible through a deliberate effort to demonstrate empathy, cooperation, and accommodation across local racial and linguistic divides. As she further explained, "This mix of language just shows how much . . . we try to understand each others' race and how much we incorporate each other in our daily lives."

Alongside Nur's translingual understandings and uses of language in Malaysian sociolinguistic landscapes, there seemed to be a pull in the opposite direction in other domains of her life. For instance, Nur recounted memorable literate encounters with educational practices of linguistic separation where the languages she was taught at school were thought of in a container-like, bounded sense. Forced to cope with the messiness and unexpected material effects of an abrupt language policy reversal institutionalized by the Ministry of Education in her senior year of high school, Nur described the challenges of developing scientific and mathematic literacy after tumultuous language policy changes where the teaching of English was relegated from its role as medium of instruction throughout her primary and secondary education to a compulsory language subject and *bahasa Melayu* became designated as the medium of instruction for all content areas. The socially and politically constructed nature of these established structural boundaries that separate between English and Malay in academic literacies based on organized class times and specific spaces became especially visible in the context of such sudden shifts in national language policy orientations. The image of her daily experience working on, between, and across languages as dynamic, mobile, and fluid resources in space and time was pitted against one of working "within" languages as static, distinct entities, easy to pin down and segregate into discrete curricular spaces and time schedules.

Nur had similar influential experiences with such socioculturally motivated ideas about and expectations concerning language fixity, uniformity, and separability, but this time these ideas were rooted in her own home environment. She was constantly cautioned by her mother that she needed to stick to a "correct" and "specific grammar and . . . vocabulary" in her compositions because "written English or academic writing require[d] this formality and this specificity." Following her mother's advice "took a toll on" Nur as she struggled to make "a mental note in [her] head" that she could no longer "mix and match" her language and semiotic resources. Forced to negotiate the contradictory representations of and practices with English at home, at school, and in daily urban life, Nur became more aware of the workings of power and perceptions of cultural and symbolic values in the global linguistic marketplace, whereby the locally legitimized ways of using the language of British colonizers as permeated with chunks of Malay, "a dash of Chinese, and a dash of Indian" were clearly proscribed in her academic literate learning.

As a senior manager of a government-affiliated communications agency who was responsible for writing press releases for Malaysia's prominent politicians and public speakers, Nur's mother played a leading linguistic-ideological brokering role in her daughter's language and literate education, that of reproducing and disseminating a dominant ideology of language and the appropriate language practices that should be mobilized for it in her undergraduate writing. Thanks to regular and improved transnational communications through low-cost voice or video chats, the way Nur's mother continued to review and mark up the work she produced in her FYW course for language errors impacted Nur's conviction that for her academic language and literacy practices to be deemed appropriate and successful, they were "supposed to be rigid," "neat," "understood internationally," and "not really influenced by any voices around" or inside her. Clearly placing the ways of using English expected from her in FYW in a relatively restricted domain, Nur argued that those ideals, deeply "instilled" by her mother, could only be achieved through a conscious effort to "remind" herself that she needed to "segregate these two, um, different kinds of English that [she's] been using [her] whole life." Seen from this angle, her engagement with a growing understanding of the dynamics of language sanctioned by the fluidities of her sociolinguistic realities and her subsequent ability to seek or even imagine opportunities to enact this understanding in practice became constrained by monolithic conceptions of language, its use, and its learning perpetuated jointly and severally in her secondary school and home language and literacy educational practices and policies.

"You're not gonna use slang around me!"
Malika spoke of similar experiences of moving between apparently contradictory yet coexistent views about language and language difference. A freshman biochemistry major, Malika is a Seattle native who briefly studied Spanish in middle school and took four years of French in high school, though without the approval of her mother who couldn't see

the value of Malika's French foreign language education, especially for building a competitive advantage in the US workforce. As a student of color with superior intellectual and creative abilities enrolled in accelerated programs throughout her primary and secondary education, Malika was adamant about distinguishing herself from the majority of her peers who adopted, as she put it, a "credit-based, you just fulfill your requirements and you're done" approach to foreign language learning. Malika's French learning process moved beyond the traditional learning of fixed forms and structures to portray universal meanings and instead incorporated a way of knowing "people holistically" and connecting with the complexity of "their heritage, culture," and social lives embodied in and through the new language. Despite feeling burdened by her academic studies at UOS, Malika expressed her intentions to further develop her expertise in French "above and beyond a high school setting," with the hope that her mother "doesn't get too upset."

Like Nur, Malika seemed to be sensitive and well attuned to the true character of English, which for her was a living, "constantly changing," and "not stagnant" language with new lexis and meanings noticeably being generated and appearing even in standard English lexicography. As Malika further illustrated, seeing how African American R&B group Destiny Child's vernacular coinage "bootylicious," not normally perceived as "a real word," officially made it into Merriam-Webster's Collegiate Dictionary and hence straight into the wider academic and literary promised land reinforced her current belief that "our language does change with the people who use it" and reinvent it across the United States. Her "potpourri kind of ideas" about language and its relation to cultural, classed, and racial aspects of one's identity, as Malika described, have been perpetually mediated through a range of literate experiences and interactions with a local and transnational network of cherished individuals, most notably her high school French teacher, her host family in France, her "artificial" grandmother who raised her while her mother worked hard to make a living, and her "real" ninety-seven-year-old grandmother.

Malika owed the way she positively oriented to foreign language learning to her French teacher. She described her fondness for her teacher's inspiring method of teaching, which steered away from "memorization and repeat" techniques and was "contradictory to the whole banking concept of education" Malika had learned about in her FYW class. In addition to having her class pledge to commit from day one to learning French, the fact that Malika's high school French teacher provided plenty of classroom opportunities for collaboratively creating their "own little France within a classroom environment" where language and culture became inseparable sparked a lot of interest in the language and pushed Malika and her classmates to "take it seriously": "Listening to French music, reading French literature . . . we cooked our own French meals and we had a four-course dinner like a French family during a special occasion would . . . just very much stimulating." According to Malika, this particular teacher had the greatest influence in encouraging her to "put language to practicality" by joining the school's French summer abroad program and in helping her recognize that though the use-value of her working foreign language competence may not always be visible in "Federal Way, Washington, it doesn't stop at the border." With the generous financial and moral support her teacher helped secure, Malika was able to travel to France after graduation, and she lived an hour away from Lyon for a month and a half with a host family with whom she remained in touch. Malika particularly recalled the intellectually stimulating interactions she constantly had with her host mother, who happened to be a middle school English teacher. This cross-cultural and cross-linguistic experience was a source of "enlightenment" for Malika in that it opened her eyes to how English along with French were being taught, learned, and used differently in the French context. It also came in handy for interacting with the hundreds of tourists who flooded into the frozen yogurt shop at Seattle's famed Pike Place Market where she worked for the summer.

Another person Malika described as being directly involved and having "a big part" in shaping her ways of thinking and talking about language and language difference was her best friend's grandmother, whom she kept referring to as her own "artificial" grandmother. An African American woman born into a Spanish-speaking family of immigrants, her "artificial" grandmother was an English teacher at a high-poverty high school in Seattle. In Malika's opinion, she was not "your stereotypical" high school English teacher, enforcing blind mastery of and conformity to language standards and "negating the creative aspects of the student or their personal backgrounds," but rather she had "a more wordly view of what English is." Growing up around "an activist" like her "artificial" grandmother, who moved in with the family right before Malika was born, she reported that a lot of her articulated ideals regarding the flexibility and hybridity of language and its use even in academic contexts and the importance of maintaining such "radical views" for social justice and change originated from the exciting stories her grandmother shared on road trips or while picking her up from school. These were stories about how her grandmother motivated her own high school students from diverse sociocultural and linguistic backgrounds and low-income families to improve their academic achievement by tapping into their interests and "accommodating the languages they use[d] in their personal lives in the classroom." With most of those students frequently dropping in for after-hours support, Malika got to witness firsthand how her grandmother effectively made room for hybrid language practices in the design of her teaching materials and accordingly worked with her students as they composed and revised their texts.

These dynamic translingual orientations to language and language relations were given materiality in Malika's formal and informal language socialization ecologies as well as through the wealth of her experiences negotiating language and cultural difference in transnational exchanges with her host family members and, more locally, with people on campus and in her bustling workplace. This individual, biographically organized patchwork of brokerage activities fostered Malika's strong view of and relation to her arsenal of diverse language and semiotic resources as fundamentally fluid, modifiable, and "intertwining" in relation to the diverse urban spaces she occupied and actively gave meaning. As she noted: "All these experiences with these different types of backgrounds of people who have studied English in college or me going abroad and seeing how English is taught there, it's just led me to formulate the hypothesis that it's [English] just, it's gonna change eventually, just seeing how many, how much ties French has to English and how much English has relied on French and English has relied on Spanish." As indicated in her remark, Malika made an insightful observation that language features and practices traditionally understood as belonging to a posited language-as-entity constantly echo, have traces of, and, as she put it, are "pieced" from other forms and practices in other so-called languages. In addition, the enriching experience of living abroad, albeit briefly, seemed to have opened up an opportunity to negotiate and put her ongoing learning of French "to the test against the teenagers who use[d] it" on French ground, thereby helping her recognize that "their language is changing as well" and that the inevitable practice of refashioning and transforming language, be it English (as used in the United States or beyond) or French, was happening "all around" the globe.

This pluralistic view of English and how it actually worked seemed, as she described, to be "totally contradictory" to the more static and deterministic view of English and the learning of reading and writing in English that appeared to be valued and reinforced by her actual grandmother. Upon her own confession, Malika declared that she was inevitably "a mixture of both" conflicting orientations to language, language use, and language relations, each of which accentuated a different aspect of her literate identity. As "the only person of color" in her FYW classroom with concerns that her language usage may be constantly and "silently judg[ed]," hence having "so much to prove" academically, the way her "real" grandmother upheld English-language standards was a constant reminder that her language resources and the way she deployed them may get treated as "ghetto or too opinionated, loud." At the same time, her "artificial" grandmother's "more worldy" stance toward language difference allowed Malika to "go against the grain and question" taken-for-granted assumptions in oral and written communication. In stark opposition to her "artificial" grandmother's accommodative, progressive stance, Malika's "real" grandmother, a retired English professor closely affiliated with a historically black liberal arts university, was "very critical" of Malika's "ability to speak English and the way in which [she] use[d] English" in her writing. In fact, as an academic professional invested with an institutional responsibility, Malika's grandmother appeared to share with Nur's mother the same deep-seated tendencies to treat Standard English as a sanctified object not to be adulterated through contact with substandard language practices and eventually always felt the need to correct Malika's "improper usage" of words and sentences. As Malika reported, "It's always a correction because she believes that I should be upholding the standards." Though her grandmother never quite uttered those scolding words, Malika could almost sense her reacting furiously, condemning her violation of standard language practice: "You're NOT gonna use slang around me!" She perceived Malika's alternative language practices as "disrespecting" the English language, its rules, and its standards as enduring idealizations firmly enshrined in the same dictionaries—regarded as tangible artifacts for supposedly regulating and fixating English—Malika herself invoked earlier to exemplify the fluidity and changeability of the language.

Contesting the monolingualist logic of the universality, rigidity, and timelessness of English-language standards that her grandmother championed, Malika firmly asserted her strong sense of agency over a language she conceived of as always changeable and adaptable: "I kinda twist and mold it [English] into whatever I feel is necessary, and to her, it's some kind of set thing that you should respect and learn . . . I believe that the standards change for the occasion." Calling herself "the queen of code switching," Malika not only "s[aw] things differently" but, more important, was "very responsive to the environment" and its changing demands while moving with dexterity among her African American

Vernacular English (AAVE), the ways of using English deemed acceptable by the academy and its numerous gatekeepers like her "real" grandmother, and her growing expertise in formal French and the French slang she acquired abroad.

When it came to learning academic written English, the only possible approach Malika could imagine taking to follow her grandmother's advice to "respect" this "set thing" called SWE was through doing her best to keep her language resources in their sociopolitically assigned places and monitor any obvious leakage across allegedly rigid, airtight linguistic boundaries. However, no matter how hard she tried to seal all the cracks, so to speak, she "c[ouldn]'t help but letting them seep into [her] papers" in FYW. Though Malika felt that the diverse values, worldviews, and discursive resources she inevitably brought to her composing processes were much more accommodated in her FYW course than in informal lessons about proper and correct usage with her grandmother, she still had to grapple with her writing teacher's comment on one of her essays that said "A little too colloquial." As she started revising this essay for her final course portfolio, Malika was forced to negotiate between a natural tendency and desire to mobilize her own understanding of her language resources as fluid and fairly borderless, on one hand, and, on the other hand, her teacher's evaluative judgment with an implicit suggestion for amendment, which according to Malika seemed to impose a disembodied intellectual experience and engagement with language use in her writing. When discussing her revision plans, Malika stated that she intended to keep unchanged those very instances in her writing marked out as needing to be reworked to sound more academic. As Malika argued, though the writing practices and conventions that maintained the unacceptability of slang and colloquialism in her written texts were conceived of as givens (as indirectly reflected in her teacher's comment and as inculcated by her "real" grandmother), she could not approach her writing as operating autonomously from the personal or socially situated character of her writerly persona.

Clearly not demonstrating the right uptake as her teacher would have expected her to, Malika confidently placed the onus of sense meaning across language difference on her readers: "I take pride in my voice no matter how flawed it might be. I am not willing to sacrifice that quite yet. I shouldn't sacrifice myself, why shouldn't my readers be more accommodating?" This deliberate lack of uptake on her part constituted strategic divergence from the long trajectory of, as Malika explained, repetitively "being a sellout" to her ethnolinguistic self throughout her English language and literacy education. Perhaps emboldened by an understanding of English as translingual that seemed to be supported by her "artificial" grandmother's ideological and pedagogical interventions, Malika was proud of her ability to "pick and choose [her] battles," and this certainly was a battle Malika was willing to fight to preserve her earned voice and agency as "the only student of color in the classroom."

"并不是一条界线划分，而是包容"

His first year in the United States and at UOS specifically, where he intended to major in materials science and engineering, was Li Ming's seventh year away from his hometown, Suzhou, in the Jiangsu Province of southeast China. As an early study abroad sojourner sent by his parents to Singapore to achieve a better high school education and gain a more global edge, Li Ming clearly had a wealth of linguistic and discursive resources at his disposal, with considerable differences in their level of development. An only child and grandson in his family, Li Ming described "a close sense of intimacy," wholeness, and attachment to his Suzhou dialect—which he used only with his parents and grandparents and in which he had partial conversational competence, as it was a considerably declining variety among teens his age—and the Mandarin he used in public spaces and had formally studied in China and Singapore. Li Ming indicated that his grasp of Mandarin academic literacies "outweigh[ed]" that of English in which "his way of phrasing may be awkward," at least according to his FYW teacher's written feedback. Given China's and Singapore's ever-deepening integration into the globalized economy and its domineering language, as Li Ming had the unique chance to experience education in both economically driven nations, the prevalence of his representation of English as an unchanging "global, international" language to be fully mastered following NES norms for its instrumental exchange value to both individuals and societies was not surprising.

As Li Ming's travels confronted him with moments of confusion and difference resulting from considerable language and cultural contact, he recalled how the "conflicts" he experienced in meaning and identity negotiations over the vibrant presence of Singlish in daily activities and interactions ultimately led to his evolving understanding that "languages are actually a form of ideologies" and to his curiosity toward learning about the intricate relations among ways of knowing, thinking, living, and languaging. Informed by Michael Byram's (1997, 1–2) theorization of intercultural communicative competence, I earlier ascribed the role of "sojourner"—potentially more complex and valuable than that of an unaffected traveler—to Li Ming mainly because his ability to reflect on, assess, critique, and destabilize "unquestioned and unconscious beliefs, behaviours, and meanings" in transnational space became apparent and intensified in his engagement with the requirements of one of his major writing projects, and "his own beliefs, behaviours, and meanings [we]re in turn challenged and expected to change."

In response to a prompt that asked students to come up with accessible and relevant ways of re-presenting selective core academic concepts or themes explored in the FYW classroom to their local community and compose a detailed statement of their rhetorical decisions, Li Ming chose to introduce his parents to the theme of "linguistic identity" as it emerged in his own reading of and collective class discussions around Anzladúa's essay and Pacita Abad's artwork. Knowing that his parents had "little English proficiency" and "limit[ed] mastery" to effectively communicate in the language of the academy, Li Ming opted to tackle the peculiar weave of linguistically and culturally based terms, metaphors, and meanings in those verbal-visual texts first through a letter he composed in Mandarin and then in a follow-up phone interview. Mindful of time zone differences and established sociocultural perceptions of politeness, Li Ming argued that his strategic choice of writing genre provided the necessary degree of formality his parents expected of him and sufficient time to execute and "craft out the best translation" before undertaking the complex on-the-spot translation and interpretation required in a phone conversation. Because of his conviction (in contrast with Malika's) that the labor and responsibility of meaning making is attributed solely to the writer/speaker, in order to accommodate potential non-intelligibility by his non-Chinese-speaking teacher and peer-review partners, Li Ming provided his own Chinese-English translations of the formal letter and of selections from the phone call transcript.

Despite the added difficulty of having to translate academic English discourse to Chinese and then back to English, Li Ming recognized the value of such complex cross-language work in helping him approach the concept of linguistic identity in his writings from multiple vantage points and bring a new insight "different from what [he] receive[d] from [his] teacher and peers." As his parents pointed out that his and his classmate's sole focus on the costs of transnational mobility was simply part of the story, this encouraged Li Ming to construct a stronger counterargument to the prevalent narrative of loss elucidated in his class discussions and instead to highlight in his writing the potential rewards and productive challenges of literate negotiations across linguistic and cultural difference. Prompted by Anzaldúa's and Mali's (in Abad's work) experiences of chafing friction, Li Ming shared emerging concerns with his parents about how to define and maintain his own cultural and ethnolinguistic identity as he straddled diverse language and cultural worlds. In response, his parents were quick to contest popular views of "natural" dividing lines on the basis of cultural or linguistic criteria and argued instead that "人类的共性，无论东西方，并不是一条界线划分，而是包容" 'There is no clear cut line of eastern and western culture; it is all mixed and blended' (Li Ming's translation). This cognitively challenging cross-border exercise allowed Li Ming to complicate and "refine the definition of language identity" he was exposed to in class. In addition, experiencing firsthand the complex realities of thickly interpreting and recasting academic concepts gave rise to Li Ming's break from a one-to-one approach to translation and to his changed beliefs that "there is no exact translation from a word from a single language to another language."

Thanks to his FYW teacher who provided a hospitable environment for the vexed issues of language and cultural diversity, Li Ming was able to "reap the opportunity" and consciously "take actions" to engage in this sort of back-and-forth movement between and across language resources, cultural contexts, and meanings. Upon his own confession, he would not have thought about "going this direction" of drawing on his reservoir of linguistic and cultural knowledge on his own accord because in his mind, effective academic English writing practices required remaining "confined inside" this "extremely neutral," English-only, translation-free "zone." Li Ming identified these perceptions as originating in what he referred to as the "general academic environment" in his prior and current literacy education. Based on the way he was taught English in China and then Singapore, he relied on monolingualist conceptions of the mastery of normative spelling, grammar, and punctuation as "the first priority" in writing, sometimes even "before the content." These deeply embedded and implicitly assumed ideas about the fixity, givenness, and universality of language standards and conventions that have moved with Li Ming from abroad seemed to also be confirmed and reinforced in the context of his FYW class with the occasional emphasis on "*the* standard" language practices in academic writing as invulnerable to change and on the students' sole responsibility to "get these things right" (repeated twice in transcript) and produce "grammatically correct" writing.

As is apparent in the interview exchange[14] below, when I pressed Li Ming to elaborate on his perceptions of such imposed neutrality and fixity in language and literate practices in hopes to deliberately challenge them, particularly in relation to the new possibilities of language and cultural identification his translation exercise opened up, he acknowledged the contradiction I was trying to point out in his assertions by referencing his original definition of language as an ideological construct:

> 1 L: I have to be extremely neutral in the sense I bring—**I do not bring ANY cultural aspect into this, into my writing itself** because . . . I'm not being neutral anymore . . .
>
> 2 N: Who taught you to think of Standard English that way? Where did you get these ideas from?
>
> 3 L: I think it's from, uh, I wouldn't say WHO taught me but **the general, um, academic environment.**
>
> [. . .]
>
> 4 L: I know academic is supposed to be shared aCROSS groups. So I'm afraid that what I'm writing may not [be] understood by the—so I'm trying, uh (.) [to] **hide my own like understanding and trying to provide what THEY** [native-English-speaking audience]—**what I understand that they can understand.** Yeah.
>
> 5 N: But if as you mentioned earlier, language use is not neutral but echoes different ideologies, cultural values, and worldviews, don't you think that even in your attempt, um (.), Li Ming, to be neutral, you cannot separate language from the identities of its learners like yourself. Is that even possible? . . .
>
> 6 L: Yeah, but I, I I know it's imPOSSible to be neutral, but **for academic, it has to be neutral**—as neutral as possible. Yes.
>
> [. . .]
>
> 7 N: What about the languages that are in your possession? The way you work with Chinese and English? Especially after an assignment like this? Do you ALSO see them as you see your cultural identity; you know that you can't really draw a dividing line? This is where MY CHINESE ends and this is where my ENGLISH begins.
>
> 8 L: **They're more blended**. It's like both of them are part of me. I can't say this is the Chinese part of me, this is the English part of me. I can't really tell. **Everything is is integrated as a whole.**
>
> 9 N: So in other words, even when your teachers are not pointing out that you could tap into your knowledge of English and your Chinese, even when you haven't thought of using translation in a writing assignment like this, these languages are ALREADY blended and in translation when you're writing?
>
> 10 L: Yes. Yes. **That was some kind of like instinct. Natural instinct.**
>
> [. . .]

11 L: Because when I like drew on the content, I have to go back to my Chinese culture, that education I received from childhood. So it already touched on my, uh, Chinese culture, the Chinese part of this academic term.

12 N: . . . So in other words, no matter how neutral we try to be, even in academic writing situations, our cultural background, the languages that we already know always come into play.

13 L: In a way or another.

Under this "general academic environment," Li Ming seemed strongly socialized into accepting the established norms of what Yasemin Yildiz (2012, 207) refers to as a dominant language and literate "economy of 'in' and 'out,'" where effectively participating in and generating academic written knowledge meant that one would have to adopt a seemingly simple "substitutional logic," that is, "eject" and "keep out" the diverse language and cultural resources picked up in the course of a lifetime and then "make room" solely for what a monolingual English-only ideology counts as standard language practice. At the same time, in line 8, Li Ming perceptively spoke of the "natural" character of his unevenly developed language resources as "blended" and "integrated as a whole" and of the supposedly visible line conventionally separating them under a monolingualist mind-set as increasingly blurred. Despite my efforts to bring to his attention that written communication, even in academic situations, without difference and translation was "inconceivable, a *non-sens*" (Cronin 2003, 90) and though he had already been thinking along similar lines throughout our conversation (see line 10) in relation to his language resources and his ways of putting them into useful practice, he seemed to push such a position aside (lines 1, 6, 13) when discussing his academic literacies. This may be a product of years of exposure to prevailing monolingualist language representations and practices in daily academic life and work across various institutions and geographic locations and perhaps, as a result, he did not feel entitled to question and defy such schooled language representations.

It was the same "general academic environment" that seemed to constrict, control, and block from view the complexity and potentiality of the cognitively taxing practice of double translation he engaged in in his writing project. At my question about the transversality or the difference in meanings and rhetorical effect created through such intense cross-language work and about moments of untranslatability—most particularly Anzaldúa's metaphor of taming tongues, which, as he admitted, passed uneasily into Chinese—that he intriguingly left out when cataloguing his translation choices in his reflection statement, Li Ming explained that "it's not talk about translating academic to non-academic. It's basically, uh, a linguistic translation. Like from English to Chinese. So I didn't include that in detail." To successfully complete the task at hand, Li Ming had to negotiate the perceived value of his cross-language work with his explicit knowledge of the writing prompt and assessment rubric, which constituted, in Anis Bawarshi's (2003) words, "genred sites" of articulation and consequential linguistic and literate action. He also had to take into account his perceptions of what such genred sites revealed about the local discursive and ideological structures already in place in his FYW classroom and institution at large and how they variably positioned his language resources and situated practices. In other words, though Li Ming's work presented the possibilities of borderless, flexible cultural and linguistic crossing, it still had to rub against dominant valuations for the fixity and boundedness of language norms and conventions as reflected in his course documents.

Unable to locate the "extra work" across language and cultural difference he put into meeting the requirements of this assignment in specific language from the rubric criteria, Li Ming assumed that the fruits and labor of moving across linguistic, cultural, and ideological landscapes seemed to be overwhelmingly subordinate to negotiations across audiences, registers, genres, or media and not constituting as much "real" intellectual work within his FYW classroom's and his institution's political economy of language. Though he "benefited from a closer connection" with his parents, who didn't always get a chance to learn about the particularities of his academic work, Li Ming complained about the disproportionate demands imposed on him compared to his NES peers who didn't have to go through the same trouble of translating to and from English.[15] On top of having to work with what he regarded as the already highly demanding task of learning university-level academic English writing and reading practices, the actual increase in cognitive complexity and intensity involved in producing and analyzing his English-Chinese-English translations required considerable energy and "double the time," yet both the material demands and potential intellectual heft of his cross-language work remained unaccounted for in the assessment of his writing project.

SUMMARY AND CONCLUDING REMARKS

As Nur, Malika, and Li Ming moved among the fundamentally conflicting monolingual, multilingual, and translingual understandings and usages of language, which existed simultaneously and in perpetual tension in various domains of their literate lives, they had to navigate complex language relations characterized by both fixity and fluidity, territorial assertions and flows, insularity and permeability, English-only and cross-language work—key features of a postmonolingual state variously defining their language and literate engagements and negotiations. These student writers with widely diffuse literate experiences and capabilities were coming into the FYW curriculum with a range and sophistication of highly specific linguistic and semiotic resources and variable in-school and out-of-school socializing practices for the values and meanings attached to those resources in their academic literacies. More precisely, the ubiquitous sets of representations they brought to their dealings with language and language difference in their literacy learning were mediated through a messy configuration of social networks within which these representations traveled.

Conversations with Malika, for instance, indicated that contestation in language representational practices existed even within the same family circle, as different prominent professional black women in her surrounds have had conflictual histories and life experiences involving cultural and linguistic plurality and hence differently socialized her into viewing and using language for competing social goals. Both grandmothers were immersed in the English-language teaching and learning industry to which they each brought contradictory intellectual and ideological concerns and aspirations: the "real" grandmother grew up during the economic hardships of the Great Depression, hence she perceived and treated full native-like proficiency of mainstream English in the higher education sector as guaranteeing and sustaining employment amid significantly reduced socioeconomic mobility among African American communities at the time; on the other hand, the "artificial" grandmother had a generational experience of coming of age in an era where creating social change was deemed possible thanks to the Civil Rights Movement and ultimately put her own English-language teaching policies and practices in the service of revising and altering these sweeping master narratives in secondary-level education of blindly "adopting the standard" and "having to conform," as Malika explained. Around her actual grandmother, Malika was exposed to passionate beliefs about the importance and significance of achieving perfect mastery of the standard language of the "culture of power" (Delpit 1988) for the family's full and effective participation in mainstream American life and to strong views about violations of its grammatical and mechanical rules as the "number one cardinal sin," as Malika reiterated on several occasions. Concurrently, spending much more time at home and on the road with her artificial grandmother had a compounding effect on Malika's decision to strategically align herself in her revision of her FYW portfolio with being and doing "black" as a "resistant" female student writer through performing her written English "against the grain."

Telling us something about the translingual language representations she had taken up through repeated informal brokering encounters with her artificial grandmother, Malika demonstrated how her linguistic expertise and attachment to AAVE could not be so easily discarded in her written text. However, she seemed to subscribe to a reductive view of successful written communication as a matter of choosing between either submitting to dominant demands on her language use in writing the way her real grandmother and her university writing teacher would want her to or affirming her individual language and cultural differences. As such, she treated her translingual practice as only a right for voice and criticality that she couldn't and "shouldn't sacrifice," as she put it. Particularly because the pedagogical rationale for her FYW class did not scaffold translingual meaning making, Malika was unprepared to move forward and put her written English into work as a mobile resource for active meso-political negotiations with conventional readers like her teacher and real grandmother who commit to opposing language representations, values, and practices (I will elaborate on such translingual-oriented pedagogical goals in chapter 5).

International students like Nur and Li Ming seemed to also be as translingually disposed as Malika toward English and their other language resources as inseparable from and in a "permanent state of indebtedness to" (Cronin 2003, 171) other openly flowing language and cultural resources and practices. Though dismissed by her mother as a clear sign of linguistic imperfection and incompetence, Nur was most expert in and affiliated to what she named "slum" English, characterized by amalgamating together and renewing features drawn from vernacular Malay, English, and her rudimentary knowledge of Tamil and Mandarin in sociolinguistic landscapes. Li Ming emphasized his view of the inseparability and complexity of language, culture, and identity to which he naturally brought his multiple investments, alignments, and desires. However, when it came to their literate transactions in the FYW classroom, we witnessed the reduction of English in their imagination to an identifiable, immaterial, and impenetrable entity surgically removed from their ever-evolving contexts and agentive doings as if it really existed independent of them. Their assumptions about language fixity, isolationism, and purity were mainly enforced by external policing and verbal hygienic practices—explicitly exercised by Nur's mother, and in Li Ming's case, these were not fully traceable to specific human agents but instead functioned tacitly through a collective intellectual environment that traversed national-cultural borders (in his case, China, Singapore, and the United States).

We've seen Li Ming claim a certain degree of ownership and authority over English and his other language resources in one of his writings in response to an oral invitation by his teacher permitting him to do so. Pursuing the full complexities and possibilities of his labor, however, was impeded by his felt need to censor what he depicted (and tossed aside) from the "collaborative hybridization" of his text in its "production and understanding" (Cronin 2013, 40) with the aid of his Chinese-literate parents (and potentially his writing teacher and peers), based primarily on his representations of his hybridized English as less meaningful and relevant in relation to what dominant monolingualist assumptions have predisposed him to place more weight on.

Though also influenced by similar dominant monolingualist representations through social engagements with her real grandmother, Malika's case is a bit different from Nur's and Li Ming's in that her artificial grandmother, yet another educational authority figure, instigated an alternative practice-based view of language that directly and openly challenged such deeply held assumptions about language use, language relations, and language difference in writing imposed by educational institutions and their various gatekeepers (including her actual grandmother). With a widened and diversified repertoire of language representational practices, Malika was determined to continue treating her meaning-making resources, even in educational landscapes, as strategic advantages in her literacy learning and development. However, for a more rhetorically effective realization of her translingual practice, Malika still needed to more seriously explore and experiment with multiple ways of achieving the performative meanings and voice at which she was aiming in her writing. In this sense, she would have benefited from more pedagogical guidance on how to act strategically on her refined language representations in academic writing through considering whether and how to cue her eventual readers "for encountering different, unexpected uptakes when these readers might not be prepared for, interested in, or tolerant of difference and when uptakes are subject to power imbalances" (Bawarshi 2016, 248).

There appears to be an obvious connecting thread between the analysis I've offered here and what we've observed at the level of language representations and practices in Beirut, in that a climate of postmonolingual language-ideological tensions seems to cut across national, cultural, and linguistic boundaries and forces itself on the teaching and learning of university-level writing in both writing program ecologies. In her cross-cultural analysis of French and US student writing, though interested in the side of language practices more than representations of them, Tiane Donahue (2013, 156; see Donahue 2008 for a further discussion) makes a similar observation that becoming and "being a 'first-year' student doing" academic written work while attempting to reconcile individual desires with shared expectations and values "might trump" cultural, sociolinguistic, and political landscapes. In comparing student writers' representational practices from different parts of the world, one would expect to find more differences than commonalities. After all, Lebanon and the United States are the most distant of nation-states in their economic and geopolitical standing and the concomitant management of and responses to language diversity. Given the nation's current status as the global superpower, for instance, the US's unmatched language heterogeneity and plurality in terms of both intensity and complexity have altered constructions of Americanism and American cultural identity at the level of statistical significance but not collective social consciousness. The ideological dominance of English-only monolingualism, which further tightens an already strong Herderian weave of language, culture, community, and a bounded nation-state in social perception and public discourse, has created a historical cultural barrier to the acceptance, promotion, and learning of language resources other than standard English (Gal 2006; Ricento 2006; Wiley 2000). As meso-level implementations of Washington's language policy suggest, pervasively naturalized monolingualist representations of language and language difference in literacy education continue to thwart the state's progressive and accommodative policy agenda. In a developing country like Lebanon, on the other hand, a strong dependence on regional and transnational relations for continued banking- and tourism-driven prosperity has rendered language diversity not only a statistical norm but also a sociocultural and national ethos, explicitly articulated in its official language and language-in-education policies.

Despite these noticeable differences in macro-level (geo)political, socio-historical, and economic conditions and ideologies, a postmonolingual reading of the language representational practices revealed in the accounts from both research sites point toward more parallels than divergences. Equally struggling to make sense of the multiplicity, ambiguity, and contradiction of language representational practices as they related to their local writing ecologies and material conditions, FYW students in both locales had to push through, with varying degrees of successes and failures, the constraints and affordances that surrounded their understandings and subsequent usages of English in their language and literacy learning experiences. Overall, the experiences recounted by my participants in Lebanon and the United States pointed toward the extent to which the inherent characteristics of English as dynamic, mutable, and negotiated in their sociolinguistic landscapes clashed with powerful monolingualist conceptualizations of English in educational landscapes as an orderly, standalone system, located and kept firmly outside the putatively well-defined boundaries of their changing literate resources, identities, and realities. Their felt sense of the fixity, neutrality, and universality of standard English writing practices and conventions and the tensions this produced in their FYW coursework placed a stranglehold on their understanding of what might be linguistically possible in their written texts and hence on their ability to productively utilize the full range of language and semiotic resources at their disposal.

With established views of English in educational landscapes as a discrete, autonomous entity, students like Nathalie, Naser, Lucas, and Nur could not even consider the option of reshaping and modifying English and their other resources to meet their changing goals and desires; and those like Diva, KAPPA, Malika, and Li Ming, who chose to mobilize and capitalize on the various language resources and practices they ideally perceived as most valuable to their personal, academic, and intellectual development, still felt they could not openly and fully exercise their translingual orientation in their writings at all times and in all literate situations. Metaphoric articulations among student writers in Beirut of an obsession with the interiority and unbridled agency of English as in and of itself producing performative effects along with frequently repeated phrases among FYW students in Seattle in reference to putatively fixed, universal language practices and conventions in their academic work (e.g., "it's a given," "it is expected," "it's supposed to be," "it is obvious," or "taken for granted") are all indicative of the forcefulness of these historically held monolingualist assumptions and their perceived naturalness as uncontested truths about language and language practice in writing and its learning.

Interestingly, similar dynamics with regard to working across language difference were in play within the more open and accepting atmosphere of Seattle's FYW program and the less tolerant writing program ecologies in Beirut. For these students, translingual language relations, sanctioned in both Beirut's and Seattle's superdiverse sociolinguistic landscapes, had to be pursued either under the noses of their writing teachers (as in the cases of Diva in Beirut and Malika in Seattle), after asking for their blessing (as with KAPPA), or only in response to pedagogical invitations that unfortunately remained shallow in their commitments to language difference (like Li Ming's case). Full deployment of language and semiotic resources among students like Diva, KAPPA, and Malika who nimbly worked between the cracks of imposed English-only imperatives or among those like Li Ming who chose to take advantage of classroom affordances was confined by monolingualist English-only representations, which admit to no leakage or traffic across putatively tight linguistic boundaries. The assumption that a "clear line of demarcation" and containment (Mangelsdorf 2013, 113) can and should be traced around idealized, pure, authentic, and differentiated language entities seemed to hold strong and heavily informed their language and literacy learning experiences. For instance, Diva was forced to suppress her code-meshing practices in high-stakes writing situations; KAPPA was unsure how to address the challenges of working with Italian sources in his research writing tasks in light of a sole focus in his FYW class on conventional English-only academic research and citation practices; Li Ming sensed that he could not effectively develop in his writing assignment the difficult translation choices he made and what his experience of translation suggested about the possibilities and problematics of working across language and cultural difference; even Malika, who seemed the most determined among the four to turn dominant language relations in her FYW course to her own advantage, still had to pit her alternative representations and subsequent practices against her writing teacher's (and her real grandmother's orally conveyed) strict expectations and valuations. What is significant, however, is that the translingual orientations toward English and other vibrant language resources in Malika's repertoire that she confidently subscribed to in literate interactions with an actual English teacher like her artificial grandmother had a fundamental influence on how far she was committed to manifesting them in her own language practices even in high-stakes writing.

This general tendency to sidestep the concrete, inevitable labor of reworking English in written texts as "always-already translated" and translating (Cronin 2013, 38)—which is part and parcel of these students' translingual meaning making—in both writing program ecologies that appear to be pervaded with monolingualist English-only representations and those that do not philosophically subscribe to such blinkered representations but instead enact more accommodative multilingualist orientations is telling. The possibility of mobilizing and transforming students' deployed resources, including and especially English, and what they might imagine to be the discrete, stable nature of these resources is unimaginable under the dominant English-only orientations to teaching writing we've seen in Beirut and is also not seriously considered under the multilingual-oriented pedagogical approaches prominent in Seattle's writing program (and less so in Beirut). Still not aimed at confronting, problematizing, and potentially transforming (subtly or dramatically) the monolingualist language representational practices that seem to have a strong grip over FYW students' language resources and practices, these traditional multilingualist orientations to teaching writing through creating textual and pedagogical spaces for a multiplicity of language resources, however good the intent may be, do not cut very deep. Instead, they remain anchored in the same long-standing language ideologies they are designed to get beyond, thereby inflecting the way these resources are themselves configured, perceived, and put into literate practice in relation to one another as wholly separate and circumscribed categories.

Recall here Louis-Jean Calvet's (2006, 151) formulation that representations concerning language resources, language relations, and language difference in writing determine the nature of practices of these and, at the same time, are the "driving force of change" in local language and writing ecologies. Having a strong "retroactive effect" as they do on "usages" and "being capable of modifying them" considerably, Calvet's (2006, 131) work therefore prompts us to pay attention to FYW students' socioculturally constructed and transmitted understandings of language, which are important aspects of their literate learning and constantly guide their practices. With language representations playing a fundamental, if often implicit, role in the dynamics of language fixity and fluidity in literate situations, I discuss in chapter 5 initial pedagogical efforts to counter-socialize students by dislocating language standards and conventions from the fixed, neutralized status in time and space attributed to them in monolingualist and multilingualist approaches to teaching writing and instead relocating them within the logic of critical translation. In fact, it is crucial to start sensitizing current and new generations of FYW students, albeit slowly, to the fact that the dominant language representations, which clearly demarcate a particular standard of language usage in their writing as static, timeless, and uniform, are not really divinely created and mystically infused with value, hence irreversible, for they emanate—just like the lines of demarcation they imagine—from social material practice that can be reworked and re-created. As Juan Guerra (1997, 251) points out in early work, the college writing classroom cannot continue to serve as "a mere port of entry" into a putatively stable academic discourse community with likewise fixed language and literate practices but rather can and should become a key site for powerful "initiation" and brokerage into a more complex "way of looking at language," into its active naming and subsequent doing both locally and in the rest of the world. We therefore cannot ignore the fact that the *invention* of English itself, the set of descriptive and analytical terms for *referencing* it, and the ways of consequently *acting* on particular situations involving its presence "constitute an intervention in and [can significantly] modify" the postmonolingual realities of our and our students' "ecolinguistic niche" (Calvet 2006, 248).

While we are led to believe that a monolingualist version of English is what students actually want and need to succeed in American or American-style universities, a lot of our students (as we have seen with students like Diva, KAPPA, Malika, and Li Ming and shall see in the next chapter with students considered both linguistically and socioculturally marked and unmarked in the US educational system) do find on their own or can potentially find with our sustained guidance, scaffolding, and support real value in experiencing and working with English as a language always and already in and undergoing critical translation (Pennycook 2008; Cronin 2013). The analysis I present in chapter 5 offers a glimpse of the potential yield of presenting a more complex and intricate view of written English, as both a constituent and an embodiment of perpetual "tensions around the politics of translations across spaces, times, ideologies, [language resources,] and cultures" (Ramanathan 2006, 224) at local, regional, national, and international levels.

5

TRANSLINGUAL ACTIVISM
Turning up the Volume of Critical Translation in Writing Pedagogy

Representations of and resulting practices with English in mainstream writing pedagogy as an autonomous, discrete entity with stable, distinct, and clearly defined frontiers impervious to foreign influence have contributed to the reduction or at times even elimination of potential opportunities for student writers in the national and international locales explored in this book to take part in a globally powerful translation traffic.[1] Falling outside the monolingual English-only norm of erecting walls and constructing language fortresses, situated translation practice and the degree of "*opacité*" (Bernabé, Chamoiseau, and Confiant 1989, 52) involved in its production and interpretation have generally provoked concerns about the "distortion, contamination" of putatively fixed academic conventions (Venuti 1998, 31) and about meddling with a dominant valuation of efficiency and transparency in meaning transmission. Under the dogma of English-only monolingualism and its concomitant shunning of translation inquiry and practice,[2] the traffic in meanings, interpretations, texts, resources, and practices in the writing classroom has remained decidedly one-sided—always and only into a presumably autonomous entity called English—and ostensibly smoothly running, mess-free, and devoid of full-fledged cross-border exchanges and transformations.

Contesting such normative representations and treatments of language generally and English specifically that have come to characterize conventional conceptualizations of translation and the nature of literate work enacted under their auspices, we have been witnessing a revived scholarly interest in the place and role of translation[3] in language and literacy learning and instruction, though not the reductive version of translation that has proliferated since the advent of old-fashioned grammar-translation methods and practices.[4] This growing recognition of the value and relevance of translation is informed by convergent perspectives in complementary language- and literacy-related fields advancing the (re)appraisal of translation as lying at the heart of all meaning-making and negotiation practices in our contemporary superdiverse world, where engagement with diverse circles of transcultural and translingual flows is becoming increasingly inescapable. Critiquing a long history of "translation eschewal" in mainstream English-language education, for example, Alastair Pennycook (2008, 33) argues compellingly that "if students are to enter into the global traffic of meaning, translation has to become central to what we do." Rendering translation as key to understanding the full depth and complexity of language-in-use, Sinfree Makoni and Pennycook (2007, 36) likewise suggest that "all communication"—both written and spoken, between or across languages, and inside the same language, as conventionally perceived—encompasses and "involves translation." In a similar vein, the MLA Ad Hoc Committee on Foreign Languages, in its 2007 report, calls for treating translation not as a peripheral but a principal meaning-making practice, part of a broad traffic of languages, ideologies, and cultures. Supporting pedagogic translation as a resource for language learning in its own right, the MLA Ad Hoc Committee (2007, 242, 236–37, 238) reasserts the centrality of translation as "an ideal context for developing translingual and transcultural competence," which places value on literate individuals' ability to "operate between languages" and across "differences in meaning, mentality, and worldview."[5]

Taking up similar lines of argument in composition studies, Bruce Horner and Laura Tetreault (2016, 20) have recently called for embracing translation as an "analytical tool" for developing translingual orientations to language and language relations as always emergent, fluid, hybrid, and intermingling. Such a focus on the actual and necessary labor of translation in writing pedagogy, Horner and Tetreault argue, activates deliberations over the complex negotiations of language difference in writing as well as the conflicting language ideologies driving or hindering them, explorations that lie at the heart of a translingual approach to writing and its teaching. This perspective, as Horner and Tetreault (2016, 14, 18; emphasis added) observe, necessitates reintroducing into writing pedagogy translation in its full complexities, "not merely as a distinct form of writing but also as a [constant] feature and outcome of *all* writing," writing that produces obvious surface-level as well as concealed, less remarked difference (with the latter deserving of our attention as much as the former) through the reproduction and "reworking of common language practices" and conventions.

The current chapter aligns with and builds on these and many other voices in their contestation of a dominant monolingualist English-only ideology that has kept labor with writing and translation in and out of English apart. I've elaborated in depth in the previous two chapters the significance of representations in effecting any changes on practices and realities involving language and its difference. With this in mind, critiquing a dominant monolingual mind-set or its much vaunted multilingualist variant and simply calling for a translingual approach in composition seem to be insufficient if such calls are not rooted in a sustained investment in confronting, unsettling, and recomposing the very notion of English itself and its sanctioned relations to and discrete operations with other language resources and practices. As a powerful corrective to this actual and potential tendency to continue laboring with language difference from within the same epistemological framework of language we've set out to challenge, Pennycook (2008, 44), citing Michael Cronin (2003), calls for taking up a project of "translingual activism" as a form of collective "political action" and engagement with the sociocultural politics of translation as a central aspect of social and literate life in the national and international arena. From this perspective, then, I argue that translingual activism for teaching English in the writing classroom as constantly and inevitably operating in translation can provide a condition of possibility for intervening in and opening up much-needed explorations of the kind of present-day postmonolingual tensions FYW students are constantly coming to terms with. As I demonstrate in this chapter, if we wish to take seriously the problems of dominant and residual language representations constraining and interfering with students' meso-political negotiations (as textual and interview-based data from superdiverse cities like Beirut and Seattle have brought to light), we are called on as writing teacher-scholars to more openly tackle and interrupt the institutionalized language representations associated with the imposed separation between the roles of (re)writer and translator, which students are, willingly or not, bringing into their academic written work. In the next section, I briefly take up unpacking the notion of translation and the still dominant language representations at the very basis of its theorization and practice before I discuss, with an extended example, some of the potential possibilities and problematics of foregrounding writing-translation connections in writing pedagogy.

RECLAIMING THE 'TRANS-' IN TRANS-LATION

Under an activist dimension to translingualism, which necessitates a serious, open engagement with the representations and subsequent practices concerning language that are grounded in and emergent from students' diverse localities, the notion of critical translation I am interested in here is not so much concerned with conventional approaches to translation as with the neutral, transparent, and linear flow or mapping of lexical or structural items from one code into another. Translation, in this classical sense, has been treated as an exact mirroring of an original or source text/language with full equivalence in meaning, one that is "mandated by the original" (Weinberger 2000, 8), thus rendering any deviations from it undesirable and reprehensible.[6] Driven by a hallowed search for "*un meme contenu selon un code different*" (Bénard et Horguelin 1979, 17), this particular way of thinking about translation maintains and fortifies monolingualist and disguised multilingualist representations of language and language relations in that it is essentially concerned with "original" and translated texts as presumably belonging to and composed in what are believed to be stable, autonomous, bounded, and discrete non-traversing languages-as-entities.

Contrastingly, under a translingual orientation to language resources as intertwined and interstitched and themselves traversed by ineluctable relations of difference and heterogeneity, all that talk about and meticulous attention to privileging the clear linguistic parallelism and symmetry between texts and their translations does not make much sense. In fact, Anthony Lewis (2005, 22) argues that an alternative "view of languages as interacting and mixed rather than distinct and homogeneous systems has very specific consequences for a conception of translation." In this sense, under an activist translingual framework—which unsettles and contests monolingualist assumptions about languages as pre-given, unitary entities existing in separation from the agentive subjectivities that produce and partially sediment them, from the world, and from each other—normative conceptualizations of translations become hard to maintain. The dynamic *trans-* take on translation I adopt in this chapter, or what I'm referring to as critical translation, foregrounds the symbiotic interpenetration and intermingling of the "original" as conventionally conceived and the translation, much like the fabric of the banyan tree with its roots, trunk, and branches confused and enmeshed, hence nullifying origins/starting points and targets/endings in all meaning-making practices and literate transactions. Critical translation is thus construed as an ongoing rhetorical, contingent form of "re-writing," as translation scholar André Lefevere (1992) calls it, or, as Sujit Mukherji (1994) describes it in Indian literary criticism, "new writing," which emerges in response to various social, linguistic, cultural, historical, (geo)political, and economic relations of power and difference. As Susan Bassnett and Harish Trivedi (1999, 2) explain, critical translation is never "an innocent, transparent activity but is highly charged" and charging with significance and difference at every stage and every encounter, rarely, if ever, involving "a relationship of equality between [sic] texts, authors, [readers,] or systems." What gets minimized or overlooked by traditional understandings of translation is exactly what is specific to critical translation as a point of entry into and departure—but never an endpoint—for sustained engagements with the language and "cultural transactions, the appropriations, negotiations, migrations, mediations, recodings, and transposings" (Pratt et al. 2010, 96) involved in and giving rise to its practice in diverse literate contexts.

FROM BEIRUT TO SEATTLE: TRANSLATING WRITING-TRANSLATION CONNECTIONS INTO VISIBILITY

"Remember that writing is translation, and the opus to be translated is yourself."

E. B. White, in a letter to a college student
(Sims 2012, 27)

"Translation has been too long in exile, for all kinds of reasons which . . . have little to do with any considered pedagogic principle. It is time it was given a fair and informed appraisal."

(Widdowson 2003, 160)

The idea of the rehabilitation and revival of critical translation in writing pedagogy that is behind this chapter was first conceived after I experienced an apparent discordance during my fieldwork in Beirut between the nature of language relations and the treatment of English in first-year writing (FYW) courses, on one hand, and, on the other hand, in undergraduate-level courses on the theory and practice of translation taught by the same teachers. While the English writing and translation teachers I interviewed approached English in their introductory translation classes[7] as bound up with the dynamic materiality of students' locality, always in relation to vibrant language resources (mainly Arabic and sometimes French), these same teachers switched to focusing on English in their FYW classrooms in its own presence and as having status outside the bodies, identities, translingual realities, and local contexts in which it is situated. When I pointed out this lack of synergy between the FYW and translation classes I observed them teaching and invited them to consider whether and how they might potentially harmonize these pedagogies and toward what goals, the teachers reported that they had not previously been aware of this as a possibility in the first place.

As I further explored this mismatch in the nature of language representations and practices between FYW and translation pedagogy in Beirut, student participants who were simultaneously enrolled in both courses seemed to confirm these observations. For instance, in his attempts to contrast the way he experienced and put language into work differently in his FYW and translation classes, one student pointed out that "instead of working with English separately and with Arabic separately, [he] can now think about the relation between the two languages in this [translation] course." While this student described imposed treatments of his available language resources of English and Arabic as operating in FYW in isolation and devoid of any interactive influxes, he was able to infer for himself, in a conscious way, how translation-oriented pedagogy helped establish the presence, relevance, and interaction of the full multiplicity of his vital language resources in concrete intellectual labor. That is to say, as a central aspect of students' ordinary social, academic, and global life, the opportunity to rework English along with other vibrant language resources (for instance, Arabic in this student's case) in translation-related coursework challenged the very monolingualist representations of languages in FYW and their discrete operations as reified, immobile systems with hermetically sealed boundaries. One of the translation teachers I interviewed further explained that because students of translation in these classes are prompted to "think about and work with English and Arabic simultaneously," they develop into textual "detectives with a profound critical eye" and increased "sensibility" toward language difference, constantly deliberating over content, style, diction, coherence, and voice in relation to cultural context, historical period, physical space, and ideological and sociopolitical entanglements in their interpretation and creation of translations.

In the translation classes I observed in Beirut, the assigned translation tasks, activities, and projects enticed first-year students and kept them busy like bees around a honey pot. As the translation students worked their way across an extensive range of translation options, they carefully negotiated the breadth of meanings, registers, and usages, sifting through the choice of every punctuation mark and sentence structure, of words and their neighboring descriptors, local cultural associations, metaphors, and idiomatic expressions, and constantly adding, omitting, clarifying, and making all sorts of linguistic changes and textual adjustments. While these students' language and discursive resources were stowed out of sight in separate compartments as is the dominant norm in their FYW classes, the messy and forked path of doing cross-language work in the translation classes triggered voracious negotiations and multiple (re)readings, (re)writings, and (re)translations, opening up various interpretive doors and sensibilities and at times closing others. This demanding labor of translation was evident, for instance, in one group's prolonged deliberations over the loss and gain of meanings resulting from a rhetorical decision to rework references to the month of May, its "rough winds," and its "temperate" climate in an Arabic translation of Shakespeare's Sonnet 18 and thereby rewrite moderate and pleasant English summers against the backdrop of the geography and cultural specificities of some neighboring Arab countries with long, hot, dry, and humid summers. Extending a classic text like Shakespeare's sonnet beyond its spatial and temporal limits, critical translations in such coursework were not "subsidiary, passive or parasitic" (Guix 2007, 97) but rather active, re-contextualized (re)readings and (re)writings that dared to question, complicate, and leave their own mark even on already well-known texts. As these first-year students kept (re)translating and (re)writing, their labor brought to light how one practice inevitably led to the other, and in their continued practice, the two became interdependent and inseparable.

The more the starkness of Beirut's translational writers' decision-making was laid bare for me to observe, the more I sensed the possibilities of this serious intellectual undertaking, which brought to the fore the "indivisibility between writing and translating" (Bassnett 2011, 52; see also Bassnett and Bush 2007), and the more this made me determined to transport the same level of commitment and complex engagement with the fluidity of language and its workings to my own FYW students' composing processes. Knowing that the term *translation*, as I've cautioned earlier, runs the risk of reinforcing the monolingualist language representations and practices I seek to challenge, I adopt the notational practice of italicizing the prefix *trans-* as a continual mental reminder for approaching '*trans*lation' in the alternative sense of translingual meaning making and interpretation across boundaries of knowledge and understandings of language and being. I follow this practice throughout the chapter and the rest of the book in my pedagogical descriptions of and references to the critical writing-*trans*lation connections I've deliberately created in my own writing classrooms.

In the remainder of this chapter, I present accounts from a *trans*lation-oriented writing assignment design (summarized in figure 5.1) that I've piloted at my home institution in Seattle with both a mainstream and another specialized section (designed separately for self-identified L2 writers) of the required, credit-bearing FYW course.

ASSIGNMENT 1: (RE)WRITING ACADEMIC TENSIONS

Using their language and literacy profile as a chance to revisit, think through, and continue the work already begun of identifying language and cultural resources valuable to meaning-making and social relations, writers-*trans*lators:

- locate tension-filled moments in academic work where perceptions about the institutionally-defined and sanctioned "ways of using English" in writing seem to constrain and stand in the way of effectively mobilizing resources and expressing intended meanings and relations.
- explore and experiment with a range of possible alternative *trans*lations.
- showcase personal annotations of previous work along with its *trans*lation(s).

ASSIGNMENT 2: WRITER-*TRANS*LATOR'S COMMENTARY

Writers-*trans*lators offer a detailed retrospective insight into critical points of decision-making:

- reasons for selecting to *trans*late and cull specific word(s), phrase(s), sentence(s), or entire passage(s) while intentionally leaving out others.
- alternative ways of *trans*lating the existing elements chosen.
- what to selectively retain, omit, add to, substitute, rearrange, recast, or alter from their main written texts.
- intended social and rhetorical effects on various elements of their writing (e.g. organization, meaning [both explicit and implicit], authorial presence and voice, inter-textual links, [counter]argumentation, supporting evidence).
- the uncertainties and messes of planning and executing their *trans*lations as new writings and how exactly those were navigated and handled.

ASSIGNMENT 3: MESO-POLITICS OF *TRANSLATION* AMID READER EXPECTATIONS

Retracing previous steps, writers-*trans*lators explore the following set of questions:

- What specific role(s) did they want what kind of readers to adopt as they read their *trans*lation(s)?
- What local framing strategies did they opt for (or intentionally withhold) in order to signal (or not) such desired role(s)? When adopted, where in the text, and crucially, why did they position these frames?
- What parts of their *trans*lations did they deliberately choose to elaborate on for the sake of successful negotiation and mutual intelligibility?
- Alternatively, what parts of their *trans*lations did they expect their readers to fill in or struggle with? To what specific purpose(s)? And at what cost(s)?
- What was their sense of the specific nature of the language-ideological orientations and social positioning(s) informing each of these individual rhetorical choices as well as their readers' expectations and interpretations?

*Figure 5.1. Summary of writing-*translation* connections sequence*

All students in my specialized FYW course were international visa-holding Chinese students with only one from Taiwan, all of whom had advanced Mandarin Chinese academic literate abilities. As for the mainstream FYW section, of the twenty-three students enrolled, the overwhelming majority of students who identified as belonging to the sociolinguistic mainstream described having studied but not being comfortable with any language other than English, and only three reported having an intermediate to advanced command of Spanish. Nine students in that class were generation 1.5 students of Latino, Vietnamese, Filipino, and Filipino-Chinese descent, with varying degrees of familiarity and experience with a language other than English.

Built around a critical writing-*trans*lation connection where academic writing meets and becomes enmeshed with critical *trans*lation, the assignment sequence I describe below is aimed at engaging students in the following course outcomes: (1) negotiating and experimenting with a wide range of options when working across diverse practices with language, not for correctness, accuracy, and quality writing but rather for rhetorical effectiveness in conveying intended meaning(s) and function(s); and (2) demonstrating rhetorical awareness and responsiveness in creating texts through articulating, assessing, and acting on understandings of the impact of specific choices and decisions. Most obviously, these targeted outcomes are aligned with the essential fundamentals of nationwide FYW curricula outlined in the WPA Outcomes Statement for First-Year Composition (see Yancey 2001) and the Framework for Success in Postsecondary Writing (2011), developed and endorsed by the Council of Writing Program Administrators (CWPA), the National Council of Teachers of English (NCTE), and the National Writing Project (NWP).

Like any other writing class invested in developing students' rhetorical and metalinguistic awareness, the first half of the course focused explicitly on the complexity and heterogeneity of culture, English, and other vibrant languages and the imagined boundaries separating them. We started the course with a close reading and analysis of Amy Tan's essay "Mother Tongue," with its combination of the re-localized Englishes of first- and second-generation female Chinese immigrants. We then moved on to consider iterations of similar and other writing practices and conventions in selections from Haunani-Kay Trask's *From a Native Daughter*, which is marked by the complex blending of English and Hawaiian expressions, chants, personal stories, and reflection but also scholarly research and argumentation. We also read a chapter titled "The Veil" from Marjane Satrapi's graphic memoir *Persepolis*, with the artistic crossing between text and black-and-white illustrations and images. In class discussions, I focused attention on sensitizing my students to relations of *trans*lation and difference in these various texts, but I was also aware that I needed to do so while transcending some of the problematic assumptions (as I discussed extensively in chapter 1) in American popular imagination that exclusively tie such hybridity and fluidity in language usage to non-mainstream sociocultural identities. Toward that aim, I introduced texts authored by those who represent the universal "norm" for all writers, such as British literacy scholar and educator Roz Ivanič and classic white American male writer Henry David Thoreau. I specifically selected Ivanič's (1998) unconventional opening chapter in her book *Writing and Identity*, which blends auto-ethnographic writing into rigorous ethnographic research and analysis, along with the first chapter from Thoreau's *Walden* titled "Economy," in which he inserts Greek and Latin usages, archaic references, semantically dense passages, and poetry into his nineteenth-century prose, thereby rendering his writings impenetrable for modern-day readers. Our talk around this wide variety of texts was not focused on their lexical, syntactic, and rhetorical peculiarities but rather on the kinds of transversality they accomplish, that is, the complex meanings and relations that are being borne by specific practices, and on the cultural politics of academic and social life (at local and [trans]national levels) enabling and disrupting these intended meanings and relations and the uptakes necessary to secure them.

There is neither space nor special reason to explicate the actual writing assignments and projects students worked on in the first half of the course, since similar engagements have been thoroughly described in FYW pedagogies focused primarily on language-related issues (see, for example, Lu 2010; Mangelsdorf 2010; Lu and Horner 2013; Bizzell 2014; Canagarajah 2014). Instead, I will briefly describe here the second half of the course, which was dedicated to introducing and exploring *trans*lation practice as translingual meaning making. Thinking about English written texts as, in a sense, already in relations of *trans*lation, which had slowly begun in the first course sequence, was more directly scaffolded in the second sequence through a collaborative writing project.[8] I encouraged students to choose one of the reading selections we'd already closely examined and that intrigued them the most. To engage students in critical reflections on the uses and limitations of particular language and writing practices and conventions, I asked them to write a brief version of select passages from their chosen reading in which they deliberately excluded one of its linguistic and textual choices, whether seemingly conventional or not. As such, they had the option to exclude characteristics that appeared to be either (semi-)scholarly research and argument, verse, graphic, reportorial prose, autobiographical narratives, anecdotal evidence, or code-meshing practices. In a short essay, they compared the effects of what they'd rewritten to the class's interpretation of these texts while considering what differences in content, form, and purpose seemed to result from excluding these language and writing practices. As such, individual students needed to be judicious in their group negotiations of possible renderings while remaining mindful of their chosen author's purpose, argument, and style. This interactive group writing activity allowed students the opportunity to begin their consideration of the notion of *trans*lation as "re-writing" and to explore how meaning(s) and understanding(s) might be shaped and reshaped through their and others' purposeful use and reuse of language. It led to very vibrant in-group and whole class discussions and reflections on why each of these authors strategically chose to incorporate those specific language and writing practices and not others in composing his or her piece.

These invigorating conversations contributed to generating a wide range of linguistic and rhetorical strategies students might potentially experiment with for diverse performative effects in their own writings. Only after my students had gained some familiarity with the negotiability and translatability of the language and writing conventions and practices expected of them in FYW did I expose them to select texts on *trans*lation theory and practice and introduce them to some basic *trans*lation concepts, all of which I myself use and hint at in this chapter's discussion. With an enhanced awareness of the complex relations of *trans*lation already at work in various academic written texts, those both exemplifying and falling outside the dominant norm in the social imaginary, my students were ready to attempt their own individual *trans*lations through the writing-*trans*lation assignment I describe below.

In the first assignment in the critical writing-*trans*lation sequence I designed, I had asked students to reread existing academic pieces they had already written early in this or any other course and identify moments in their writing where they felt that they did not sound like their true, authentic selves,[9] that they had to overcome a paralyzing sensation as writers, or that their meaning construction was confined or hindered. These particularly difficult, unsatisfactory, or unnatural moments in their written work could take the form of single term(s) used, phrase(s), sentence(s), or entire section(s). Early in the course, students had composed a narrative of their language and literacy learning and development in which they explored and reflected on the actual language and literate resources available to them both inside and outside academic settings, how these connected (socially, culturally, emotionally, somatically, professionally, or intellectually) to their own sense of self and ongoing literate work, and how these resources have shaped and been shaped by their bonds to influential individuals or social institutions in their local surrounds. This language and literacy profile assignment, which is typically incorporated into FYW curricula, served as a reminder to my students of the wide range of language and literate resources they brought and drew on the most, consciously or otherwise, in their effort to learn the kind of academic written English they felt was required of them to survive and thrive in today's academic and business world.

As figure 5.1 shows, in the first assignment in this critical writing-*trans*lation connection sequence, I invited students to consider alternative ways of rewriting the instances of dissonance or inauthenticity they were able to identify in their written texts while still preserving the meaningfulness of the situated experiences, resources, relations, and desires touched upon in their language and literacy profile assignment and which they felt have been overlooked, trivialized, excluded, concealed, or even silenced by a dominant valuation of transparent, translation-free, accurate, neutral, and "correct" academic language and writing practices. Along with their rewritings/*trans*lations, the second assignment in this sequence asked students to compose a writer-*trans*lator's rationale in which they identified the particularities of their *trans*lation choices and analyzed with concrete examples from their efforts at *trans*lation the kind of difference made to meaning or understanding.

After a back-and-forth movement through the different possible renderings of their existing written work and an exploration of the forms of knowledge, meanings, and practices made possible or eliminated through their *trans*lations, the third follow-up writing assignment in this sequence triggered a sense of responsibility toward potential readership among my students and encouraged them to take ownership of the choices they made in their *trans*lations by acting on an understanding of all written communication as social transactions and negotiations. With an intention to immerse students in the complex endeavor of investigating the promise, stakes, and problematics of *trans*lation in the specific context of their actual and imagined personal, civic, academic, and professional life and work, I prompted them to consider issues of readability and intelligibility as they pertained to their *trans*lations. This final and crucial step helped touch on students' false sense of their powerlessness—hence deprived right to even consider to negotiate—in academic reading and writing situations and provided the occasion to revitalize and reinforce their dynamic role as critical (re)*trans*lators, (re)writers, and negotiators of meaning and difference. Engaging them in such an intellectual exercise helped draw their attention away from thinking about their meaning construction practices in writing in terms of the binaries of correct/incorrect, right/wrong, standard/non-standard, norm-conforming/norm-flouting, and more in terms of textual responsibility, intentionality, and agency and how these core elements got played out differently in their own translations.

In her application of narrative theory to the practice of *trans*lation in and through sociopolitical and hence ideological conflict, Mona Baker (2007, 156; emphasis in original) assigns a central place to the concept of "framing," which, in her words, is "part and parcel of the phenomenon of activism" in that it crucially entails the deliberate, agentive act of "setting up structures of *anticipation* that guide others' interpretation . . . usually as a direct challenge to dominant interpretations of" and narratives surrounding a patchwork of written and spoken texts. Building on Baker's (2007, 156) framework of *trans*lation as (re-)narration in relationships of ideological tension and struggle and particularly her "activist sense of framing," the final assignment in this sequence invited my students to approach their *trans*lational choices and the (re)framing strategies they drew upon (maybe at a variety of points or sites within or, alternatively, around their actual *trans*lations) not only as local, immediate linguistic and discursive practices but also as contributing directly and actively to the larger cultural and ideological structures and concrete material realities in which their *trans*lational written work was embedded.

As my students embarked on their own *trans*lations, they were compelled to painstakingly reconcile what academic institutions and their gatekeepers have established as fundamentally unquestionable and untouchable rules and conventions of appropriate English writing with their *modi di dire*, which felt more relevant and necessary for their active construction of meaning(s) in and out of English(es) and other language and cultural resources. Encouraged to unpack and reflect on the complexities of these tensions and their direct effects, students were able to situate their specific *trans*lational choices in relation to broader norms and ideologies shaping their language negotiations without losing sight of their individual texts and the nuances of local meanings, values, and relations. To further contextualize this discussion, I share three concrete examples[10] that seriously engage and reconfigure the postmonolingual tensions and turbulences that pervaded my students' academic writing experiences and labor and which gesture toward the active and conscious decision-making that went into the composition of their individual inter- and intra-English *trans*lations.

Translation 1:

One student writer, Ryan, who self-identified as belonging to the mainstream of American society, wrote in his writer-*trans*lator's memo: "I chose this specific work . . . because I found this whole paragraph to be worded awkwardly. Generally, when going through my past writings . . . I did find that one factor consistently got in the way of my academic writing: the inability to use personal pronouns (such as 'I,' 'my,' 'mine,' or 'me'). This restriction on my choice of words forced me (especially in the case of this section) to reword thoughts I wished to communicate on paper in a way that may seem disjointed or convoluted." Lying among what Ryan described in the same memo as "the established and agreed-upon laws of writing," such as "no contractions" or "do not begin sentences with 'And,'" dominant representations of personal pronoun usage as generally frowned upon in academic prose were repetitively "engrained in [his] mind" by his fifth-grade English teacher. He recounted moments of embarrassment when his well-meaning teacher anonymously displayed on a large screen excerpts from his written work to advise against using first-person pronouns in academic written English, yet his identity was accidentally exposed on the basis of his poor and peculiar handwriting. As he further explained, after that upsetting incident in which his "inappropriate" personal pronoun usage in formal academic writing served as a cautionary tale for the rest of his class, Ryan became determined to resort to various lexical and syntactic means, such as using the passive voice or attributing an agentive role to readers, characters, or the text itself (for instance, his adoption in the excerpt below of phrases like "the marlin and Santiago's 'deaths' show . . ." and "after reading the book, the audience can reflect on . . ."), as an alternative to claiming ownership of his own interpretations and understandings through explicit self-references. The kind of explicit teaching of the features of formal academic discourse and texts as depersonalized and objective that Ryan was exposed to in his early years of schooling have instilled ideas about the necessity for evacuating his personal voice for successful writing and contributed to this reticence to individualize his claims or arguments. Forced to "check it [his personal voice] at the door" throughout his years as a student and novice writer, as he put it,

Ryan, in response to the current sequenced assignment, chose to reclaim his authorial presence and agency in a "new, restructured version" of a concluding section from his high school report on Hemingway's novel *The Old Man and the Sea*:

> Main Writing
>
> Hemingway's novel, "The Old Man and the Sea," is a very interesting tale with a small cast of characters. Rather than depending on characters to make a message, Hemingway uses the environment surrounding his protagonist to tell a tale . . . After reading the book, the audience can reflect on Santiago's interactions with nature to derive a message about nature itself. The marlin and Santiago's "deaths" show a lack of anything good being derived from the conflict. Ultimately, if a battle with nature is taken too far, nobody wins.
>
> Translation
>
> How "The Old Man and the Sea" could create an interesting tale with such a small number of characters fascinated me.[1] Due to the lack of characters, Hemingway used the surrounding environment (rather than actual characters) to present his message . . . Reflecting on Santiago's interactions with nature, I argue that it presented a deeper message about nature itself. More specifically, I contend that Santiago's and the marlin's "deaths" showed that if a battle with nature is taken too far, nobody wins.
>
> Footnote
>
> [1] Typically, inserting the self into one's academic works is frowned upon by academia. Some critics may say that "it could inadvertently lead to an insertion of bias" or that "it could weaken the impact the work may leave upon the reader." However I would argue that, if done correctly, it could add to the work . . . If the audience feels like they are hearing from an actual person (through the flavor provided by the insertion of the self) rather than an anonymous sterile voice, they may be more inclined to consider the author's argument. The added layer of (what can only be described as) "humanity" adds a certain air of likeable authenticity to the argument.

As Ryan experimented with the real possibility of expressing his own voice in his *trans*lation, the generic, impersonal construction "the audience can reflect on" in his previously written book report was rendered as "Reflecting on . . . I argue that." To better foreground his contribution in the active reading and interpretation of Hemingway's literary work, "the marlin and Santiago's 'deaths' show" became "I contend that Santiago's and the marlin's 'deaths' showed that." Although Ryan was keen that the addition of the first-person pronoun in his *trans*lation might impart a conversational and colloquial tone to his formal academic writing and hence be perceived by some conventional academic readers as jeopardizing "the impact" or validity of his argument, he insisted that this devalued practice projected a much-needed authoritative and authentic stance. In his reworking of the academically sanctioned practice of strictly avoiding personal subjects, references, and tone in prior English academic work, Ryan made a deliberate choice to insert a footnote into his *trans*lation as a meta-text, in which he alerted his readers to his decision not to comply with their demands, explained the rhetorical impact of his choice, and ultimately added a sense of legitimacy to such literate practices without disrupting the central stream of the text. In essence, Ryan's footnote served a vital rather than peripheral function in his *trans*lated text in that it interrupted and diverted the dynamic of authority and agency in his actual *trans*lation. He actively negotiated with conventional readers who might be sticklers for punctilious compliance with academic English writing conventions from and through his insurgent footnote—the so-called marginal space for scholarly practice and labor. In this sense, Ryan strategically incorporated into his *trans*lation a counter personalization element, which in effect exerted a centrifugal force pulling readers away from the personal proper, thereby underscoring that the regularized features and conventions that supposedly make up an academic English text may not be as stable, secure, unified, and easily separated from the *trans*lations of them over and again as his readers might have imagined.

Exploring the specific moments of difference and tension that pervaded particular writing situations in his language and literacy learning and development both inside and outside FYW, Ryan wrote:

> I sometimes struggle to word things in my papers; perhaps this could be rooted in a **subconscious rule** to not personalize my essays (emphasis added). As I progress through college and beyond, perhaps this will go away. I am (hoping) to pursue Computer Science as my major. Since this does not heavily require strict academic writing rules, perhaps my writing voice will begin to become more personal. Lately, I have been finding myself (for classes and otherwise) to be writing more papers, project proposals and reports, and letters that require some degree of personalization and the pronoun "I" more than before. This could be leading to a future evolution in my prose. Ultimately, I could write in **my** voice rather than **a** voice (emphasis in original).

Ryan's use of the phrase "my voice" in opposition with "a voice" in this last statement is particularly significant here in that it signals his willingness to reinterpret and rework his relation to the established academic stance he seemed to perceive earlier as existing in a seemingly neutral, contextually and personally evacuated state. As demonstrated by this excerpt, Ryan made his own connections between this heavily sedimented, "subconscious" language practice of pronoun usage in his accumulating experiences of learning academic written discourse, on one hand, and, on another hand, the actual and conflicting language practices that seemed to be required to demonstrate disciplinary knowledge and participation in other domains of his academic college life, that is, his major courses in the hard applied sciences. For a young prospective computer programmer like Ryan, this movement toward a stronger projection of individual voice and identity would likely be gradual, messy, and rather complex as he continues to shape knowledge and meaning throughout his undergraduate studies by extending the use of first-person pronouns beyond its associated narrative-like genres to his discipline-specific genres and practices.

Translation 2:

For another student in the same class section, who moved to the United States from Venezuela at the age of four, this *trans*lation-oriented writing assignment allowed a reflection on and confrontation with relationships of tension underlying his initial composing process of his language and literacy profile and ultimately a critical questioning of the larger ideological orientations and histories that might have shaped his language and discursive practices early in the quarter. In his writer-*trans*lator's memo, Mateo described his lived experiences negotiating what he has come to discern as school-based and home-related language resources (i.e., English versus Spanish) as he moved between the appropriate, discrete spheres of usage allotted to each by a dominant sociocultural imaginary. More specifically, Mateo wrote extensively about succumbing to forceful representations and treatments of such resources and discourses and the sociocultural identities and domains linked to them as stable, neatly segregated, and homogeneous to demonstrate proper social and civic engagement:

> Although English and Spanish are like two equally comfortable suits for me, it took a while to get used to **shedding one and donning the other**. English was for school, and Spanish was for home: in both places **I would be criticized if I slipped into the inappropriate language unprompted**, so **it was necessary throughout my youth to define them as two separate spheres and states of being if I wanted approval**. As someone who prides themselves on being studious and respectful both at home and in school, **disobedience** rarely crossed my mind, and this process of compartmentalizing who I was became **almost second nature** (emphasis added).

This socially regulated practice of "shedding one" language resource and "donning the other," deemed more appropriate and legitimate in specific social spheres and sites, has become sedimented through time and turned into Mateo's "almost second nature" in his language and literacy learning and development. In these remarks, Mateo seemed to tap into his imposed role as an ideal, obedient literate individual involved in the (real or perceived) reduction of language difference and consequential cross-border traffic and in the production of recognizably normative definitions of and practices with language and meaning. This is testament to the strong grip dominant monolingualist representations of languages as isolatable and compartmentalized entities have on Mateo's inability to recognize how these so-called givens about language are, in fact, discordant with and removed from his language resources as actually practiced—always already hybrid and involving movement within and across their defining boundaries—or even to consider any alternative except as "disobedience" and "inappropriate" language and literate labor.

Alternatively, approaching critical *trans*lation in his written work as an interpretive frame for recognizing, interrogating, and contending with such moments of language ideological tension and conflict in writing brought about some changed representations and treatments of the language resources in Mateo's repertoire and their conventionally delineable boundaries, both in the linguistic and geographical sense. For instance, exploring the actual fluidity, instability, and intermingling of the language resources he has gotten into the habit of viewing as split into either everyday or curriculum-based and mobilizing them in the enactment of the kind of critical writing-*trans*lation connections this assignment sequence seemed to encourage, Mateo produced the following *trans*lation densely packed with code-meshing, which he characterized as "an uncensored jumble of language and culture":

> Viviendo en los Estados Unidos, todavía hablaba español en la casa, pero el mundo exterior me estaba forzando a hablar *English*. This new language was overwhelming and everywhere—despite the fact that home was familiar, everything else was foreign, and oddly enough I absolutely loved it. I dove into learning English as fully as possible, y desafortunadamente me olvide de continuar a enfocar me en el español. En la escuela siempre tenía que tomar una clase de español, simplemente porque no quería perder mi lengua maternal mientras que aprendía otras—cuando minha familia se mudo a Brasil eu tuve o mesmo desafio. Amei o Portugués, e atentei de aprender lo con tudo meu coracao, mais no podía dechar que esta nova lingua borraria meu español. So many languages in so many new places—it was a challenge to keep everything aligned in my head,

and over time I lost a lot of my lexicon in Portuguese because of disuse, but I refused to let Spanish slip away. Nunca dejaré que se desaparezca el español de mi mente.

What is noteworthy about Mateo's *trans*lation is the uses he chooses to make of code-meshing and the valued subjectivities, meanings, and investments such informed uses are intended to activate. After considering various ways of *trans*lating the English-only introductory paragraph of the auto-ethnography he composed for this class, Mateo chose not to provide direct or loose *trans*lations or interpretations of his non-English constructions and instead composed entirely in "every language resource at [his] disposal"—that is, English, the language he "rapidly became enamored with," though learning it "overwhelmed him and took up all of [his] energy and focus"; his Spanish mother tongue, which he did not have "the best grasp of" but had "no intention of giving up," as it created an exclusive link to his Venezuelan identity; and the little bits and pieces of Portuguese he learned during his brief residence in Brazil. With this amalgamation of language resources in mind, Mateo started his above *trans*lation by moving back and forth between Spanish and English as a way to emphasize the continuity of grappling with language difference, which sets the stage for the piece's central motif of colliding language affiliations and orientations. In the third sentence, the use of Spanish text, though not *trans*lated, assists the English text it is contextualized by in making his point about the pressures of striking a balance between a preoccupation with access to English academic literacies and an ongoing desire to further and sustain Spanish literacies. The subsequent Spanish and Portuguese text (in the fourth and fifth sentences, respectively) exist alongside the English text (in the sixth sentence) to summon memories of long and painstaking processes of language learning as Mateo traveled across various moments, stages, and geographical realities in his literate life. This progression, which weaves together the full multiplicity of Mateo's language resources, sets up the *trans*lated paragraph for the concluding statement, which indirectly circles back to references about the imposition of English in public and educational landscapes of American society made in the opening statement and asserts Mateo's active resistance to the subtractive effects of such English-dominated ideological structures. Here, more specifically, the final Spanish statement allows Mateo to shift the tone of the entire section from personal reflection and narration to a more confrontational claim-based language usage in which he firmly declares his insistence on marshaling his Spanish-language abilities and literacies.

This sense of active negotiation does not exist as distinct from transformations in Mateo's own perspectives, ideas, and understandings of language and its working in the everyday FYW classroom. This is demonstrated through the newly developed descriptive and analytical representational practices Mateo adopted in his above *trans*lation and the accompanying reflective piece. More specifically, while Mateo initially constructed his Spanish language and literate practices as "separate spheres and states of being" and performing (in equally distinct, discrete contexts of his life), which can easily "slip away," be "taken from" him, simply erased (see his use of the Spanish verb *borraria* to mean "expunge" in his above *trans*lation), or even effortlessly "shed," he shifted into writing in his *trans*lator's memo about his language practices and resources in terms of "fluidity," "lack of strict boundaries," "neither entirely in [one code] nor in [another code]," and, most important, avenues for "open[ing] up" and "tapping into" the potential for self-exploration and learning of how "the meaning of what [he's] rewriting itself changes." The pedagogical opportunity to mobilize and harness his Spanish-, Portuguese-, and English-language resources and affiliations as requiring an engagement with *trans*lation appears to have triggered such substantive changes in Mateo's initially reported language representations and ultimately his meaning-making practices, as indicated by the following remark in his writer-*trans*lator's memo:

> Before this class I had believed that the only entirely monolingual situation I found myself in was that of academia: apart from actual Spanish language courses, every single lesson I learned and paper I wrote had to be **100% English**. The opportunity to open up that space in this translation to every tongue I know brings in a wonderful freedom to my life: **all of my language resources are something I can dip into now . . . My mind, like my life, is neither entirely in Spanish nor in English**. Different parts of my story are narrated in different languages in my mind, and in this translation I simply let that **fluidity** transfer into my writing . . . Allowing myself freedom from academic boundaries not only gives me access to these language resources, but **tapping into those language resources allows me to speak my mind in more ways than one: my grasp of Spanish is a huge part of my identity, and when I can incorporate it in my work I feel I am truly myself** (emphasis added).

As a young transnational migrant student writer, Mateo has been exposed through dominant social and educational practices to tenaciously held understandings of languages in terms of segregated, monolithic entities easily identifiable as "100% English" at different times of the day and in specific spaces (for instance, in his AP English-language and composition course or in his current college English course) or even 100 percent Spanish (primarily in the Spanish-language classes Mateo opted to take in high school). In contrast to these dominant language-as-entity constructions, Mateo's comments about his new experience of composing the current *trans*lation seem to pinpoint a growing recognition of the actual "fluidity" and permeability of the strict spatiotemporal borders and boundaries traditionally established between his various language resources. Mateo could sense that by holding on to rather rigid views on the language resources in his repertoire as static and discrete entities, he had placed himself in an isolated "entirely monolingual" space and had, to a large extent, limited his possible labor and practices with written English. In response, Mateo sought out opportunities to perform English and his social identity in his writing as indelibly tied to *trans*lation and difference. Rather than feeling pressured, as he put it, to "limit [himself] exclusively" to what I referred to in chapter 1 as a specific insular and pure code-island (a 100 percent English, 100 percent Spanish, or even 100 percent Portuguese island) under relatively unproblematized monolingualist orientations to language, Mateo started exploring the many possible identities, histories, and meanings that can be reclaimed and potentially flow in and out of the full range of language resources he felt inclined to tap into in his *trans*lation. Reflecting on his emerging representations and subsequent practices mediated by the current pedagogical affordances (as Mateo expressed in the above excerpt) created in him a sense of substantial learning about the actual character of the language resources in his repertoire as not static, neutral, neatly ordered, or pure but rather as constantly in a relationship of complexity and contention, a new relationship he had not experienced or perceived before in the production of his putatively "pure" English-only texts for past English classes (and of the initial version of his language and literacy profile assignment for this class). As he further analyzed his *trans*lation choices, Mateo explained:

> When I allowed myself to write about the problem with learning other languages in these other languages I found that the words I set forth were far more truthful: . . . Spanish made it a lot easier to articulate my thoughts as to why using Spanish felt so odd when I was younger, and throwing Portuguese into the mix brought me back to Brazil in a way that simply was **not possible with a purely English text**. Writing in these languages helped project me back into the past when these languages were everywhere and overwhelming, and analyzing why I had to frame them in English only [in the original version] helped remind me that even now **these languages were always fighting** to try and get as much of a grasp in my mind as others (emphasis added).

It is exactly those tension-filled moments of working with and across difference and the constantly "fighting" language ideologies in his surrounds that Mateo wanted to re-create in his translation for his readers and their interpretive experience, as is evident in his brief *trans*lator's note that prefaced his actual *trans*lation, wherein he wrote:

> This is the story of me, [his full name]. I intend with it to put my life into words, and a great deal of the words I use are in languages other than English. I am not a native English speaker, and recreating my tale exclusively in a foreign tongue would be an injustice both to myself and to **anyone who truly wishes to understand me**. Spanish and Portuguese are major parts of my identity, and if you do not comprehend them, a significant amount of the story will be lost, so **I encourage anyone interested to make an effort. I understand not everyone will be willing to make that effort. I have never been brave enough to ask anything of my readers, but to accomplish what I hope to with my writing, demanding compromise will be necessary**. Who I am is not going to be easily understood by everyone, but that does not mean I should change who I am. If you wish to see me as I am, this is your chance. **There are plenty of ways to translate the text into something more tenable for you . . . but ideally a reader would consume the words exactly as I wrote them**. Otherwise, something will inevitably be lost in the shift. **If there is a gap between you and I, then this is your opportunity to cross it; I am inviting you to do so if understanding is truly your intent** . . . I will set up a landing platform for you, but **the bridge-building is your responsibility**. Getting to the island of my identity was not an easy struggle, and I will not give up ground (emphasis added).

In this mini-introduction to his main *trans*lated text, Mateo's use of the second-person singular or plural pronoun (as in "you and I," "If you wish," "more tenable for you," "your opportunity," "your intent," "your chance," "your responsibility") to directly address his readers marked a more conversational register and a higher degree of involvement with his addressees and the kind of ceaseless interpretation and *trans*lation labor required of them. As this prefatory note makes clear, Mateo challenged his readers to construct meaning across emerging communication gaps and to face exactly what resonated with his own literate experiences of enduring and grappling with difference somatically, intellectually, and linguistically. Given Mateo's "mixed upbringing" and his experience growing up in the United States as someone who self-identifies as a gay, bilingual Venezuelan male with a patchwork of language resources and competencies in his repertoire, preserving and openly performing his evolving gendered, ethnic, linguistic, and sexualized identity has never been "an easy struggle" for Mateo and hence, in his own words, is "not something [he or his readers] can or should overlook" or deny in his actual *trans*lation. Such a messy, labor-intensive engagement on the part of his readers, as Mateo argued, is fundamental to a nuanced understanding of his writing as critical *trans*lation, partly because his own cultural, national, linguistic, gendered, or sexed affiliations (and the literate repertoires and practices cultivated from them) are never pre-given, friction-less, or transparent but always transitory, sticky, opaque, and locally contingent. In this sense, Mateo composed what Suresh Canagarajah (2013b, 142; emphasis in original) has described as "a *writerly* rather than a *readerly*" *trans*lation, which compels, "not just expects or invites," a less tolerant readership to seek out and actively invent the desired meaning—which in this case is not easily given or handed over but requires challenging co-construction, reciprocity, or what Mateo has referred to as the "responsibility" for "bridge-building."

According to Mateo's note, in this *trans*lation process where his language and identity are constantly being socially negotiated and renegotiated, made and remade, there is no room for readers' conventional valuation for a flat, smooth, neutral, and undisrupted transmission of meaning. He is, however, aware that such a serious sociopolitical undertaking, which comes at the cost of his readers' inward ease, might not gain positive reader uptake and, as he put it, "is not without a consequence," which would be even bigger upon engaging with academic writing genres and contexts beyond this particular assignment and this FYW class. In fact, working through similar writing-*trans*lation decisions, whether small or significant, with efforts toward voice and agency in academic text and knowledge production involves, as Jakob Arnoldi astutely points out, "constantly accept[ing] and/or tak[ing] risks" and "necessarily entails risks of all sorts" (cited in Canagarajah and Lee 2014, 62).

Translation 3:

I'd like to direct your attention once again to the excerpt from Ruijia's writing that I first presented in this book's introduction. The *trans*lation, which Ruijia produced in my specialized FYW course section, of interest here is the following:

> Once my teacher told me that language was power. I did not understand her at that time. Several years later, when I look back at my 18 years of language learning, I gradually understand the spirit of language. **I know that most conventional academic American readers expect me to explain my main argument at the beginning of my essay. However . . . I choose to write this essay following a Chinese writing style that keeps the main**

argument at the end of a writing piece. Due to the complexity and richness of my experiences, **readers of my essay need to be a patient** because my deep feelings that have changed over time cannot be captured by a single statement or two. **I hope this decision would encourage my readers to focus more on my personal experiences and collaborate with me** in order to grasp my conclusion about the power of language in expressing one's feelings and emotions and bringing different writing styles and cultures together (emphasis mine).

Ruijia's *trans*lation of the introductory paragraph in the language and literacy profile she composed for this class might at first glance be dismissed as deceptively devoid of relations of powerful difference, as ideologically neutral and *trans*lation-free in that her writing didn't appear to traverse what is conventionally recognized as clearly demarcated language boundaries the way Mateo's most obviously did. However, what might give us pause in Ruijia's text is the textual material she deliberately inserted in the middle of her *trans*lation, which served a particular framing function of encouraging her readers to see her work as a form of give and take even before they delve into reading it. Worried that some readers may not even bother to read a separate prologue (like the one we witnessed in Mateo's *trans*lation) or accompanying footnotes (as in Ryan's case), Ruijia explained in her critical writer-*trans*lator's rationale that she chose to engage in the body of her actual *trans*lation with readers who might be intolerant and too fussy about knowing immediately what her written text was about and set out to accomplish. With this paratextual intervention realized *within* her written text, Ruijia's introduction clearly elaborated a narrative in which she was making deals with readers about her intention to broaden dominant organizational conventions and re-create a space for valued Chinese rhetorical traits and practices, thus setting the scene for a reading of every other section in her essay from the perspective of this active re-positioning.

As a first-year international Chinese student still navigating her valued Chinese rhetorical traditions and reasoning patterns in her new literate realities, Ruijia's *trans*lation was the result of her attempt to reconcile academic demands that a writer's thesis appear at the beginning or end of the introduction in expository writing—as prompted by my own written feedback in relation to an earlier version of her text—and a desire to experiment with the indirectness, ambiguity, and complexity she found evident in the writing practices of modern Chinese writer Xun Lu. Though her nontraditional opening to her essay might be viewed as unruly or in need of substantial revision, she indirectly declared that it was the result of her own negotiations as a writer working across multiple language and cultural resources imbued with diverse rhetorical traits and traditions. She was particularly keen to highlight in her *trans*lation that she was inserted into the academic discourse community and was in effect negotiating with its members by expressing her awareness of the unquestionable rhetorical moves of an academic essay. More important, her implicitly apologetic introduction to a conventional academic readership whom she might have let down aided in foregrounding the kind of textual authority we normally see in a professional *trans*lator's statement or an established writer's note, as it included reassuring agentive statements, such as "I know that . . . expect me," "however . . . I choose," "readers of my essay need to . . . ," "I hope this decision would encourage readers to . . . ."

In doing so, Ruijia managed to unsettle the very definitive expectations readers (myself included) might have brought to the scene of reading and interpreting her academic written work by forcing them to question and reassess the potential usefulness of single, streamlined, and fixed rhetorical patterns and conventions for all writers and all occasions of writing. She deliberately disrupted and recomposed her readers' own normalized reading habits by echoing a refusal to offer a labor-free, *trans*lation-free, and friction-less reading experience. Assertively asking them to be "patient," "collaborate with" her, and meet her halfway, she purposefully brought her readers face to face with the reality of difference and *trans*lation, thereby transforming her text into a space of multiplicity, ideological contestation, renegotiation, and discontinuities. Ruijia's critical *trans*lation immersed readers in a more complex network of literate labor and relationships, under which the traditional, neatly demarcated discursive practices of (re)reading, (re)writing, and *trans*lating become seen and enacted as multifaceted, overlapping, and collaborative. As such, however, there was a risk involved, of which Ruijia was aware and explicitly tried to respond to. She was upfront about her decision that this was a risk worth taking in her essay in order to preserve and capitalize on "the complexity and richness" of her transcultural and translingual literate experiences and realities.

UNFINISHED REFLECTIONS: POTENTIALITIES AND CHALLENGES OF CRITICAL WRITING-*TRANS*LATION CONNECTIONS

These student *trans*lations put on display the postmonolingual tensions, contradictions, and turbulences that pervaded the different deployments of language and semiotic resources for the realization and assertion of voice and agency. As Ryan, Mateo, and Ruijia put their written English into complex and sustained relations of critical *trans*lation across power hierarchies and difference, they took a first step toward recognizing and foregrounding their multiple, shifting, and ongoingly negotiable (re)positioning in relation to their written texts, readers, competing language ideologies and epistemologies, and actual sociocultural and political realities. In doing so, they also took an initial step toward moving away from treatments of the navigation of their writerly voice and agency as a fait accompli, that is, as largely trapped in fixed polarities[11]—of personal versus academic, authentic versus inauthentic, alternative versus socially and institutionally sanctioned, or creative versus constrained—in their language and meaning creation over which they appeared to have no control. In this extended example from two FYW classes, the active roles my students took on as critical writers-*trans*lators became visible in their *trans*lations through the intricate means by which they negotiated their way around particularly sticky and volatile aspects of their writing and had to oscillate between and select from a wide range of possible *trans*lation choices and strategically frame them in their *trans*lated text. It is this series of purposeful decisions surrounding the depth of critical writing-*trans*lating connections in the FYW classroom that we need to optimize for our students for the sake of directing their attention away from the seeming universality, definiteness, certainty, and fixity of language and meaning in academic writing toward a truer sense of "the impossibility of perfection" (Bassnett 2011, 73) in all language use and of the illusion of the unmediated, un-*trans*lated written word.

I have argued in this chapter that there has to be a more engaged, activist dimension to translingualism in writing pedagogy, which moves beyond the logic of *Ideologiekritik*,[12] or only exercising a critique of dominant monolingual ideologies, and toward a more deliberate intervention in taken-for-granted monolingual and multilingual language representations and subsequent practices that all our students alike—whether mainstream or non-mainstream—are, knowingly or unknowingly, exposed to in their ongoing work with written English. In fact, if all we do as current or aspiring translingual writing teachers-scholars-administrators is merely critique dominant English-only monolingualism and its reductive treatments and reifications of language, language learning, and language difference in policies and practices, then we end up, as Linda Adler-Kassner (2008, 83) has argued, "position[ing] ourselves as agents who can only refute analyses that lead to this 'reduction'" at the expense of addressing the equally urgent task of taking specific actions in mediating and transforming our own language representations and practices and those of others. I have specifically called for taking critical writing-*trans*lation connections seriously as one possible activist engagement in the FYW classroom that can encourage a translingual orientation to language, language difference, and language relations.

This renewed attention to *trans*lation, much like the MLA Ad Hoc Committee envisaged in its 2007 report, can provide a condition of possibility for opening up much-needed explorations with students of the opacity of written English as constantly leaking into and out of all other language resources (including but not limited to languages [native, heritage, foreign, second, third, and so on], dialects, registers, and English-/non-English-based creoles) at their disposal for each occasion of reading and writing. We can challenge students to more openly work through the perpetual postmonolingual tensions they see themselves subjected to in their own language and literate learning experiences by bringing them to the table in all in-class discussions, activities, readings, one-on-one conferences, and writing assignment prompt design. Rather than keeping them purged or in stagnation and suspension, as a dominant English-only monolingual ideology would urge us, complicated moments of local language-ideological tension and the decisions involved in resolving them when *trans*lating their own or others' texts can become available for collaborative inspection in ways that help students see that their developing practices in reading and writing and the language representations guiding them are limited, unfinished, and provisional—situated in changing economies, ideologies, and political histories of academic knowledge production and reception (Venuti 1996, 1998; Tymoczko 2006; Hrach 2013; Wittman and Windon 2010). In terms of the metaphorical framings I have presented in the course of my explorations in chapter 2, this entails engaging students in critical investigations of how and toward what end their (actual or projected) *trans*lations and the deliberate negotiations necessary for producing and interpreting them serve to enter, disrupt, or reconfigure the global transdirectional flow of charged and charging meanings, language resources, social relations, and subjectivities.

Those of us who wish to truly take on this challenge of pursuing translingualism in composition work, however, need to come to terms with the fact there is "no soft landing" (Dasgupta 2005, 47), neither for students nor their writing teachers. In fact, while for most of my students working on and through such unfamiliar writing-*trans*lation connections in academic literacies work made an intellectually satisfying endeavor, a few went no farther in their translations than swapping terms with synonyms or mere equivalents in a language/language variety they knew without rhetorically engaging with their own and their readers' social (re)positioning or with the kind of transversality such choices might potentially yield. In addition, not all my students, especially in my mainstream course section, were comfortable with such alternative orientations to language in writing and the nonconventional intellectual labor those orientations required of them. In fact, I received comments from three different students in the end of the quarter formal teaching evaluations complaining that this type of work was in their mind "*not* English composition" (emphasis added).

As ethnographic fieldwork in both Beirut and Seattle seemed to portray following the analyses in chapters 3 and 4, it is my contention that these students' comments echo what past language and literacy education and brokering activities might have trained them to recognize and name as legitimate engagements with academic English literacies and subsequently dismiss the actual and necessary critical writing-*trans*lation connections this assignment sequence activated as aberrations or at least annoyances. As these comments (however misguided) from only a handful of students suggest, my attempt at pedagogic intervention might not have been successful in encouraging changes in the language representational practices of these particular writers. However, the fact that the current assignment design and the kind of intellectual labor it demanded triggered such bursts of annoyance indicates that it has indeed placed their taken-for-granted and definitively naturalized representations of the "English" in their imagined "English composition"—as a static, bounded entity with an un*trans*latable core, separated from its natural belonging in the realm of situated practice—face to face, in collision, and in confrontation with the kind of translingual-oriented representations and subsequent practices this pedagogical design aimed to develop. In other words, while we may not necessarily succeed in reconfiguring *all* our students' tenaciously held beliefs and familiar ways with language in writing, the necessary labor for engaging such critical writing-*trans*lation connections in the FYW classroom can at the very least help create an appropriate dose of productive tension, thereby allowing some degree of awareness and recognition of the nature and working of local language ideologies and representations as "normally" multiple and competing rather than singular and unified within the same college "English composition" classroom space to start germinating.

Such anticipated moments of resistance from students suggest that in an alternative pedagogical orientation built around the ideology of writing as critical *trans*lation, the burden lies in destabilizing the specific representations that might be at the basis of our students' treatment of language and *trans*lation and in bringing critical *trans*lation in its full complexity more deliberately to the forefront of their consciousness. For example, recognizing that the common reduction of *trans*lation to the perfect mastery of linguistic skills might be tempting to many of my students in both mainstream and specialized FYW courses, I announced to my students early in the course that advanced competence in a language other than English as traditionally conceived was helpful but not necessary to perform the kind of labor this particular assignment sequence demanded of them. Despite my reassurance, making *trans*lation central to our conversations and explorations initially seemed startling and unusual for most, if not all, students identified as Anglo-American native English speakers to whom *trans*lation practice was generally perceived as deserving little to no investment, notice, or concern. For instance, Ryan wrote in his commentary about "wrestl[ing] with the issues of translation." In his mind, he did not "often (or at all) communicate in languages other than American English, so initially it did not seem too apparent to [him] that [he] may occasionally speak or *write in ways that can or must be translated*" (emphasis added). Another student from a predominantly white neighborhood in the eastern part of Washington state, for whom English was also the primary and only language and negotiating the heterogeneity of languages and cultures on campus was a relatively new phenomenon, stated that he originally thought he "d[id] not have the most racially, linguistically and culturally diverse background" he felt would be necessary to successfully participate in these *trans*lation activities, but the type of literate engagement this critical writing-*trans*lation sequence invited brought back to life a more complex view of academic written "English as more diverse than it seem[ed]" and hence as constantly rewritten by rewriters like himself.

Even students seen as socioculturally and linguistically "Other," to whom negotiations across difference, arguably, came more naturally, also brought their unique set of assumptions about language relations and *trans*lation labor. Some of them, for example, reported having been warned by previous English teachers against the problems of literal translation in writing and of strong dependence on electronic translation technologies like Google Translate, Babylon, and Yahoo's Babel Fish without being presented with more productive translation strategies. Buying into such traditional understandings of translation as mechanical linguistic transposition and the deep academic suspicion surrounding the fruits of this labor, some of my non-mainstream students started out with the assumption that something will eventually get lost through their process of translation and that the quality of their writing will consequently be diminished; however, a lot of them described experiencing for the first time through these writing-*trans*lation activities that there might be a process of gain as well. For instance, Yuran, an international Chinese student, wrote about tremendous shifts in his views of translation and English writing as he transitioned from a long-standing culture of learning English in China as a set of fixed linguistic and notational rules and conventions following dominant transmission models into the unfamiliar (and seemingly new) translingual meaning-making orientation adopted in my specialized FYW class section:

> Back then, when I tended to write something, I would write a Chinese draft then translated it into English word by word. I became a translator who merely changed the shape of the words into the form of "English." . . . The difference between "translator" and "writer" was sort of obvious at that time. I now, however, find this opinion shortsighted . . . as a Chinese who need to write in English, this obvious difference becomes dramatically weak because I, as a Chinese whose mother tongue is Chinese also, write in a language that is different from my mother tongue is really close to what translators do. Then, in this class, I was re-thinking about the actual difference of "translator" and "writer" in my special identity—**I am a Chinese English writer and translator. The true translation as far as I know now is when a writer could feel and use English as a transforming language—the hybrid of power, strength, identity, culture, and passion.** But the "young me myself" did not notice this point (emphasis added).

As this remark suggests, Yuran has started recognizing the impossibility of treating *trans*lation, writing, and the language resources of Chinese and English engaged in these practices as fitting neatly into separate compartments, as he encountered in his past language and literacy learning experiences. The act and experience of writing his English texts for this class became an operation of *trans*lation, with English itself seen as a transformed and "transforming language" inhabited by plurality and difference.

These examples of some of my students' initial, nebulous set of representations and treatments of translation (also shared by the social imaginary at large)—as irrelevant to English composition work, as of little practical value, or, when not entirely written out of the picture, as nothing but mechanical, transparent, and meaning-fixating practice—that have come to the fore during individual or group conferencing sessions can serve as teachable moments for unsettling the institutionalized monolingualist language ideologies circulating around and among our FYW students. As writing teacher-scholars, we can contribute to denaturalizing the hegemony of such language ideologies and epistemologies through engaging students in pursing fundamental questions of why, in what ways, and at what cost have these precluded their potential for recognizing, engaging in and benefiting from such *trans*lation labor in their past or current experiences of learning English composition. In fact, the same methodological tool of thinking and "talk around" written-*trans*lated texts that is core to much of the research presented in this book can itself serve as a productive "pedagogic resource" (Ivanič et al. 2009, 122) for initiating these much-needed conversations with students and unpacking some of the complexity and contestation of language representations and practices shaping and shaped by their own academic literacies work.

To aid in such explorations, we might also consider introducing students to critical theorizations about *trans*lation in the burgeoning field of translation studies (much of which I've cited in the previous pages and hence does not require repetition here), which can help supply them with a basic set of vocabulary and conceptual tools (some of which I've presented in my analysis, such as transversality, [re]framing, paratextual commentary, [re]positioning) for shaping the composition and impact of their *trans*lations in conjunction and negotiation with multiple others. More important, this translingual-oriented thinking and labor can push them toward a deeper attention to and continual engagement with how *trans*lation and difference operate not merely in writing between or across language resources and practices but also in rewriting language itself. With all the challenges and possibilities involved, the centrality and complexity of critical writing-*trans*lation connections I am advancing in this chapter can and must become more visible, explicit, and significantly regarded, especially in the context of US college composition where our and our students' learned inclinations often lead us to make *trans*lation an issue only when working across or between languages (or cultures) but not within the same language (or culture).

(RE)WRITING *TRANSLATION* INTO THE FUTURE OF WRITING PEDAGOGY

Translingualism from an activist perspective, as I have tried to indicate, necessitates a serious engagement from the outset with meaningful writing-*trans*lation connections in the FYW classroom not as another discussion topic tackled through a simple circular arrangement of chairs but, most important, as an alternative way of thinking, doing, and learning academic English literacies in which our students continue to invest their linguistically and ethnically imprinted, nationalized, raced, classed, gendered, sexualized, and abled selves and desires. Without suggesting that combating and intervening in our students' monolingualist language representations and practices in learning academic writing is bound to happen overnight or will be an easy, labor-free feat or claiming that only one writing class or one writing assignment design (like the one I've presented here, though not meant as a perfect curricular blueprint either) can single-handedly achieve such desired effects, the kind of intellectual engagement critical writing-*trans*lation labor demands puts on display students' everyday experiences of postmonolingual language ideological tensions, which have generally remained implicit or unarticulated or have been dismissed as students' sole responsibility to properly diffuse and resolve. Seriously engaging students with the complex postmonolinguality that pervades their (as well as our and colleagues') experiences and labor in college composition can begin to raise their awareness of how the deliberate writing-*trans*lation choices they or others make in their academic texts are embedded in, contributing to, and unsettling particular ways of thinking about language, language usage, and language difference. Allowing such critical writing-*trans*lation connections to thrive in our students' literate engagement involves encouraging them to fully explore how these ever-present postmonolingual tensions get mediated in terms of the selection of texts/parts of texts to be *trans*lated, the specific *trans*lation strategies adopted, the compromises made, the various "paratexts" (e.g., introductions, separate explanatory prefaces, footnotes, afterwords, glossaries, and many other rhetorical and interpretive aids) exploited as available sites of framing *trans*lations and (re-)positioning oneself and readers in time and space (see Baker 2006, 2007), and finally, the actual and desired effects on written texts, readers, writerly identities, immediate life-worlds, and social futures.

Strengthening such critical writing-*trans*lation connections in the FYW classroom allows students to start viewing and implementing their reading and writing as ongoingly embedded in and contending with crisscrossing, even competing, language ideologies and representations (themselves understood as practices) and *not* bounded, static, and chained by the inarguable givens of academic discourse. Rather than continuing to be frustrated by and complaining about the shortcomings of some of our first-year students' incoming writing practices (to name a few, frequently adopting the five-paragraph essay structure, weak personal stance and authorial presence, heavy dependence on colloquialisms) and how fossilized these practices seem to be in their resultant (flat, predictable, and safe) written texts, we can engage them in critically interrogating and reworking their existing values and practices with language and writing.

Under this focus on translingual activism, through intensifying critical writing-*trans*lation connections in writing pedagogy, the goal hence becomes that of reclaiming the social situatedness and constructedness of these academic writing practices and conventions from their projected state as absolute linguistic monuments or impenetrable real estate. With critical writing-*trans*lation connections brought concretely and repeatedly, again and again, to their attention in every reading and writing situation, students can start accepting the "imperfection" and "incompleteness" (Müller 2007, 212) of their own written-*trans*lated texts and those of others and ultimately put their unattainable quest for stabilized, intact, and value-free language standards, practices, and meanings to rest. As the examples of some of my students' *trans*lation and interpretive work have demonstrated, foregrounding critical writing-*trans*lation connections allowed them more opportunities to start de-centering and de-automating their habituated patterns of thinking about whatever language resources they brought with them and chose to tap into (including English, if at all there indeed is an identifiable, neatly bounded entity called English) as impregnable, zip-locked entities best kept in their place in their written texts and instead helped reveal the traces of traffic and flow. Explorations of the meso-politics and problematics of producing, analyzing, and interpreting *trans*lations can provide sustained invitations for student writers-*trans*lators to become more astute listeners to and readers of the actual flow of traffic in the entire congested highway and not just the one-way monolithic traffic of language and meaning they have been forced into—a traffic whose desired characteristics and conditions from path, direction, headway, speed, and density to boundaries have been clearly mapped by a dominant monolingual English-only ideology. Thanks to such critical writing-*trans*lation connections where writing and *trans*lation are conceived as intertwined and mutually enriching forms of translingual meaning-making practice, all our students—whether institutionally or self-identified as US mainstream, US resident generation 1.5, or visa-holding international—are brought face to face with the reality of *trans*lation and the complex layers of difference beneath the apparent homogeneity of written English that, as most of my students pointed out, they did not even know existed.

As we continue to consider locally effective ways to reconcile writing and *trans*lation in our writing pedagogies on firmer ground for the years to come, it is worth keeping in mind that the reigning exclusion and invisibility of the labor and fruits of translation in FYW renders students' written texts, as Lawrence Venuti (1996, 331) has so succinctly put it, "free-floating, unmoored from history, transcending the linguistic and cultural differences that required not merely their translation but their interpretation in the classroom." Both shaping and taking shape within opaque relations of power among texts, contexts, writers, readers, or language and cultural resources, all written communication both in and well beyond the FYW classroom needs to be seen as a sustained act of translating "translations of translations," because as Octavio Paz (1992, 154) has argued, "language itself [and English included], in its very essence, is already a translation." From this standpoint, the agentive role of FYW students as critical writers-*trans*lators co-constructing and co-negotiating with equally responsible readers the broad range of meanings, interpretations, texts, identities, languages, discourses, and Englishes needs to emerge from underneath the cloak of imposed, institutionalized invisibility.

It is unfortunate that the biggest responsibility confronting us as we move into a world of heightened translingual and transcultural flows is in promoting and reviving the normality and necessity of *trans*lation, especially when working *within* English, in the eyes and minds of our FYW students—the very literate group that can indeed claim much more expertise than we can in naturally and constantly thinking, languaging, reading, writing, and living in and through continuous movement between and across various contexts (home, school, work, the internet, and so on) and transitional phases in their life-worlds (from adolescence to adulthood, secondary to postsecondary education, academic to professional realm, and the like). The task ahead, as I see it, lies in combining our organizational, administrative, scholarly, and pedagogic productivity under an activist translingual approach where, as postcolonial translation theorist Sherry Simon (1999, 72; emphasis added) describes, critical "*trans*lation and writing become part of a single process of [inter- and intra-lingual] creation" and transcreation, with many hidden potentialities yet to be fully unearthed in our local writing programs and classrooms.

Conclusion
LESSONS ON THINKING AND DOING TRANSLINGUALITY *WITH*[1] BEIRUT AND SEATTLE

The local language and writing ecologies in different parts of the globe that have been the particular focus of *Toward Translingual Realities in Composition* seem to be breathing with movements, mixtures, contradictions, and complexities in which the monolingual, the traditionally multilingual, and the translingual in language representations and practices constantly coexist and reconstitute contemporary language and literate identities and realities. This push and pull of competing representations and subsequent practices involving language and literacy, certainly unique to the specific ecologies explored in this book, nevertheless spans geographical space and permeates, in one form or another and to differing degrees, the teaching and learning of college composition nationally and internationally. The extent to which particularly forceful abstractions and mystifications of English academic literacies as putatively fixed, autonomous entities for universal transmission and consumption have placed powerful constraints on the language negotiations and practices of young university-level writers in both countries and on their pursuits of furthering translingual inter- and intra-linguistic relations forces us to take them seriously and acknowledge their lived materiality. Significantly, accounts from both superdiverse port cities like Beirut and Seattle serve as immediate reminders that the complex disharmony and contestation at the level of language representations and practices in our local writing program ecologies need to become a more firm and enduring part of our ongoing re-envisioning of various aspects of theoretical and practical work as potential sites for translingual activism, be it curricular infrastructure, pedagogical approaches, assessment instruments, composition teacher-preparation programs, or campus-wide partnerships. Drawing perspectives from within and across linguistic, cultural, and national worlds together, *Toward Translingual Realities in Composition* foregrounds several interrelated observations regarding the nature and workings of language representations, summarized as follows, with some pertinent

DOI: 10.7330/9781607329046.c006

insights into how we can and must (re)locate, understand, and enact future intellectual work in composition:

First and foremost, *just like the construct of language they stand for, name, and describe, language representations are grounded in material experiences and socially interactive processes of negotiation and renegotiation within and across a complicated constellation of significant brokers.* The rival local language representations circulating around and among FYW students in our programs and courses, guiding their academic literacies work, and determining their level of engagement with or resistance to aspired translingual practice are not inert, isolable, and abstract complexes of ideas occurring and existing 'out there'. Instead, their representations about language, language relations, and language usage in academic literacies co-emerge as the product and modality of expression by a valuable network of multiple (active and/or implicated, formal and/or informal, local and/or translocal) language ideology brokers with different power positions. In fact, it is doubtful that the socially agreed-upon values the FYW students portrayed in this book attached to specific practices with certain language and semiotic resources and not others and the strong ideas they voiced about the nature of successful academic language and literate practices as characterized by purity, rigidity, complete self-censorship, and loss of writerly voice and agency came from nowhere. As we have seen in chapters 3, 4, and 5, when the interplay among dominant monolingual, residual multilingual, and counterhegemonic translingual tendencies in their daily literate lives was laid bare, many student participants were prone to link their shifting management and navigation of those tendencies, sometimes directly and immediately, to memorable everyday or school-related literacy events or particular literate communities or individuals with whom they were in contact, in tension, or both.

Some of the similarities and divergences I've highlighted in the language representational practices of university-level writers in Beirut and Seattle were inevitably products of a range of language socializing and language ideology brokering activities. More precisely, their highly individualized ways of thinking and doing language were reinforced and at times complicated to a large extent by the positioning of various stakeholders in past or current language and literacy learning experiences—including, but not limited to, language policymakers and implementers at the national, state, institutional, or programmatic level, teachers, parents, immediate or extended family, peers, and others. For example, Nathalie, induced by her father's popular imagination of English as a durable commodity for social and economic mobility, seemed to endorse a norm-based view of near-native academic English competence abstracted from its contexts of use and *trans*lation across and against her working literate knowledge of French. In an opposite part of the globe, Nur primarily called on her geographically distant mother's expertise and advanced knowledge of English professional writing to directly monitor her academic textual production and help "fix" her word- and sentence-level "errors" through numerous email consultations and phone and Skype calls. Reductive official language and educational policies in her native country that have kept English and Malay language entities apart according to assigned curricular space and time have also influenced much of Nur's perceptions of her everyday *rojak* English as "out of place" and irrelevant in educational landscapes, hence untapped as a mobile resource for her learning and meaning making in FYW. As the dominant US culture and its myriad collaborative institutions have deterred the mixing and meshing of clearly demarcated home-school boundaries and their associated language usages and identities, Mateo described working very hard to maintain those discontinuities in his literacy practices. Ryan was able to trace back an uneasy yet automatic adherence to valorized practices of removing all traces of the authorial subject in his academic written texts to prior language and literacy learning experiences as early as middle school.

Even in FYW ecologies, accounts of academic frictions (from Lebanese students like Nathalie, Naser, Lucas, Diva, and KAPPA; from international students like Nur, Li Ming, and Ruijia in the United States; from students like Malika and Mateo who belong to the racial, ethnic, and linguistic minority and those like Ryan marked by the sociocultural imaginary as mainstream) have pointed toward our roles and responsibilities as writing teachers in propagating reductive representations of Standard Written English (SWE) and its traditionally identified conventions as fixed, pure, and abstract entities in our pedagogies and assessments. As Joseph Sung-Yel Park and Lionel Wee (2012, 110) argue compellingly, sustained, collaborative recognition of and reflection on how "it is our own doing that offers the space for this cyclical [discursive] reinforcement to take place" is a powerful starting point for identifying key points of critique and intervention in our subjective and embodied views of English in composition so that eventually "this chain may be broken." We can begin by taking small, local, and manageable initiatives that help make students' sense of their negotiations of the perpetual language-ideological tensions they find themselves compelled to tackle in their academic literacies work an open question and always available for critical inspection in the writing classroom.

In doing so, we can encourage students to tap into the heterogeneity and often disjuncture and contestation in terms of the explicitly "verbalized" as well as the unstated "implicit understandings and unspoken assumptions" (Gal 1998, 319) about the ways of thinking about English and its doing, teaching, and learning across the literate worlds of their homes, local communities, sociolinguistic realities, primary or secondary-level education and training, local writing classrooms, actual or aspired academic disciplines, and imagined professional futures. We can engage them in critical explorations of how they have been subscribing, and continue to subscribe, and give life to particular ways of thinking about English and ways of putting it into actual literate practice in relation to other vibrant yet unevenly developed language resources in their repertoires and of how these understandings and practices can be mapped onto or get entangled with socially relevant identities and stances—such as complying with tacit/explicit (nation-state, school, or home) language policy, adhering to specific pedagogical agendas (mine in chapter 5 included), maintaining possibilities for selfhood (e.g., Lebaneseness, a pan-Arab identity, Spanglish identity, or a hybrid/hyphenated sense of belonging and loyalty), showing signs of good citizenship, demonstrating a strong cosmopolitan outlook, and so on. The fundamental focus of such explorations, however, becomes not so much on tracing and spelling out the pedigree of the vocalized language representations, both at the folk and institutional level, as much as critically reflecting on what possible meanings, functions, social relationships, and identifications get opened up, excluded, or shut down by them and, more important, what agentive roles might be available for students within ongoing processes of language ideology brokerage to productively and meaningfully interrogate and reconfigure such representations in their new university literate life and prospective social and professional future.

Second and following from the above, *language representations are dynamic, in a state of flux, and constantly shifting with ever-evolving mobilities, desires, identities, macro- and micro-sociopolitical contexts of English academic literacies work.* Regardless of their many and diverse origins or discursive modes of construction, activation, propagation, and appropriation, language representational practices are not essentially stable, discrete entities residing in the minds of literate individuals but are rather variable, contingent, and fluctuating as part of the embodied refashioning of their lived realities, identities, and social relationships; therefore, they can be challenged and, over time, reconstituted and transformed. These young university writers' narratives from both countries point toward the need to support just such efforts. As they aligned with and positioned themselves differently in relation to various brokering practices across key literate situations and moments, they took up and applied contrasting ideas, images, and symbolic associations about their language resources, with potentially significant consequences for their patterns of use and development in their academic work. Though Naser, for instance, primarily echoed counterproductive representations about the fixity and uniformity of language use triggered by his sense that his valued language and visual communication resources were disqualified in his experiences of learning academic English literacies, as he moved into graphic design educational landscapes, we could sense some degree of fluctuation in how he viewed and ultimately mobilized the full multiplicity of his Arabic linguistic and typographic resources in his disciplinary compositions. Naser's reinterpretation of his perceptions of his resources as peripheral and immobile in school literacies and his subsequent translingual and transmodal performances of those resources in graphic design work were prompted primarily by a classroom environment that offered meaning and semiotic potential for disciplinary learning and by a personal desire to bridge the gap between his growing knowledge of the fundamentals of modern graphic design and his strong ethnolinguistic identity.

Like Nathalie's father, who associated no valuable capital to the commodity named French in the international linguistic marketplace beyond his daughter's high school education, Malika's mother assigned little to no exchange value to French in the urban US workplace, where English was deemed the sole high-mobility language resource. However, despite Malika's constant concerns about going against her mother's wishes, these reductive monolingualist English-only orientations toward foreign language learning were weakened by her alternative perceptions and lived experiences of transnational mobility and networking; instead, a desire to further expand and diversify her current French repertoire in college and beyond was invigorated thanks to her high school French teacher and continued transnational communication with her French host family. Even when Malika was bombarded with her real grandmother's ideals that the alternative language resources critical to her sense of self would not allow mobility, especially to a young African American female expected to mimic socially and culturally mainstream English-language practices, her stronger ties and meaningful communication with her other grandmother, who treated her own students' linguistic and cultural resources as valuable to knowledge production in a high school English classroom, opened up more useful ways of thinking about

English in local writing ecologies. Such counter language socialization resulted in a significant change in Malika's doings of the language in ways that deviated from her real grandmother's (and her English writing teacher's) prescriptive instructions even in high-stakes writing. The voices and experiences of these young writers from tremendously diverse backgrounds in *Toward Translingual Realities in Composition* highlight how the dynamic language representations they have brought with them into their literacy learning pursuits are not necessarily permanent but rather context-dependent and have the potential for gradual change sometimes even for the same individual under highly specific situations, thereby giving us more reason to remain hopeful.

Unraveling and rewriting popular and institutionalized ways of construing English, other vibrant language resources, and their concomitant doings in educational landscapes that have become deep-seated, heavily sedimented, and routinized is indeed challenging—though probably not more than sustaining an old cultural artifact like the invention of fixity, discreteness, immobility, and purity in language, usage, and meaning that, arguably, no longer has the same convincing and realistic resonance it once had in eighteenth-century Europe. For those of us who wish to truly take this challenge seriously, the academic and professional development of novice writing teachers can and should serve as fertile ground for unpacking, intervening in, and reworking (again and again) the tension-filled "languages on language" vibrant in local institutional and writing program ecologies. In fact, as Sidney Dobrin (2005, 5; emphasis added) has argued, the introductory composition practicum is indeed "the *very* location—if not the only location—through which composition studies as a discipline, as theory, as practice, is constructed for the newest members of the field and, perhaps more important, for many who will never identify themselves as compositionists" but end up staffing most writing-related course offerings. Aligning with a substantial body of work affirming the crucial role of intensifying critical language-related knowledge in graduate-level education and training (see Kilfoil 2015; Mangelsdorf 2017; Canagarajah 2016; Varghese et al. 2016; Tardy 2017; Preto-Bay and Hansen 2006; Shuck 2006), I would argue that reform energies and efforts in composition under the translingual rubric need to be channeled more toward the preparation of current and future generations of the teachers of the compulsory FYW course among other writing courses who will, it is hoped, remain in the field (or at least affiliated with its teaching component) and will have to deal with the multifaceted, ambiguous intensities of its perpetual postmonolingual frictions for the longer run. It behooves us, as I have stated elsewhere, to provide constant occasions for existing, new, and incoming writing teachers to openly talk about and carefully examine among themselves and their students the complex web of institutional, programmatic, and individual documents[2] (Bou Ayash 2016; also see Wible 2013; Tardy 2011; Dryer and Mitchell 2017), much like the ones I've examined in the previous chapters of this book, through which overt and covert representations of language, language competence, language standards, language errors, and language difference in writing mainly "travel" and end up shaping their own and their students' attendant practices. Often, these documents inadvertently foreground, recycle, or leave unproblematized the very same dominant monolingual ideologies and epistemologies with cloaked connections to multilingualism we seek to unsettle and disrupt.

Third and perhaps most fundamental, *language representations and the embodied literate practices they directly influence have a complex trajectory permeated by change and refinement in response to particular contextual affordances and meaningful, conscious reflection on practice.* We have seen particularly with struggling student writers like Naser and more accomplished ones like Diva, KAPPA, and Li Ming that their language representations are emergent and situated and follow a complex, messy trajectory, often revealing tremendous or subtle changes throughout their negotiations of various contextual contingencies. Again, it is relevant here to reference how the pedagogical spaces graphic design professors created for Naser's linguistic and semiotic resources gave rise to the emergence of representations of language usage as heterogeneous and hybrid and of the full range of resources in his repertoire as meaningful and accessible in academic contexts. In fact, such pedagogical affordances offered opportunities for Naser to change his language representations and fueled his affirmative thinking about his language abilities and agency in making meaning and design. The way Diva, KAPPA, and Li Ming navigated their perceptions of the true translingual character of language, identity, and culture in the complex postmonolingual space of the FYW classroom in their corresponding localities indicates that they deftly assessed and worked through the possibilities and constraints of local pedagogical and assessment sites. While Diva embraced and enacted translingual writing practices in low-stakes writing, she felt the need to censor her sustained engagement with such practices in high-stakes writing assessments. Similarly, KAPPA felt under-prepared to meaningfully handle foreign language sources in his written work and, like Li Ming, felt underappreciated for his tedious and time-consuming *trans*lation labor. However, KAPPA's decision to continue working through such challenges was responsive to the kind of intellectual profundity he was confident cross-language relations granted his academic work. When reflecting on the meaningfulness of literacy learning events surrounding the making of his written work, Li Ming attributed his active participation in *trans*lation to his teachers' invitation to tap into valuable language and cultural resources; nevertheless, his perceptions of such translingual work as not central, hence not mattering, when demonstrating effective English academic abilities and practices prompted by his felt sense of the primacy of English-only imperatives in the assignment expectations and grading rubric prevented him from sufficiently engaging with such work in its full complexity.

As they emerged in this study, these writers' voiced representations of language relations and language difference in academic writing were mediated by critical reflection and assessment of the affordances of social and ecological communicative contexts. I turn once again to the work of Louis-Jean Calvet (2006, 247), who insists on the fact that social interactions and situations repetitively and firmly "construct these representations, but that they can at the same time be modified by them." Put differently, with the nature of language representations and their workings on subsequent practices being relational and responsive to classroom contextual influences, offering meaningful and relevant pedagogical support, scaffolding, and facilitation—which seems to be within our power and control as writing teacher-scholars and writing program administrators—can potentially play a pivotal role in enabling and fostering a translingual orientation to language and literacy learning among university-level writing students. We can and should provide classroom affordances for stretching and broadening our, our colleagues', and our students' representational landscape of English in the FYW classroom as continuously evolving—even as I write this passage—impregnated with nuances, and "'cultured' . . . in our minds . . . in our bodies, our practices, our doing" (Park and Wee 2012, 120). For these jointly constructed translingual-oriented representations to become an integral part of students' knowledge reservoir as resources for literate interpretation and sense making, they also need to be acted upon repeatedly and consistently in writing pedagogies and assessments as well as in affiliated language socialization sites operating outside but alongside the bounds of the FYW classroom. As I have suggested in chapter 5, sustained commitment to giving voice and volume to critical writing-*trans*lation connections in the writing classroom is a good first step for introducing more productive, fine-tuned language for students to qualitatively understand and construct their language resources, their actual labor with these resources, and their own identities in increasingly complex and dynamic literate lives. A serious advocacy for critical writing-*trans*lation connections in composition pedagogy can be an opportunity for our students to further engage and engage us and one another in explorations of the problematics and potentialities of critical *trans*lation in academic literacies and the representational practices involved in making such deliberately slow, circuitous intellectual labor (im)possible.

As for issues of assessment, with the advent of a translingual turn in composition, we've already started to see an insurgence of scholarship (see Inoue 2017; Dryer 2016; Lee 2016) that directly confronts the many hidden agendas, interests, and complicities behind writing placement and assessment tools in higher education, which serve to activate and resuscitate English-only monolingualism assumptions about language and its learners and writers. Calling for creating more favorable conditions for translingualism in writing assessment ecologies, Asao Inoue (2017, 132–33), for instance, argues that rather than becoming objects of uninformed recycling in assessment tools, dominant monolingualist demands for language efficiency, accuracy, correctness, clarity, precision, and persuasion need to be treated as "having particular class, racial, economic, and historical origins" and "being idiosyncratic in readers," hence susceptible to "mutual interrogation and negotiating judgments."

While there is much talk (to be applauded) in composition studies about accommodating, honoring, and legitimating (through textual and pedagogical spaces) the full range of students' existing and vibrant language and semiotic resources, there is still little corresponding talk on the representations of these resources, whether directly or indirectly, in curriculum expectations and course outcomes, in writing assignment prompt design, in written feedback and assessment practices. As Dylan Dryer (2016, 279) notes, the nature of language relations and practices emphasized in our local writing assessments needs to align and work "with, rather than against," efforts at translinguality in writing instruction and the translingual character of the checkered complexes of "our and our students' language resources more generally." From this perspective, I would argue that exactly "what is devalued or ignored" or perceived as 'weightless' under the auspices of English-only monolingualism and its traditional multilingual surrogate—namely, "the effort, the difficulty and, above all else, the time required to establish and maintain [translingual] linguistic (and by definition, cultural) connections" (Cronin 2003, 22, 49)—is what needs to become a central, "weighty matter" in our writing assessment ecologies. In fact, it is necessary to make explicit (again and again) to students attempting the cognitively fulfilling yet taxing translingual labor the fact that the added complexity and requirements (including high mental, emotional, and time costs) placed on them are fully taken into account. Such labor needs to get "rewarded for its ambition" (Barnard 2010, 447), persistence, and intellectual heft, for its challenges to both writers and their readers, and for its imbrication in and production of transversality and a much more congested traffic in meanings, resources, ideologies, and worldviews.

In addition, the kind of labor happening or needing to happen in FYW programs and individual classrooms is influenced, according to Mary Jo Reiff and colleagues (2015, 305), "in consequential ways by their interaction with and interdependence on the kinds and structures of third spaces available to students" and is uniquely situated and "operating 'outside and alongside' writing programs" and classrooms. These meso-spaces—including but not limited to writing centers, writing studios, libraries, and academic support programs—can, I argue, facilitate our writing students' complex negotiations of the competing language representations and practices central to their academic knowledge production and consumption as they move into and across diverse local institutional writing contexts. While it might be beyond our scope to tinker with the hegemonic assumptions about language usage and language difference among the rest of the campus intellectual community, we can at the very least start by collaborating with library liaisons on incorporating cross-language work into information literacy sessions specifically designed to provide research assistance for FYW courses and on directly addressing the logistics of locating and properly citing foreign language sources as well as maneuvering the complexity of the back-and-forth movement the work of *trans*lation demands. In our ongoing, much-needed campus-wide partnerships with these "liminal, in-between" (Reiff et al. 2015, 305) institutional sites, we can start considering, with the help of students, how language, cultural, national, even disciplinary boundaries as traditionally conceived can and should be reworked and redrawn in researched writing within larger institutional ecologies to support the kind of translingual language (but also transmodal, transnational, and transdisciplinary) relations integral to their personal, intellectual, and future professional success.

TRANSLINGUAL REPRESENTATIONS-IN-THE-MAKING: AVENUES FOR MOVING FORWARD

As writing teacher-scholars and writing program administrators, together with our students, both graduate and undergraduate, we have been old and expert members of the monolingualist imagination of

English—studying and teaching it as a discretely circumscribed entity in allegedly pure form, interlocking snugly without any overlap or leakage with other equally definable and fixed language entities—for years (and will continue to be for many more years to come), but we are still "young" and "apprentices" when it comes to confronting, re-examining, and rewriting our habitual construals of and written practices with college English. As we begin engaging in such labor, I have argued that representations of language (including English) and its difference in acts of composing, themselves understood as local practices rooted in highly specific life biographies and experiences that play a significant role in shaping other practices with language and literacy, contain within them the potential for aspired change and transformation in composition research and pedagogy along translingual lines. With learners of academic writing in the United States and elsewhere equally contending with postmonolingual academic frictions to varying degrees of successes and failures within the changing mobilities of their lives and work, we need forms of scholarly inquiry aimed not only at demonizing monolingualism or its pluralized reproduction through traditional multilingualism or at eulogizing translingualism any more than composition scholarship has done thus far. Instead, it would be more fruitful to turn our ethnographic gaze toward *local language representations and practices* in diverse writing program and institutional ecologies as a central analytic pairing that could potentially move our ongoing disciplinary dialogue and labor over correcting the real, detrimental consequences of institutionally sponsored English-only monolingualism further forward.

If we truly seek translingual realities in composition, it would be crucial to continue to combine a multiplicity of ethnographic perspectives that trace and theorize the intricate linkage between local contextual sets of language representations and their subsequent practices that *Toward Translingual Realities in Composition* has started tapping into but has only scratched the surface of this tremendous complexity. At present, my own thinking (and indeed that of the field as a whole) regarding how language representations and mediated practices interconnect and interrelate with each other in increasingly superdiverse ecologies of teaching and learning university-level academic literacies, just like the core concept of language itself, is provisional and still work-in-progress. Accordingly, I invite my readers to work jointly on refining and further expanding our current understanding of the descriptive terms, ideas, images, or metaphors (about English[es], other vibrant language resources, and the relations among them) our writing students frequently entertain, defy, and disrupt in their academic literacies work as part of their local histories, lived realities, and projected social futures. With an eye toward their dynamicity and complexity, future composition research could throw further light on the precise nature of and possible changes in first-year writers' language representations and practices as they move across different physical and social spaces and ensuing language-ideological brokering activities in the daily routines of their literate lives. There is a growing need for sustained investigations of the successes and challenges of negotiating the multiplicity and contradiction surrounding local understandings and mobilizations of language as young writers strive to strategically position themselves and their own academic texts in relation to diverse interactional and institutional histories, economies, inequalities, and affordances. Getting closer to the messy complexities and entanglements at the level of local language representations and practices that constitute our and our students' contemporary postmonolingual realities necessitates more robust multi-sited/multi-scape ethnographic fieldwork that moves the study of writing and its teaching and learning in higher education amid language and cultural difference beyond traditional single-site locations (e.g., single writing program or classroom, single institutional setting, or single national-cultural context) and beyond dominant US-centered traditions of "intellectual tourism" (Donahue 2009, 236). Taking up a project of translingual activism in composition can prove to be consequential in nuancing the field's level of preparedness for its necessary and perpetual questioning of the lack of continuity between the sociolinguistically relevant co-constructions of English and its academic performances through the constant work we do, in concert with the writers and writing communities we are meant to serve, both locally and in different parts of the world.

Appendix A
AN ETHNOGRAPHY OF LANGUAGE REPRESENTATIONS AND/AS PRACTICES

RESEARCH SITES

This project combines ethnographic accounts from Beirut University (BU), a prominent teaching-centered and research university in the Middle East region, and the University of Seattle (UOS), one of the oldest urban research universities on the US West Coast. Table A1.1 summarizes some of the characteristics of each research context. The specific selection of these urban institutions of higher education mainly coincides with my own transnational mobilities and personal connections and is not intended to suggest that the increasing complexity of the concrete labor of sense making amid ideological difference is central and exclusive to cityscapes (or institutions of higher education within them)—hence leading to their romanticization and idealization—and, by extension, less visible or significant in rural language ecologies.[1]

As a private American-style university, BU bases its educational philosophy, standards, and practices on the American liberal arts model of higher education. Its local students are drawn from various religions, strata, and areas of Lebanese society, but with a predominance of middle to upper socioeconomic classes. In addition to the local English- or French-educated student population, there is an increasing number of international students, which makes the language situation complex. Its international student population is from seventy-three different countries, with the majority coming from neighboring Arabic-speaking nations, such as Jordan, Syria, Saudi Arabia, and other Arab Gulf states. Twenty-two percent of students enrolled in fall 2014 were foreign student visa holders. Though its students are predominantly Lebanese (as shown in table A1.1),[2] it is very common for them to have dual citizenships, having been born and raised in countries where their parents had emigrated (especially the United States, Canada, Australia, Venezuela, Brazil, the United Kingdom, and France) because of changing political and economic conditions.

UOS is a public, world-class research university. It is largely a commuter school, with 79 percent of its students coming from diverse areas

Table A1.1. Characteristics of research contexts

	Beirut University[a]	University of Seattle
Size (undergraduate enrollment)	6,837 students	31,525 students[b]
Demographics (national origin; ethnic/ racial distribution)	78% Lebanese 22% international students	41.4% Caucasian[c] 24.9% Asian 7.7% Latino 2.7% African American 2.0% Filipino 0.4% Native American 0.5% Native Hawaiian or other Pacific Islander 1.1% not indicated 14.3% international students
(gender distribution)	52% female 48% male	51.7% female 48.3% male

[a] *Based on fall 2014 enrollment figures; source: Enrollment Statistics and Management Unit.*

[b] *Based on headcount enrollment trends for fiscal year 2014–15; source: Office of Planning and Budgeting.*

[c] *Source: Office of Minority Affairs and Diversity Factsheet (fiscal year 2016–17).*

within Washington state. Nearly three fourths of its graduates remain in the state. About 57 percent of UOS undergraduates receive some form of financial aid, and 27 percent of its freshman students are the first in their generation to attend college. Like most large university campuses in the United States, along with the presence of US resident language minority students, there is a considerable and quickly growing population of newly arrived international students at UOS from eighty different countries. In fact, the number of international students, mostly from mainland China, Korea, India, Taiwan, and Saudi Arabia, has tripled over the past decade.

RESEARCH PARTICIPANTS

For this project, I recruited undergraduate student participants at both institutions based on the following criteria: (1) enrolled in a universally required first-year writing (FYW) course at the time of research and (2) self-identified as having working knowledge of one or multiple languages in their repertoire besides English. The student participants recruited at both research sites represented a diversity of disciplines, educational and linguistic backgrounds, nationalities, ethnicities, religions, and gender (see appendix B for demographic information on featured student participants). Many of my student participants at both sites were involved in different types of dwelling and traveling and hence self-consciously reflected on their experiences of working across language difference, which affected them and their literate lives in motion. In fact, the experiences of navigating geographic and linguistic mobility that I shared with many of my research participants contributed to establishing strong rapport and subsequently greater levels of openness and cooperation.

Students in Beirut were very eager to participate in my study and have their voices heard, though I offered no tangible compensation for their time and energy. I could sense that for some of them it was an opportunity to practice their English-language conversational abilities, while others felt there was some value in expressing and sharing their concerns and needs grounded in lived and embodied academic literacy learning experiences with a center-based university writing specialist who was also familiar with the specificity of the local context and had knowledge of its locally vibrant languages. Working with, learning from, and listening to my student participants was immensely rewarding in so many ways that I cannot render in ink. Sometimes our conversations continued during on-campus literacy-related events (such as "The Celebration of Student Writing," a university-wide showcase of student writing and research projects) and outside the school context (while traveling on buses or in taxi cabs; at nearby restaurants, coffee shops, or the campus dining commons, to name just a few). The overwhelming majority of participating students were native Arabic speakers. There was only one native Armenian speaker with advanced literacies in Arabic, two who moved from Venezuela and self-identified as native Spanish speakers with a limited speaking knowledge of Arabic, and two who were native English speakers (one coming back from Canada and the other from Abu Dhabi) who possessed truncated Arabic comprehension skills.

It was much more challenging to recruit student participants in the US research site without financial compensation, and some teachers (of their own accord) were gracious enough to offer their students extra credit for participation. Of those students, 2 were African Americans, 1 was Native American, 2 were Pacific Islanders, 20 were Generation 1.5 students (of Vietnamese, Indonesian, Chinese, Filipino, Eritrean, Iranian, Korean, and Japanese descent), 15 were international visa-holding students (2 Malaysians, 6 Chinese, 1 Taiwanese, 1 French, 1 Indonesian, 2 from Ukraine, and 2 Koreans), and the remaining 10 were located in the sociocultural mainstream. The overwhelming majority of participants in the Seattle context reported possessing a range of unevenly developed language resources in their repertoire. As for the handful of mainstream American students who participated in this study (upon their own confession, mostly for the extra credits) and who described themselves as having "grown up around pure English" and only English, as one student put it, they portrayed a view of English as a tradable commodity in the world's knowledge and communication economies, thus making what another student described as the "burden" of stretching their partial or minimal competence in a foreign language beyond their high school requirement seemingly superfluous. Among this group of students, only two students reported being persuaded, sometimes even forced, by their parents, who themselves have capitalized on their own linguistic repertoires, to further their foreign language abilities, though often guided by the same monolingualist treatment of languages in one's possession as products and services with capital gains in time in the local/global marketplace.

Thanking me at the end of our lengthy conversations, sometimes after I had turned off the voice recorder, several students from my Seattle site mentioned that their participation in this project was a unique opportunity for them to think more reflexively about their sense making in academic language and literacy work, hence significant in making them more aware of the extent, diversity, and complexity of the sometimes battling and overlooked linguistic, rhetorical, and semiotic resources they carried with them and often drew on, maybe in ways they were not always conscious of. For instance, one African American male student, who had growing expertise in Japanese after formally studying the language for over eight years, expressed gratitude for bringing to his attention the fact that his working relation with Japanese does not necessarily have to be seen as "dormant" and less relevant to his public life and identity when compared to his other language resources (e.g., standard English, African American Vernacular English [AAVE], southern accent), hence "giving [him] some insight," as he put it, into his evolving linguistic self. Throughout our exchanges, I found myself forced to take a more deliberate role in raising his awareness of the potential value of his expertise in Japanese and its place as an actual resource in his own ongoing language and literacy learning and development.

In writing about the teachers' take on local and global language politics in teaching postsecondary-level writing in this study, since my purpose is to keep the central focus on the writing students at both sites and their changing moments of literate struggle and triumph, the actual perspectives of the small number of writing teachers I've interviewed constituted only a brief part of the overall discussion in this book. As I knew some of the teachers who agreed to work with me in both research sites (when they had been my own FYW teachers or colleagues during my teaching career in Beirut or when they had been my students in the graduate program in Seattle), I remained attentive to what they hoped their students would get out of this research and what they themselves hoped to gain that would potentially mobilize them professionally. The majority of writing teachers in Beirut were Lebanese nationals trained in applied linguistics and English-language teaching methods at the current research site, with four having received their professional training abroad (in the United Kingdom, the United States, and Canada) in either TESOL or creative writing, and only one was an American-born native English-speaking teacher with no special training in second/foreign language teaching issues. Two of those instructors were teaching writing and translation courses simultaneously (see chapter 5). Women represented a significant majority of my teaching participants at both research sites (with only one male in Beirut and three in Seattle), maybe reflecting a common trend in these writing program ecologies in particular and the English-language teaching profession in general. All the teaching participants in Seattle were graduate teaching assistants (GTAs) (training in TESOL, rhetoric and composition, or literature and cultural studies) who were receiving at the time of research or had already received in previous years their teacher training through the introductory composition practicum course (see discussion in chapter 4). Five of those GTAs were international, one belonging to the ethnolinguistic minority, and the rest were mainstream Americans.

DATA COLLECTION AND ANALYSIS

The data I discuss in this book were collected over a considerable period, from 2006 to the present. In the initial phase of the project, I was mainly collecting during my three-year teaching career in Beirut[3] and later in Seattle what Jan Blommaert (2013, 16) calls "linguistic landscaping" materials. These included diverse popular culture texts and artifacts, photographs of moments of language-in-use in public cityspaces (ranging from signage in the city to graffiti), communication tools of advertising and publicity, cultural and mass-tourism products (e.g., personalized T-shirts, greeting cards, license plates), local newspaper and magazine clippings, and so on. These linguistic landscape texts representing different genres served as chronicles documenting how the flow of language and semiotic resources participates in the making and remaking of Beirut and Seattle cityscapes and the lived realities of the people who inhabit and fashion them. Put differently, the superdiverse sites explored in this book should not be seen as inert, static geographical spaces simply existing somewhere out there but are instead mobile and actively given meaning and design (and ultimately transformed) with and through language by diverse social actors in shifting spatio-temporal domains (cf. Pennycook 2010; Pennycook and Otsuji 2015). In addition to my local "collectibles," I was simultaneously keeping a journal on the various academic and professional writing courses I was teaching at the time in Beirut—though written with a critical gaze mainly on my own pedagogical practices for self-assessment and self-revision. It was not until the spring of 2012, upon my brief return to Beirut as a US-based researcher, that I started combining the linguistic landscape data and teaching notes I've kept with more structured and rigorous forms of ethnographic inquiry, but this time turning my critical lens toward the language perceptions and practices of other writing teachers and their students.

Identifying and further exploring the distinctive features of the language ideologies—as well as their scope, force, and diverse manifestations—employed by both national-cultural contexts under study in this book, the two selected institutions of higher education within them, and even the main literate agents and decision-makers at those institutions called forth special attention to macro-level language policy texts and discourses. For that purpose, I reviewed and conducted a close rhetorical analysis of various language policy documents, with an eye toward the hows and whys, if at all, of the particular stated and unstated views, attitudes, and perceptions toward language and language relations that surfaced in those texts and the ideologies of language closely tied to and motivating them. In the case of Lebanon, I traced the ideological, cultural, (geo)political, and economic underpinnings of the historical and contemporary development of national language and language-in-education policy documents. With the absence of a codified language policy in the case of the United States, I focused on how a tacit monolingual English-only policy as the de facto cultural norm and specific Washington state–endorsed language policies get interpreted, appropriated, and re-contextualized by various identifiable agents who are expected to follow them at the micro level. In addition, I examined official university-wide and program-specific webpages, mission statements, university presidents' messages, policies and guidelines involving language usage, and student catalogs and faculty handbooks at both research sites while paying special attention to how they impacted the way writing students and their teachers oriented to the ebb and flow of language resources and practices on their campus grounds.

Knowing that writing curriculum design and classroom writing pedagogies are additional evident embodiments and products of educational language politicking and socialization practices, I focused on the particular language norms and practices that core components of the design and implementation of a FYW classroom—for example, assigned writing textbooks, course syllabi, lesson plans, handouts, writing assignment prompts, teachers' markings on student texts[4]—have institutionalized, protected, promoted, (de)legitimized, and contested, thereby setting the stage for and contouring writing students' language representations and actions in their own academic written work. In sum, I have approached various textual materials written for public or institutional consumption at both research sites as the most visible vehicles by means of which language ideologies are locally (whether implicitly or explicitly) (re)produced, enforced, transmitted, problematized, destabilized, and transformed.

At the research site in Beirut, I met with one focus group composed of seven students enrolled in various sections of FYW courses to get a general sense of (1) the nature of students' language perceptions and beliefs both inside and outside the FYW classroom, (2) how they used language in academic and non-academic writing situations and to what specific ends, and (3) how well they thought their university teachers responded to their language and writing needs in the FYW classroom and beyond.

In both geographic locations, I conducted more focused individual student interviews in English and surrounding the same themes (refer to appendix C for interview protocol). These semi-structured interviews were an opportunity to inquire in more depth about student writers' specific family history, stories about language and literacy practices and values, schooling experiences, and memories of language use and learning with influential individuals. More particularly, these student interviews helped in exploring their varied representations of their relation with academic English literacies and other language and literate resources in their repertoires while still being rooted in their material localities—particularly their immediate family environment and experiences, the wider cultural and ideological structures of their postsecondary-level (sometimes even secondary- and primary-level) academic institution(s), and the larger superdiverse society and nation-state in which they lived.

In addition to conversations with FYW students, I conducted semi-structured interviews with writing teachers at both sites addressing issues of language policy and pedagogical practices in their own classrooms (see appendix D for interview protocol). These interviews were focused mainly on teachers' perceptions of their instructional practices and responses to moments of language difference in student writings and the specific nature of the teaching strategies they ideally saw as most helpful to their students. In some cases, teacher participants voluntarily offered additional data sources that I used mainly in supplementing these interviews, such as invitations to visit their classrooms, sit through oral individual student and group presentations, or attend one-day events where students showcased their writing projects to the campus community. In the case of BU, I observed one FYW class for a whole semester. These observations focused primarily on how official institutional and programmatic claims about language policy and practice along with writing teachers' articulated language perceptions and beliefs compared to the actual (re)workings of those perceptions and beliefs in the writing program and classroom ecologies.

Based on the trends gleaned from the juxtaposed voices of writing students and teachers, I used a follow-up method of "talk around"[5] academic texts in both research contexts with FYW students, whom I selected through relying on theoretical sampling.[6] Extended "talk around" drafts or final versions of texts students had written or were writing at the time this research was conducted invited a close examination of (1) how and why they prioritized particular forms and usages over others in the production of their own academic work, in which situations, when engaging (or not) with which language and semiotic resources, and for what particular purposes; (2) what/who has shaped and dictated their perceptions of these valued forms and usages; and (3) how such linguistic forms and meanings captured, suppressed, or glossed over critical moments and relations in their personal, academic, and professional life. This method of literate talk around texts, their production and potential reception, and the nature of language and semiotic resources actually deployed (or still to be deployed) to make those texts more rhetorically effective in itself served as a "useful pedagogic resource" (Ivanič et al. 2009, 122), informing my own pedagogical reflections and interventions in the workings and effects of dominant language ideologies that I present and elaborate on in chapter 5. The meaningful, ongoing personal contact afforded by a method of extended and in-depth communication helped establish comfort and trust with my student participants.

I analyzed transcripts of interviews with students and teachers following the methodological guidelines and strategies of a materialist, social constructivist approach[7] to grounded theory. After establishing some firm analytic directions through my initial word-by-word, line-by-line, and segment-by-segment coding, I began separating, sorting, and synthesizing data through more focused coding—such as "material and/or psychological investments in English," "English as a commodity," "linguistic action against English-only imperatives," "cross-border relations (linguistic, cultural, rhetorical, disciplinary, etc.) in academic writing negotiated," "management of foreign language source use," "contradictions of language orientations between disciplinary and academic English literacies," "(in)visibility of translation," "fluidity and fixity," "distinctness and relatedness," "boundedness and flow," "uniformity and hybridity," and so on. I kept successive analytic memos that elaborated on emerging patterns, themes, and categories; described their underlying properties and characteristics, and identified relationships among different themes and categories as well as existing gaps and divergences. Aiming toward an investigation of participants' representations in connections with specific contexts of language use and learning, I supplemented basic grounded theory practices of coding and extensive memo writing with a context-/situation-centered approach aimed at elucidating the increasingly "messy complexities" (Clarke 2005, xxxv, 53) of situated action involving language and literacy at the "meso-level." More specifically, I pursued "big picture" (Clarke 2005, 203, xxxv) situational maps that laid out possible human agents involved—both individuals and collectivities—and amplified the full array of major and pertinent "discursive, historical, symbolic, cultural, political," geopolitical, and economic elements of the particular language- and literacy-related situations and their "dense relations and permutations." Doing situational maps and analysis offered rich possibilities for a more enhanced understanding of the ways ideologies and representations of language in both research sites were being generated, coerced, interpreted, negotiated, valorized, complicated, or disrupted in various literate situations—of which some of my participants were perhaps completely unaware. As more perspectives came into analytic purview, my data analysis process was not entirely linear but rather entailed multiple goings back and forth among coding, memoing, and mapping to create new threads of analysis that might have been glossed over or unapparent initially. Upon conducting multiple interviews, I shared with interested participants my description and analysis of the perspectives and experiences they shared during our previous sessions and elicited their responses. The written confirmations they have provided of the interpretations offered in drafts of chapters 3, 4, and 5 served as a form of member check.

Appendix B
PROFILES OF FEATURED PARTICIPANTS

Participant	Academic Discipline	Language Resources	Educational Background
Nathalie	Computer communications engineering; math and business (minors)	French, Lebanese Arabic, Arabic, English	French Lycée, Lebanon
Lucas	Pre-med sociology	French, Arabic, English, Lebanese Arabic	French Lycée, Lebanon
Naser	Graphic design	Arabic, Lebanese Arabic, English, French (working knowledge)	English-medium public schools, Lebanon
Diva	Business	English, Greek, Lebanese Arabic	Private primary and secondary schools, Greece; IB Program, Lebanon
KAPPA	Landscape design (transferring to graphic design)	Italian, French, English, Latin, *modo di dire*	Private school system, Italy (early law specialization)
Nur	Oceanography	Vernacular Malay, *bahasa Melayu*, English, *rojak* English, Mandarin, Tamil	Public school system, Malaysia
Malika	Biochemistry	English, AAVE, French (advanced knowledge), Spanish (working knowledge)	Public schools, WA, United States
Li Ming	Materials science and engineering	Mandarin, Suzhou dialect, English	Public schools, China and Singapore
Ryan	Computer science	English, Spanish (advanced knowledge)	Public schools, WA, United States
Mateo	Linguistics	Spanish, English, Portuguese	Primary school, Brazil; primary and secondary schools, United States
Ruijia	Business	Mandarin, Shanghai dialect, English	Public school system, China

Appendix C
STUDENT INTERVIEW PROTOCOL

GENERAL

Can you tell me a bit about your educational background, your current (prospective) major, your hopes or desires for your future career?

What/who do you think might have influenced this academic and prospective career trajectory?

LANGUAGE AND LITERATE REPERTOIRES

Is English the language you use at home?

Do you identify yourself as competent in other languages or language variety/ies?

How do you use these, where, when, with whom, and to what effect?

What word, image, metaphor, or story comes to mind when you think of English, the way you use it, and its place and role in your personal, academic, and future professional life and work?

What word, image, metaphor, or story comes to mind when you think of your way(s) of using the language varieties or the language(s) other than English that you previously identified (if any)?

Describe for me something you most recently did or engaged in in your regular life inside or outside your college/university campus that you think made you feel either confident or insecure with the way you communicate and use the language(s) in your repertoire (English, one or more languages, or language variety/ies). What exactly did you do with language during this activity that made you feel that way? For what purpose(s)?

Using which language(s)/dialect(s)/accent(s)/style(s)/register(s)? Which media (speech, sound, images, text, combination of those, etc.)? Who was/were involved in that activity? How did (s)he/they respond or react to the way you acted in this particular situation? And why in your view did they behave that way? What would you have liked them to do instead?

**PERCEPTIONS OF ACADEMIC LANGUAGE
AND LITERACY LEARNING**

To what extent do you think learning academic English reading and writing in courses like (FYW course number) will help you achieve

- the personal and professional goals you've set for yourself and you've mentioned at the beginning of our interview?
- How do your English teachers define "good and clear" writing and what forms do they think it should take?
- How do YOU define "good and clear" writing?
- How do your English teachers present and define the rules of Standard American English in their courses (you might refer to them as rules of grammar and mechanics that dictate what is right or wrong, what is viewed as correct or incorrect in terms of the way you use English in your writing)?
- How much emphasis do you think your teachers give to those when commenting on and assessing your papers?
- How does that compare with your professors in your major disciplinary course(s)/other courses across campus?
- Are there any interests or areas in which you think you're an expert (e.g., varying degrees of knowledge of any of the languages or dialects that you described earlier; gaming; hip-hop music; social media networking) but that you feel get excluded and have no room in your current academic English writing course?
- How are these important to you, to your personal, cultural, national, or professional identity, maybe even to your style of learning in college, or the way you make sense of things and express your ideas?
- Do you think drawing on and working with these areas of expertise makes you feel that you are a strong reader and writer and good with language? If so, in what ways? What would be the biggest challenge for you to be able to tap into these areas of expertise? If not, what exactly would make you feel more confident as a language user and university-level writer?

SOCIAL NETWORKS

- Looking back at the several issues we've discussed in this interview pertaining to your experiences of learning academic reading and writing at and outside your university, what memorable events or specific significant individuals in your everyday literate life (e.g., family, friends, classmates, community members, past or current teachers, online acquaintances, strangers) have particularly shaped the views, feelings, positions, and experiences that you shared with me today?

Appendix D
TEACHER INTERVIEW PROTOCOL

EDUCATION AND TRAINING

Tell me about your educational background, training, and qualifications.

Do you feel confident and qualified to work with linguistically and culturally diverse student populations in your class (second language writers, basic writers, and others)?

Briefly describe the kind of resources and support, if any, you are currently offered to aid in your work with changing student demographics. Do you feel you have enough resources to tap into?

What do you think the current program administrator and course coordinators can do to help?

LOCAL LANGUAGE POLICIES AND THEIR OPERATION

What do you know about (Washington state or Lebanese) language-in-education policies? What do you know about your current institution's and writing program's language policy, if any?

Have you come across during your teaching experience here at [name of institution] any explicitly stated or maybe unwritten policies, statements or documents, or understandings regarding the preferred form of English-language use in academic knowledge production?

Do you think there should be more explicit language policies at the institutional and programmatic level?

In an ideal situation, if you had any say in the design of a potential language policy statement for your institution, writing program, or both, what shape would that policy take?

What kind of language policy/ies do you currently adopt as a writing teacher in your own classes? And why?

LANGUAGE PERCEPTIONS AND PEDAGOGICAL PRACTICES

How do you define "good and clear" writing to your students and what forms do you think it should take in student work?

How do you present and define standards and conventions of language use in your courses? Why do you approach language standards the way you do in your own pedagogy?

How would you describe your students' language practices and the linguistic resources they bring into your classroom?

- What is your sense of the impact of these language practices and resources on your students' learning, writing, and production of meaning?
- Do you make any efforts to get to explore and understand those practices and resources more? Why or why not?
- Do you deliberately make room for them in your course design? If not, what is keeping you from doing so? If so, explain how and when? And when exactly do you refrain from doing that?
- What do you regard as errors in student writing and English usage? How do you approach them in your written feedback?
- How do you perceive student compositions that pose arguments, styles, organizational patterns, language forms, and structures alternative to dominant values and practices? How do you typically respond to the presence of these differences in your written comments?
- What do you tell your students to do or not to do when you sense that they are experiencing some difficulties and moments of confusion as they negotiate (linguistic, cultural, rhetorical, and so on) differences when reading and writing for your class?
- If you were laboring under ideal political and ideological conditions, what changes, if any, would you introduce into your course design, teaching practices, and assessment tools that would most effectively harness and cultivate the kind of resourcefulness or agency you feel your students have (should have) in the way they use language in their public, personal, academic, and maybe future professional lives?
- What personal, academic, or professional experiences or maybe specific influential individuals have played a pivotal role in shaping the perspectives you've shared with me today in this interview, that is, the way you view language standards, students' diverse language resources, errors, and the way you subsequently treat them in your teaching and assessment practices and in the design of your writing assignments and projects and writing assessment tools?

NOTES

INTRODUCTION

1. This campaign was launched in a number of "Crazy Ones" television commercials, magazine ads, and billboards depicting a series of iconic figures who have left a mark in history, like Amelia Earhart, Picasso, Gandhi, the Dalai Lama, John Lennon, Muhammad Ali, and many others.
2. Here and in the rest of the book, I adopt Reiff and colleagues' (2015, 4) conceptualization of writing programs as themselves complex "discursive and material ecologies," emerging out of intertwined networks of affiliations and dynamic interactions, embodying and enacting the constant fluidity and inherent fluctuation of writing discourses and performances over time and across space. Such an ecological perspective helps situate local understandings of and practices with language resources in literate situations, which lie at the heart of this book's theme, in relation to the wider social, historical, and political forces at work within the two writing programs explored.
3. Critical ethnographic projects are particularly well-suited to provide an understanding of the ways language, literacy, and their learning are "intrinsically tied to context and human activity" and of how every situated act of linguistic and literate "production, reproduction, and circulation or consumption involves shifts in context," subjectivities, and enactments of identities (Blommaert 2008, 233, 64). Such insights can be challenging to uncover and develop under traditional descriptive ethnographic research, which presupposes the a-historical, unmediated nature of communicative and interpretive activity and practice divorced from the complex sociocultural, (geo)political, economic, educational, and ideological agendas that (re)fashion the literate lives of individual research participants and the ethnographer herself/himself. For more on common critiques of traditional ethnography in the ELT enterprise, see Canagarajah 1999; in composition and literacy studies, see Kirsch and Ritchie 1995; Horner 2002; Brown and Dobrin 2004.
4. Compare here such conceptualizations of the multiplicity of sites to the shortcomings inherent, as I highlight in the next chapter, in the "multi" of multilingualism, multiculturalism, and multimodality.
5. For more on the potentiality of sustained engagements with mixed qualitative methods or with analyses of empirical data from diverse sites, see the work of Lewis, Enciso, and Moje 2007; Ivanič et al. 2009; Lillis and Curry 2010; Coleman and von Hellermann 2013.
6. See, for instance, work aiming to contest a dominant ideology of English-only monolingualism and positing alternative neologisms: in rhetoric and composition, "transcultural literacy" (Lu 2009), "translingualism" (Horner, NeCamp, and Donahue 2011; Canagarajah 2013b; Bawarshi et al. 2016), and "code-meshing" (Canagarajah 2006a; Young, Barrett, and Young-Rivera 2014); in bilingual education studies, "translanguaging" (García 2009; García and Wei 2014; Creese and Blackledge 2010); "multiliteracies" in New Literacy Studies (New London Group 1996; Cope and Kalantzis 2000); "*creolité*" or "*diversalité*" in Caribbean literary scholarship (Bernabé, Chamoiseau, and Confiant 1989); and "plurilingualism" both in Francophone scholarship (Conseil de l'Europe 2001; Moore and Gajo 2009; Coste,

Moore, and Zarate 1997; Blanchet and Martinez 2010) and in TESOL (Taylor and Snoddon 2013).
7. For a useful overview of the plethora of such coinages with mildly or widely varying definitions, see Canagarajah 2013b, 9–11.
8. See, for example, Arnaut et al. 2016; Blommaert and Backus 2013; Blommaert 2013.
9. However, this book is not focused on urban language mobility and diversity but rather on the construction of meaning and knowledge by literate individuals in urban landscapes in light of their local understandings about language and its doing(s).
10. It is important right from the start to point out to my readers that the term *translingual*, key to this book's framework and arguments (and mentioned in its title), is itself contested as it might attract and carry utopian overtones of its own, but it serves our purposes—as writing teacher-scholars and program administrators—for the moment given its nascent nature in composition studies. In other words, the label itself is provisional and "only stabilized for [here and] now" (Bawarshi 2016, 244); in the words of Keith Gilyard (2016, 189), we might ultimately need an alternative name in the long run.
11. Just as the construct of language itself is socioculturally invented, so too is the related concept of translingualism. That being said, the term *translingualism*—like the widely used notion of multilingualism—can still retain these tendencies for the quantification of diversity, depending on the particular conceptualizations and treatments of linguality it reinforces.
12. For an elaboration on the semantic confusion attached to the prefix post, see Berger 2003; Yildiz 2012, 4–5.

CHAPTER 1: LANGUAGE IDEOLOGIES IN TEACHING WRITING

1. Language ideology, linguistic ideology, or ideology of language are all terms in play in a rapidly growing area of scholarly inquiry, which bridges linguistic and social theory. Despite my awareness of some of the key dimensions of difference signaled by these terms, with the first two predominantly invoking perceived language structures and use and the last term concentrating more on perceptions and enactments of a collective polity, regime, or institution of any scale (for more on this distinction, see Woolard and Schieffelin 1994, 56), I use these terms interchangeably throughout the book.
2. Also echoed in Irvine 1989; Irvine and Gal 2000; Gal and Irvine 1995; Kroskrity 2000.
3. The notion of "local," which immediately brings to mind the simplistic dichotomization of the local versus the global, requires extensive explanation here. My adoption of this notion in this book is not confined to only one sense of the term, which is the particular, "the small, the traditional, the immutable" (Pennycook 2010, 128, 4), but is rather simultaneously concerned with the multiple, embedded, and contextualized responses to wider matterings and happenings, on one hand, and, on another hand, the grounded "mobilizations of local movements" and resources. As Pennycook (2010, 80) argues, "The global is always manifested locally, and the local is always part of the global." In light of general concerns about the limited, narrow focus of a local view, I take this attention to the local ways of understanding and doing language in superdiverse cities like Beirut and Seattle as the starting point and not the endpoint for further in-depth analysis of their workings and manifestations in light of changing material conditions.

4. Another contested term I use repetitively in this book is the notion of "practice" (and its plural form), which has been central to contemporary theories of language and literacy, especially after the emergence of what is commonly known in the social sciences as "the practice turn" (see Schatzki 2001). Despite its popularity in such scholarship, one of the limitations of this notion, as Pennycook (2010, 8) cautions, is the potential for invoking it as merely a casual, empty "add-on" after broad, abstract concepts like community, literacy, language, and discourse that seem to carry all the weight. Though some slippage in its use is expected, my own use of the term *practice* does not only refer to a bundle of everyday activities and coherent, regulated doings but also to a higher-level combination of thought and knowledge building. In this sense, despite continuing debates across disciplines over the exact relation between theory and practice, this book builds on the idea of the inseparability of practical work by literate individuals and the potential effect of that work on the formation of language and the organizing frameworks and principles behind it. With attention to individual action but also to the social repetition of certain forms of action, we see evidence of language as a local practice in the areas of language policy, pedagogy and curriculum design, assessment, and translation—all of which receive varying degrees of attention in this work.

5. There is a profusion of competing terms used to refer to language representations, such as "folklinguistics" (Preston 1991), "folklinguistic theories" (Miller and Ginsberg 1995), *imaginaire linguisitique* (Canut 1996), "beliefs" in SLA/FLL (Barcelos and Kalaja 2011), or "*représentations sociales*" in Francophone scholarship (Py 2004; Moore and Gajo 2009). Refer to Barcelos (2006) for a more critical review of the pluralism of terms and definitions and the various analytical and methodological aspects of studies on representations of language and its learning.

6. Such Anglophone formulations surrounding the potential of representations and their possible linkages to language practice are also epistemologically shared and confirmed in Francophone studies at the intersection between educational sociolinguistics and sociodidactics (see Py 2004; Moore and Gajo 2009; Castellotti and Moore 2002; Byram and Zarate 1996).

7. See Woolard (1998, 16–17), Canagarajah (2013b, 19–24), and Yildiz (2012, 7–8) for an elaborate delineation of the rise and construction of a dominant monolingual paradigm echoing the monolingual bias of the European, specifically Herderian, thinking about language that first emerged in eighteenth-century German Romanticism.

8. The monolingualist ideology's stranglehold is not exclusive to English-language practice and education but also extends to normative, standardized, and literate varieties of other languages, such as what we call Arabic (Bale 2010) and Spanish (Menard-Warwick 2014), and even to the cross-language practice of translation (see Bou Ayash 2013).

9. A dominant monolingual ideology has produced approaches referred to in composition studies scholarship as "foundationalist" (Lu and Horner 2012; also see Dasgupta 2005 in translation studies) or "eradicationist" (Horner and Lu 2007; Horner et al. 2011).

10. Rarely is the value and "mythical nature" of the proposition that possession of native-like competence in standardized English in and of itself leads to educational success and economic prosperity questioned (García 1995, 146; cf. Horner and Trimbur 2002, 617–18). Providing sociolinguistic evidence that counters such a proposition, which has gained universal uptake and acceptance, García (1995, 142, 147) argues that (1) most African Americans and Latinos in the United States have had little economic success despite "high rates of linguistic assimilation"; and (2)

one specific Latino group of Cuban Americans has had the "greatest economic success" despite "the low rates of linguistic assimilation achieved."

11. The enumeration here is only intended to serve illustrative purposes.
12. This conventional notion of multilingualism is in stark opposition with what Horner and Lu (2007) in earlier work have termed "multilingual" approaches to language difference in student writing, what Canagarajah (2006b) has referred to as a "multilingual rhetorical orientation", and what Horner, NeCamp, and Donahue (2011) call "translingual multilingualism."
13. The notion of voice under a traditional multilingual ideology and its tangible pedagogical manifestations is seen solely from a literary lens as the presence of "force, power, energy" in written communication (Elbow 1999, 383). In contrast, voice from a social materialist perspective in an era of globalization is defined as the capacity (or its lack) for "*semiotic mobility*" or, say, the ability to generate particular functions and meanings using specific linguistic resources "across physical and social" boundaries through (re-)creating "favorable conditions for a desired uptake" (Blommaert 2005, 68–69; emphasis in original).
14. Also in this regard, see Patricia Bizzell's (2002, 2) assertion that alternative discourse practices should not be seen "simply as more comfortable or more congenial", since comfort, safety, freedom, and authenticity were not "all they provided." Rather, she argues that these alternative linguistic and discursive practices allowed literate individuals to "do intellectual work in ways they could not if confined to traditional academic discourse" and its conventions (2002, 2).
15. This is where the current book parts company with the dominant rhetoric of language rights, language diversity, and multilingualism as traditionally conceived underlying official statements of professional organizations, like the CCCC's Students' Right to Their Own Language (SRTOL) (1974), as well as the growing trend of diversity statements in US institutions of higher education where the construct of language(s) itself as a real, discrete, and reified entity remains unquestioned, hence highly suspect (also see Makoni and Pennycook 2007; Horner 2001; Pennycook 2010).
16. For a sampling, see Horner 2016; Pennycook 2010; Arnaut et al. 2016; Blommaert 2010; Canagarajah 2013a, 2013b; Ellis, Fox, and Street 2007; Leung and Street 2012; Firth and Wagner 2007; Creese and Blackledge 2010; Kramsch 2009; García 2009; García and Wei 2014.
17. Some of these language policies—most notably those developed by leading disciplinary organizations like the Conference on College Communication and Composition (CCCC) and the National Council of Teachers of English (NCTE)— include the Students' Right to Their Own Language (SRTOL) (CCCC, 1974; reaffirmed, 2003); Guidelines on the National Language Policy (CCCC, 1988; revised 2015); CCCC Statement on Second Language Writing and Writers (CCCC, 2001; reaffirmed 2014); Resolution on the Students' Right to Incorporate Heritage and Home Languages in Writing (NCTE, 2011); Resolution on English as a Second Language and Bilingual Education (NCTE, 1982).
18. For a selective list, see Canagarajah 2006a, 2009, 2013b; Guerra 2015; Jordan 2012; Severino, Guerra, and Butler 1997; Silva, Leki, and Carson 1997; Hesford, Singleton, and García 2009; Horner and Trimbur 2002; Horner, Lu, and Matsuda 2010; Kells, Balester, and Villanueva 2004; Kilfoil 2015; Horner and Lu 2007; Matsuda 2006; Preto-Bay and Hansen 2006; Schroeder, Fox, and Bizzell 2002; Smitherman and Villanueva 2003; Young, Barrett, and Young-Rivera 2014; Martins 2015, and many others.

CHAPTER 2: WORKING TRANSLINGUAL LANGUAGE REPRESENTATIONS AND/AS PRACTICES

1. Though Hymes in the introductory epigraph makes reference to linguistics and its long-term obsession with the (near impossible) study of language entities, his argument can also be extended to composition.
2. Under this critical approach to translation as a political and ideological practice, the source and the target language/text, as defined in the traditional sense, are seen as always set in motion (Pennycook 2001, 14; Bassnett and Trivedi 1999, 10).
3. For such a critique of the invocation of the tree metaphor, see Deleuze and Guattari 1987, 15; Maalouf 2008.
4. One limitation of drawing on ecological models to understand language and language relations in local milieus is the potential for confusing language(s) with biological species as static entities (for more on this, see Pennycook 2010, 94). Another critique of ecological metaphors is that they are sometimes borrowed in ways that merely acknowledge and emphasize the existence of constant and inevitable change and thus end up lacking in their analytic potential. In other words, the diverse "engines and agents of such change" as well as perpetual "changes in such engines and agents" remain to a large extent submerged (Blommaert 2010, 18). The metaphors I describe here are definitely incomplete and imperfect but might serve as a productive means for exploring, clarifying, and imagining what a translingual take on language and language relations might possibly look like.
5. The same critique of traditional multilingual approaches to language and language difference also applies to traditional multimodal approaches, which focus on modes as discrete, fixed, yet pluralized entities (see Pennycook 2007, 49; Horner and Selfe 2013).
6. The linguistic construct of a NES has been systematically scrutinized as early as 1985 in Paikeday's controversial volume *The Native Speaker Is Dead* and identified as "an ideal or a convenient linguistic fiction—myth, shibboleth . . . an etherlike concept with no objective reality to it" (107). In more recent years, scholars have put into question an idealized NES norm, its lack of correspondence to actual sociolinguistic projections on the ground, and inadequacy in accounting for the complexities of users'/learners' diverse language resources and literate experiences (see Leung, Harris, and Rampton 1997; Firth and Wagner 1997, 2007; Kramsch 1998; Canagarajah, 2006a, 2007; House 2003; Rubdy and Saraceni 2006; Parakrama 1995; Jenkins 2014; Spack 1997; Singh 1998; Shuck 2006; Matsuda et al. 2011).
7. This sense of the social materiality of error (Horner 1999) along with the value of close reading in complicating mainstream views of what counts as language errors in student writing (Shaughnessy 1977; Bartholomae 1980), which have emerged in basic writing scholarship, have paved the way for more current work on translingualism in composition despite divergences between both research strands in responses to language difference in students' language and literate practices (for more on that, see Horner 2011; cf. Trimbur 2016).
8. Similarly, outlining key principles of a semiotic and ecological approach to language teaching and learning, educational linguist Leo van Lier (2004, 92; emphasis added) argues that meaning does not reside "inside words and sentences" but is rather closely linked to "*action potential*" as it emerges from agentive interactions with diverse contextual contingencies.
9. To borrow a colleague's description in attempts to make sense of my own evolving understanding of translingualism.

CHAPTER 3: UNPACKING LOCAL LANGUAGE REPRESENTATIONS AND/AS PRACTICES

1. Here Salameh's use of "multilingualism" is not in the traditional sense of the term but rather in reference to the hybrid blending of diverse language resources at both the societal and individual level, which enables cosmopolitan orientations and relations.
2. Sitting on a peninsula extending into the Mediterranean Sea, Beirut has over its 5,000-year history seen a wealth of nationalities, cultures, languages, ethnicities, and religions throughout its Greek, Roman, Ottoman Turkish, and then French rule. Despite internal and regional political and social uncertainty and turbulence, the city remains a touristic, cultural, and intellectual center and a private banking haven in the Middle East, with a fairly sizable number of travelers, expatriates, immigrants, refugees, and Lebanese migrants (temporarily or permanently returning from the diaspora) constantly flowing through its busy streets.
3. Ras Beirut is home to several internationally recognized schools and universities and is a cultural hub for local and foreign (mainly Euro-American) professionals, journalists, artists, intellectuals, writers, and activists (Seidman 2012).
4. The oral language used at home is typically the local (urban or rural) Lebanese Arabic variety, which differs to some extent in terms of lexicon and grammatical, morphological, and phonological features from the prestigious written variety publicly recognized as Modern Standard Arabic, which takes many of its rules and norms from the classical Arabic of the Qura'n.
5. For instance, number 3 for the voiced pharyngeal fricative /ʕ/ and 7 for the voiceless pharyngeal fricative /ħ/. I myself adopt this practice in transcriptions of student interviews on pages 80 and 90. This technologically imposed way of making meaning among Arabic literate individuals, first emerging in social media and SMS writings and expanding into other writing situations, is increasingly being documented and explored in Arabic sociolinguistic studies (see Miller and Caubet 2010, 248).
6. I have cautioned in earlier work of the romanticization and commercialization of such translingual language practices, which actually drive their sales and mass production in the first place as culturally specific commodities (Bou Ayash 2014).
7. Taxis as well as other means of urban public transportation can be viewed as mobile "language laboratories" (Ogulnik 2000, 169) where travelers while in transit have the opportunity to get in direct touch with locals, actively putting all their language and cultural resources to work while on the move.
8. This video titled *Taxi* is one of a collection of several other *La France au Liban* videos (e.g., *Tante, Le Chef*) that promote a yearly cross-cultural event organized by the Paris Chamber of Commerce and Industry in the capital city of Beirut to celebrate strong sociocultural, linguistic, and economic relations between the Lebanese and French culture.
9. It would be relevant here to question the complex status of English and French in Lebanon. While French and English are officially designated "foreign" languages, many residents of Lebanon may, in fact, see them as "native," "first," or "second" languages instead.
10. Under the previous Arabic-only policy, minority ethnolinguisitic groups (namely Armenians, Greeks, Persians, and others) who lacked Arabic in their repertoire were unable to meet the institution's admission requirements, and BU's faculty members in the sciences faced serious difficulties with the unavailability of Arabic textbooks in the first three years of study in their disciplines. See Jeha (2004) for a more extensive historical account of the specific local and regional sociopolitical and material realities motivating this major shift in language education policy.

11. Though BU's writing program is designed following the larger infrastructures of North American writing programs, it still operates under the name of a "communication skills" program, originally established and directed by applied linguists. Alongside the acknowledgment of the primacy of writing-related research and instruction across the university (through the establishment and development of a dynamic writing center in 2003 and the introduction of writing across the curriculum [WAC] and writing in the disciplines [WID] courses in 2009), attention to oral communication, considered among the significant marketable skills in professional national and regional settings, still persists.
12. Here I borrow from Blommaert's (1999) early work his concept of "ideology brokers" and more recently, from Lillis and Curry's (2010) ethnographic research, their notion of "literacy brokers", which I take up as "language ideology brokers" in the context of this study's focus on language representations and practices in FYW as manifestations of battling language ideologies in the teaching and learning of writing. In this sense, I align with their preference for the value-laden, economically and politically driven practice of "brokering" over Brandt's (2001) notion of "sponsorship", which is widely adopted in composition studies.
13. Text in square brackets used here and other instances of Arabic or French textual materials in this chapter are my translations. Words or phrases in all caps are stressed as part of the transcript. Those in bold are directly relevant to the analysis.
14. For a useful analysis of dynamic constructions of subjectivities and experiences of learning foreign languages in institutional settings through metaphors, see Kramsch 2009.
15. Though Monroe's (2016) ethnographic study focuses on one specific pattern of mobility, that is, spatial mobility in the Beiruti public realm, her arguments about the collision and near collision of varied and contradictory understandings of individual and vehicular mobility can also be extended to linguistic, literate, and cultural mobility experiences and to other superdiverse cities in the rest of the world.

CHAPTER 4: UNPACKING LOCAL LANGUAGE REPRESENTATIONS AND/AS PRACTICES CONTINUED

1. Seattle's position as a trade and shipping center was a selling point in the early twentieth century to large immigrant groups from Asia, Eastern Europe, and Scandinavia. Its economic expansion continues to attract industrious and enterprising individuals and migrant workers, both foreign- and American-born. For more details on modern Seattle history, ethnic composition, and patterns of immigration and settlement, see Putnam 2008; Schwantes 1998.
2. As manifested in language-related legal cases (e.g., Ann Arbor Black English case [Ball and Lardner 1997], *Lau vs. Nichols* [García 2009], and *Meyer vs. Nebraska* [Kloss 1998; Hornberger 1990]); the controversy surrounding Ebonics and the Oakland school board resolution (Perry and Delpit 1998); continuing debates on bilingual education programs (García 2009); in news media coverage of language management practices in public and private arenas (namely, Arizona school banning Spanish [Freeman 2014], Hispanic driver fined for inadequate English skills ["Feds May Tighten English Fluency Law for Truckers" 2008], Wisconsin student's native Menominee usage punished [Hibbard 2012], and so on).
3. See García (2009) for a discussion of the ambivalent nature of bilingual education policy in US primary and secondary education.
4. Notably in the form of explicitly restrictive state-level measures, such as Arizona's Proposition 203 and California's Proposition 227.

208 NOTES

5. Enrollment figures in bilingual programs across Washington have more than doubled since 2004–5.
6. For an expanded description of the history, goals, and implementation of local program models as upheld by the official state policy, refer to Malagon and Chacon 2009, 26, 61; Malagon, McCold, and Hernandez 2012, 19.
7. These enrollments in Washington state mainly concentrate in urban areas and in a few rural areas, like Yakima Valley (Malagon, McCold, and Hernandez 2012, 11).
8. To name a few, the annual study abroad programs organized and taught by its faculty and TESOL internship programs offering mentorship and training experience for teaching English as a foreign/second language to locals in Morocco and Spain.
9. These include the Office of Minority Affairs and Diversity and the Ethnic Cultural Center.
10. Though the terms *native* and *non-native* in reference to speakers, learners, or teachers of English have long been called into question in English as a lingua franca (ELF) and world Englishes (WE) scholarship, I continue to use them in this book mainly because the suggested alternatives (e.g., "expert" [Leung, Harris, and Rampton 1997], "monolingual" versus "bilingual" versus "non-bilingual" English speaker [Jenkins 2015]) haven't gained much traction.
11. Here I adopt the same term used in the program's dominant discourse and public texts, but this is not at all to suggest that students' multilinguality (or in this sense of the term, the plurality of language resources in their repertoire) necessarily matches their ideological orientation to language.
12. Following a directed self-placement model and guided by the same learning outcomes as the mainstream sections yet with reduced class sizes, these specialized sections, taught by teachers trained in both TESOL and composition, are offered and presented to students self-identified as L2 writers as supportive placement options and not efforts to keep them quarantined from their ostensibly more proficient NES peers. The course readings, discussions, and assignments in these designated sections are more welcoming and manageable in that they focus on shared challenges and the heterogeneity of students' language and cultural resources and experiences.
13. I thank Holly Shelton for pointing me to this notion.
14. Transcription conventions are as follows:
    CAPITALIZATION: marks intensity
    (.): brief pause
    [. . .]: gap in transcript when material had no bearing on main research focus
    Sections that are directly relevant to the analysis are bolded.
15. Here Li Ming pointed out that classmates who did not pursue cross-language relations in this project did not necessarily face fewer literacy challenges but worked through different demands and constraints.

CHAPTER 5: TRANSLINGUAL ACTIVISM

1. For a useful discussion of the elision of translation and cross-language inquiry in US composition teaching and scholarship resulting from the dominance of English-only monolingualism, see Horner and Trimbur 2002; Horner, Lu, and Matsuda 2010; Horner, NeCamp, and Donahue 2011. In the infrastructure of rhetoric and composition graduate programs, such translation work is generally limited to timed exams taken in fulfillment of the nationwide foreign language requirement and is generally assessed by degree of technical replication of the original and getting the dictionary meanings and equivalences right (see Kilfoil 2015). Even when coursework and comprehensive examinations in such programs require the study and analysis of

    translated theoretical texts, these texts are rarely approached as translations, with little attention, if any, to the task and power of the translator, the theories and practices behind such translations, the situatedness of these translated materials, or the interpretations they give rise to in their own cultural, linguistic, and historical moments.
2. The persistent neglect of the value and relevance of translation, House (2012, 217) observes, is only an Anglophone but not a European tradition. EU language policies, for instance, support and promote the place of translation in the theory and practice of language learning and teaching (European Commission 2008, 13).
3. For an exhaustive survey of such contemporary resurgent interest in and revival of translation and the various ways it has been promoted in language and literacy education, see Tsagari and Floros 2013; Laviosa 2014; House 2016.
4. For more on the basic principles of monolithic grammar-translation teaching that dominated the English-language teaching industry in the early twentieth century, see Laviosa 2014, 4–6; Pennycook 2008, 35.
5. Similar arguments have also been put forward in bilingual, second, and foreign language education (Cummins 2007; Kramsch 2009; Tsagari and Floros 2013) and in translation studies (House 2016; Cook 2010; Laviosa 2014).
6. This sense of translation was promulgated during the late Middle Ages when translations of Christian scriptures into vernacular languages according to such norms were becoming increasingly popular (see Tymoczko 2006; Bassnett 2011).
7. Offered as humanities general education courses at BU, these translation courses are designed to familiarize students with basic translation theories and offer hands-on opportunities to practice basic translation tools and strategies. For more on the design of these courses, see Bou Ayash 2013.
8. This writing project is inspired by Lu and Horner's (2008) discussion on the possibilities of working with and against expectations of specific writing genres.
9. This is not necessarily a purely individualistic obsession but an engagement with local community and sociocultural values and affiliations.
10. The names of students have been changed to protect their anonymity.
11. For a useful description of such conventional theorizations of voice in composition, see Trimbur 2000.
12. I take this expression from Ross (cited in Kramsch 2006, 202).

CONCLUSION: LESSONS ON THINKING AND DOING TRANSLINGUALITY *WITH* BEIRUT AND SEATTLE

1. Refer here to the book's introduction for a detailed explanation of how and why my particular choice of preposition here ("with" rather than "about") contests dominant trade models of transnational academic exchange and research.
2. These include but are not limited to university and writing program webpages, mission statements, campus-wide diversity statements, student handbooks, teacher manuals, assigned textbooks, individual course syllabi, writing assignment or project prompts, assessment rubrics, and so on.

APPENDIX A: AN ETHNOGRAPHY OF LANGUAGE REPRESENTATIONS AND/AS PRACTICES

1. In fact, Pennycook and Otsuji (2015, 30), citing Williams (1973), have cautioned that the rustic is not "some static, immobile, timeless, traditional space, the antipathy of the dynamic urban space" as we like to think.

2. The general categories "Lebanese" (at BU) and "International Students" (at both BU and UOS) are based on official projections from each campus, which dismiss profound differences under those seemingly uniform categories across the lines of race, class, ethnicity, or religion.

3. At the time, I was a full-time writing instructor to whom research was not an integral component for career advancement and promotion, so those materials were nothing more than local "collectibles." As I began my journey through graduate studies in the United States, the fascination I've had for many years with issues involving the politics and ideologies of language in educational contexts and their interrelationship with the sociolinguistics of superdiversity in modern cityscapes grew exponentially. It was then that I started noticing that the linguistic landscaping materials from Beirut I'd casually compiled over the years were hidden gems, supporting and scaffolding many of the ethnographic observations and insights I share in this book.

4. As Bawarshi (2000, 352) notes, each of these teaching-related genres at work in the writing classroom "constructs a different sociosemantic dynamic, a particular social semiotic," which shapes how both writing teachers and their students imagine and enact their situated "identities, activities, and relations" involving language and its difference. In my negotiation of tensions between retrievability and participant confidentiality in citation practices, I deliberately omitted separate reference entries and did not offer complete in-text citations for these teaching materials and other program-related documents. Readers, however, can still identify what the exact source of information in my analysis is.

5. This widespread methodological tool of "talk around" texts has been adopted and further extended in various academic literacy studies to generate discussion about wide-ranging contextual and text-focused issues. More specifically, extended "talk around" students' written texts in this study were crucial for zeroing in on a variety of text-specific aspects in their own writing, ranging from simple linguistic features like comma usage to more complex rhetorical issues, such as (counter)argumentation, navigating multiple viewpoints, the use of colloquialisms, and working with foreign language sources. At the same time, this tool has proved useful in generating writer-focused discussions on the specific sociocultural, political, and historical contexts and institutions mediating, shaping, and shaped by their linguistic-discursive choices. For more elaborate methodological explanations and successful applications, refer to Ivanič 1998; Ivanič et al. 2009; Lillis 2009; Lillis and Curry 2010.

6. Very briefly, theoretical sampling, integral to the analytic approach of grounded theory, directly gives special attention to particular sources of data (in this case, individual students and not theories about their language/literacy learning) that can best bring to light and help explicate particular theoretically meaningful patterns and facets emerging in provisional data analysis. In other words, such a long-established, purposive strategy does not necessarily focus on drawing a representative sample of a particular researched population and its diversities; instead, it is driven especially by emergent theoretical and ideological concerns across the duration of the project (see Clarke 2005). For the purposes of this study, theoretical sampling was very crucial in explicitly pursuing and accentuating tension-filled relations of difference and heterogeneity in academic written language.

7. Grounded theory, in its essential form in the classic text of Glaser and Strauss (1967), may be among the most commonly and widely employed interpretive strategies in qualitative research studies. However, in original grounded theory texts that seem to build on the tenets of positivism, empirically grounded theories are seen as emerging from the data but detached from the putatively partial and distanced qualitative researcher and ethnographer. In *Toward Translingual Realities*

in Comsposition, I adopt a social constructivist version of grounded theory—as advanced in the works of Charmaz (2006) and Clarke (2005)—that diverges epistemologically from traditional grounded theory in its recognition of ethnographers' inevitable engagement with and critical rendering of the literate and linguistically constructed worlds they study, the empirical data they gather, and the theoretical analyses and interpretive insights they offer (also see Denzin and Lincoln 2012). As Charmaz (2006, 10; emphasis in original) argues, "We *construct* our grounded theories through our past and present involvements and interactions with people, perspectives, and research practices."

REFERENCES

Adler-Kassner, Linda. 2008. *The Activist WPA: Changing Stories about Writing and Writers.* Logan: Utah State University Press.
Agnihotri, Rama. 2007. "Towards a Pedagogical Paradigm Rooted in Multilinguality." *International Multilingual Research Journal* 1 (2): 79–88.
Ahmad, Dohra. 2007. *Rotten English.* New York: W. W. Norton.
Anzaldúa, Gloria. 1999. *Borderlands: The New Mestiza.* San Francisco: Aunt Lute Books.
"Apple Confidential—Steve Jobs on 'Think Different'—Internal Meeting Sept. 23, 1997." Online video clip. YouTube, November 5, 2013. Accessed April 23, 2016.
Arnaut, Karel, Jan Blommaert, Ben Rampton, and Massimiliano Spotti. 2016. *Language and Superdiversity.* London: Routledge.
Auer, Peter. 2007. "Monolingual Bias in Bilingualism Research, or: Why Bilingual Talk Is (Still) a Challenge for Linguistics." In *Bilingualism*, ed. Monica Heller, 319–39. Basingstoke, UK: Macmillan.
Baker, Mona. 2006. "Translation and Activism: Emerging Patterns of Narrative Community." *Massachusetts Review* 47 (3): 462–84.
Baker, Mona. 2007. "Reframing Conflict in Translation." *Social Semiotics* 17 (2): 151–69.
Bale, Jeffrey. 2010. "Arabic as a Heritage Language in the United States." *International Multilingual Research Journal* 4 (2): 125–51.
Ball, Arnetha, and Ted Lardner. 1997. "Dispositions toward Language: Teacher Constructs of Knowledge and the Ann Arbor Black English Case." *College Composition and Communication* 48: 469–85.
Barcelos, Ana. 2006. "Researching Beliefs about SLA: A Critical Review." In *Beliefs about SLA*, ed. Ana Barcelos and Paula Kalaja, 7–33. New York: Springer.
Barcelos, Ana, and Paula Kalaja. 2011. "Introduction to *Beliefs about SLA Revisited*." *System* 39 (3): 281–89.
Barnard, Ian. 2010. "The Ruse of Clarity." *College Composition and Communication* 61 (3): 434–51.
Bartholomae, David. 1980. "The Study of Error." *College Composition and Communication* 31 (3): 253–69.
Bassnett, Susan. 2011. *Reflections on Translation.* Bristol, UK: Multilingual Matters.
Bassnett, Susan, and Peter Bush. 2007. *The Translator as Writer.* London: Continuum.
Bassnett, Susan, and Harish Trivedi. 1999. *Post-Colonial Translation: Theory and Practice.* London: Routledge.
Bawarshi, Anis. 2000. "The Genre Function." *College English* 62 (3): 335–60.
Bawarshi, Anis. 2003. *Genre and the Invention of the Writer: Reconsidering the Place of Invention in Composition.* Logan: Utah State University Press.
Bawarshi, Anis. 2016. "Beyond the Genre Fixation: A Translingual Perspective on Genre." *College English* 78 (3): 243–49.
Bawarshi, Anis, Juan Guerra, Bruce Horner, and Min-Zhan Lu. 2016. "Translingual Work in Composition" [Special Issue]. *College English* 78 (3): 207–97.
Bean, Janet, Maryann Cucchiara, Robert Eddy, Peter Elbow, Rhonda Grego, Rich Haswell, Patricia Irvine, Eileen Kennedy, Ellie Kutz, Al Lehner, and Paul Kei Matsuda. 2003. "Should We Invite Students to Write in Home Languages? Complicating the Yes/No Debate." *Composition Studies* 31 (1): 25–42.

Bénard, Jean-Paul, and Paul Horguelin. 1979. *Pratique de la Traduction.* Montreal: Linguatech.
Berger, Arthur. 2003. *The Portable Postmodernist.* Walnut Creek, CA: Altamira.
Bergmann, Linda, and Janet Zepernick. 2007. "Disciplinarity and Transfer: Students' Perceptions of Learning to Write." *WPA: Writing Program Administration* 31 (1–2): 124–49.
Bernabé, Jean, Patrick Chamoiseau, and Raphaël Confiant. 1989. *Éloge de la Créolité.* Paris: Gallimard.
Bex, Tony, and Richard Watts. 1999. *Standard English: The Widening Debate.* London: Routledge.
Bizzell, Patricia. 2002. "The Intellectual Work of 'Mixed' Forms of Academic Discourses." In *ALT/DIS: Alternative Discourses and the Academy,* ed. Christopher Schroeder, Helen Fox, and Patricia Bizzell, 1–10. Portsmouth, NH: Boynton/Cook.
Bizzell, Patricia. 2014. "Toward 'Transcultural Literacy' at a Liberal Arts College." In *Reworking English in Rhetoric and Composition,* ed. Bruce Horner and Karen Kopelson, 131–49. Carbondale: Southern Illinois University Press.
Blakesley, David, and Jeffrey Hoogeveen. 2012. *Writing: A Manual for the Digital Age.* Boston: Wadsworth.
Blanchet, Philippe, and Pierre Martinez. 2010. *Pratiques Innovantes du Plurilinguisme: Émergence et Prise en Compte en Situations Francophones.* Paris: Archives Contemporaines.
Blommaert, Jan. 1999. *Language Ideological Debates.* Berlin: Mouton de Gruyter.
Blommaert, Jan. 2005. *Discourse: A Critical Introduction.* New York: Cambridge University Press.
Blommaert, Jan. 2008. *Grassroots Literacy: Writing, Identity, and Voice in Central Africa.* London: Routledge.
Blommaert, Jan. 2010. *The Sociolinguistics of Globalization.* Cambridge: Cambridge University Press.
Blommaert, Jan. 2013. *Ethnography, Superdiversity, and Linguistic Landscapes: Chronicles of Complexity.* Bristol, UK: Multilingual Matters.
Blommaert, Jan, and Ad Backus. 2013. "Superdiverse Repertoires and the Individual." *Tilberg Papers in Culture Studies* 24: 1–32. Tilberg University.
Blumenthal, Karen. 2012. *Steve Jobs, the Man Who Thought Different: A Biography.* New York: Feiwel and Friends.
Bou Ayash, Nancy. 2013. "Hi-*ein*, Hi بين or بين Hi? Translingual Practices from Lebanon and Mainstream Literacy Education." In *Literacy as Translingual Practice: Between Communities and Classrooms,* ed. Suresh Canagarajah, 96–103. New York: Routledge.
Bou Ayash, Nancy. 2014. "US Translingualism through a Cross-National and Cross-Linguistic Lens." In *Reworking English in Rhetoric and Composition,* ed. Bruce Horner and Karen Kopelson, 116–30. Carbondale: Southern Illinois University Press.
Bou Ayash, Nancy. 2016. "Conditions of (Im)Possibility: Postmonolingual Language Representations in Academic Literacies." *College English* 78 (6): 555–77.
Brandt, Deborah. 2001. *Literacy in American Lives.* Cambridge: Cambridge University Press.
Brown, Stephen, and Sidney Dobrin. 2004. *Ethnography Unbound: From Theory Shock to Critical Praxis.* Albany: State University of New York Press.
Burns, Norman, ed. 1963. *Annual Reports: Board of Managers, Syrian Protestant College, 1866-67-1901-02.* American University of Beirut Library Archives, Beirut, Lebanon.
Butler, Judith. 1997. *Excitable Speech: A Politics of the Performative.* New York: Routledge.
Byram, Michael. 1997. *Teaching and Assessing Intercultural Communicative Competence.* Clevedon, UK: Multilingual Matters.
Byram, Michael, and Geneviève Zarate. 1996. *Young People Facing Difference.* Strasbourg: Council of Europe.
Calvet, Louis-Jean. 1998. *Language Wars and Linguistic Politics.* Oxford, UK: Oxford University Press.

Calvet, Louis-Jean. 2006. *Pour une Écologie des Langues du Monde*. Trans. Andrew Brown, *Towards an Ecology of World Languages*. Cambridge: Polity.
Canagarajah, Suresh. 1999. *Resisting Linguistic Imperialism in English Teaching*. Oxford: Oxford University Press.
Canagarajah, Suresh. 2005. *Reclaiming the Local in Language Policy and Practice*. New York: Routledge.
Canagarajah, Suresh. 2006a. "The Place of World Englishes in Composition: Pluralization Continued." *College Composition and Communication* 57 (4): 586–619.
Canagarajah, Suresh. 2006b. "Toward a Writing Pedagogy of Shuttling between Languages: Learning from Multilingual Writers." *College English* 68 (6): 589–604.
Canagarajah, Suresh. 2007. "Lingua Franca English, Multilingual Communities, and Language Acquisition." *Modern Language Journal* 91 (1): 923–39.
Canagarajah, Suresh. 2009. "Multilingual Strategies of Negotiating English: From Conversation to Writing." *Journal of Advanced Composition* 29: 17–48.
Canagarajah, Suresh. 2011. "Codemeshing in Academic Writing: Identifying Teachable Strategies of Translanguaging." *Modern Language Journal* 95 (3): 401–17.
Canagarajah, Suresh, ed. 2013a. *Literacy as Translingual Practice: Between Communities and Classrooms*. New York: Routledge.
Canagarajah, Suresh. 2013b. *Translingual Practice: Global Englishes and Cosmopolitan Relations*. New York: Routledge.
Canagarajah, Suresh. 2014. "ESL Composition as a Literate Art of the Contact Zone." In *First Year Composition: From Theory to Practice*, ed. Deborah Coxwell-Teague and Ronald F. Lunsford, 27–48. Anderson, SC: Parlor.
Canagarajah, Suresh. 2016. "Translingual Writing and Teacher Development in Composition." *College English* 78 (3): 264–72.
Canagarajah, Suresh, and Ena Lee. 2014. "Negotiating Alternative Discourses in Academic Writing and Publishing: Risks with Hybridity." In *Risk in Academic Writing: Postgraduate Students, Their Teachers, and the Making of Knowledge*, ed. Lucia Thesen and Linda Cooper, 59–99. Bristol, UK: Multilingual Matters.
Canut, Cécile. 1996. "Acquisition, Production, et Imaginaire Linguistiques des Familes Plurilingues à Bamako." *Travaux de Linguistique* 7: 43–52.
Castellotti, Véronique, and Danièle Moore. 2002. *Social Representations of Languages and Teaching: Guide for the Development of Language Education Policies in Europe from Linguistic Diversity to Plurilingual Education*. Strasbourg: Council of Europe.
CCCC. 1974. "Students' Right to Their Own Language." NCTE. Accessed October 22, 2015. https://prod-ncte-cdn.azureedge.net/nctefiles/groups/cccc/newsrtol.pdf.
"CCCC Statement on Second-Language Writing and Writers." 2001. *College Communication and Composition* 52 (4): 669–74.
Charmaz, Kathy. 2006. *Constructing Grounded Theory: A Practical Guide through Qualitative Analysis*. London: Sage.
Chomsky, Noam. 1980. *Rules and Representations*. Oxford: Blackwell.
Clarke, Adele. 2005. *Situational Analysis: Grounded Theory after the Postmodern Turn*. Thousand Oaks, CA: Sage.
Coleman, Simon, and Pauline von Hellermann. 2013. *Multi-Sited Ethnography: Problems and Possibilities in the Translocation of Research Methods*. London: Routledge.
Conseil de l'Europe/Council of Europe. 2001. *Common European Framework of Reference for Languages: Learning, Teaching, Assessment*. Cambridge: Cambridge University Press.
Cook, Guy. 2010. *Translation in Language Teaching*. Oxford: Oxford University Press.
Cook, Vivian. 1999. "Going Beyond the Native Speaker in Language Teaching." *TESOL Quarterly* 33 (2): 185–209.
Cope, Bill, and Mary Kalantzis. 2000. *Multiliteracies: Literacy Learning and the Design of Social Futures*. London: Routledge.

Coste, Daniel, Danièle Moore, and Geneviève Zarate. 1997. *Compétence Plurilingue et Pluriculturelle: Vers un Cadre Européen Commun de Référence pour L'apprentissage et L'enseignement des Langues Vivantes: Études Préparatoires.* Strasbourg: Conseil de l'Europe.

Creese, Angela, and Adrian Blackledge. 2010. "Translanguaging in the Bilingual Classroom: A Pedagogy for Learning and Teaching?" *Modern Language Journal* 94 (1): 103–15.

Cronin, Michael. 2003. *Translation and Globalization.* London: Routledge.

Cronin, Michael. 2013. *Translation in the Digital Age.* London: Routledge.

Cummins, Jim. 2007. "Rethinking Monolingual Instructional Strategies in Multilingual Classrooms." *Canadian Journal of Applied Linguistics* 10 (2): 221–40.

Dasgupta, Probal. 2005. "Trafficking in Words: Languages, Missionaries, and Translators." In *In Translation: Reflections, Refractions, Transformations,* ed. Paul St-Pierre and Prafulla Kar, 42–56. Amsterdam: John Benjamins.

de Jong, Ester. 2011. *Foundations for Multilingualism in Education: From Principles to Practice.* Philadelphia: Caslon.

Deleuze, Gilles, and Félix Guattari. 1987. *A Thousand Plateaus: Capitalism and Schizophrenia.* Trans. Brian Massumi. Minneapolis: University of Minnesota Press.

Delpit, Lisa. 1988. "The Silenced Dialogue: Power and Pedagogy in Educating Other People's Children." *Harvard Educational Review* 58 (3): 280–98.

Denzin, Norman, and Yvonna Lincoln. 2012. *Strategies of Qualitative Inquiry.* Thousand Oaks, CA: Sage.

Diab, Rula. 2000. "Political and Socio-Cultural Factors in Foreign Language Education: The Case of Lebanon." *Texas Papers in Foreign Language Education* 5 (1): 177–87.

Dobrin, Sidney. 2005. *Don't Call It That: The Composition Practicum.* Urbana, IL: National Council of Teachers of English.

Donahue, Christiane. 2009. "'Internationalization' and Composition Studies: Reorienting the Discourse." *College Composition and Communication* 61 (2): 212–43.

Donahue, Tiane. 2008. "Cross-Cultural Analysis of Student Writing: Beyond Discourses of Difference." *Written Communication* 25 (3): 319–52.

Donahue, Tiane. 2013. "Negotiation, Translinguality, and Cross-Cultural Writing Research in a New Composition Era." In *Literacy as Translingual Practice: Between Communities and Classrooms,* ed. Suresh Canagarajah, 149–61. New York: Routledge.

Dor, Daniel. 2004. "From Englishization to Imposed Multilingualism: Globalization, the Internet, and the Political Economy of the Linguistic Code." *Public Culture* 16 (1): 97–118.

Dryer, Dylan. 2016. "Appraising Translingualism." *College English* 78 (3): 274–83.

Dryer, Dylan, and Paige Mitchell. 2017. "Seizing an Opportunity for Translingual FYC at the University of Maine." In *Crossing Divides: Exploring Translingual Writing Pedagogies and Programs,* ed. Bruce Horner and Laura Tetreault, 133–60. Logan: Utah State University Press.

Duranti, Alessandro. 2004. "Agency in Language." In *A Companion to Linguistic Anthropology,* ed. Alessandro Duranti, 451–73. Malden, MA: Blackwell.

Elbow, Peter. 1999. "Inviting the Mother Tongue: Beyond 'Mistakes,' 'Bad English,' and 'Wrong Language.'" *Journal of Advanced Composition* 19 (2): 358–88.

Ellis, Viv, Carol Fox, and Brian Street. 2007. *Rethinking English in Schools: Towards a New and Constructive Stage.* London: Continuum.

English, Bonnie, and Manka Varghese. 2010. "Enacting Language Policy through the Facilitator Model in a Monolingual Policy Context in the United States." In *Negotiating Language Education Policies,* ed. Kate Menken and Ofelia García, 107–22. London: Routledge.

European Commission. 2008. "Multilingualism: An Asset for Europe and a Shared Commitment." Accessed February 10, 2017. http://eur-lex.europa.eu/LexUriServ/LexUriServ.do?uri=COM:2008:0566:FIN:EN:PDF.

"Feds May Tighten English Fluency Law for Truckers." 2008. *Associated Press*, July 17. http://www.nbcnews.com/id/25716031/ns/us_news-life/t/feds-look-tighten-english-law-truckers/#.XODLlC2ZNBw.

Firth, Alan, and Johannes Wagner. 1997. "On Discourse, Communication, and (Some) Fundamental Concepts in SLA Research." *Modern Language Journal* 81 (3): 285–300.

Firth, Alan, and Johannes Wagner. 1998. "SLA Property: No Trespassing!" *Modern Language Journal* 82 (1): 91–94.

Firth, Alan, and Johannes Wagner. 2007. "Second/Foreign Language Learning as a Social Accomplishment: Elaborations on a Reconceptualized SLA." *Modern Language Journal* 91 (5): 800–819.

Foskett, Nick. 2010. "Global Markets, National Challenges, Local Strategies: The Strategic Challenge of Internationalization." In *Globalization and Internationalization in Higher Education*, ed. Felix Maringe and Nick Foskett, 35–50. New York: Continuum.

"Framework for Success in Postsecondary Education." 2011. Council of Writing Program Administrators, the National Council of Teachers of English, and the National Writing Project. Accessed September 3, 2017. http://files.eric.ed.gov/fulltext/ED516360.pdf.

Freeman, Will. 2014. "Meet the Arizona School Superintendent Who Wants to Ban Spanish." *ThinkProgress*, June 25. https://thinkprogress.org/meet-the-arizona-school-superintendent-who-wants-to-ban-spanish-c34e582bae99/.

Gal, Susan. 1998. "Multiplicity and Contention among Language Ideologies: A Commentary." In *Language Ideologies*, ed. Bambi Schieffelin, Kathryn Woolard, and Paul Kroskrity, 317–31. New York: Oxford University Press.

Gal, Susan. 2006. "Migration, Minorities, and Multilingualism: Language Ideologies in Europe." In *Language Ideologies, Policies, and Practices: Language and the Future of Europe*, ed. Patrick Stevenson and Clare Mar-Molinero, 13–27. Hampshire, UK: Palgrave Macmillan.

Gal, Susan, and Judith Irvine. 1995. "The Boundaries of Languages and Disciplines: How Ideologies Construct Difference." *Social Research* 62 (4): 967-1001.

García, Ofelia. 1995. "Spanish Language Loss . . . : Implications for Language Policy in Schools." In *Power and Inequality in Language Education*, ed. James Tollefson, 142–60. New York: Cambridge University Press.

García, Ofelia. 2007. "Foreword: Intervening Discourses, Representations, and Conceptualizations of Language." In *Disinventing and Reconstituting Languages*, ed. Sinfree Makoni and Alastair Pennycook, xi–xv. Clevedon, UK: Multilingual Matters.

García, Ofelia. 2009. *Bilingual Education in the 21st Century: A Global Perspective*. Malden, MA: Wiley-Blackwell.

García, Ofelia, and Li Wei. 2014. *Translanguaging: Language, Bilingualism, and Education*. Basingstoke, UK: Palgrave Macmillan.

Gentil, Guillaume. 2005. "Commitments to Academic Biliteracy: Case Studies of Francophone University Writers." *Written Communication* 22 (4): 421–71.

Giddens, Anthony. 1979. *Central Problems in Social Theory: Action, Structure, and Contradiction in Social Analysis*. Berkeley: University of California Press.

Gilyard, Keith. 2016. "The Rhetoric of Translingualism." *College English* 78 (3): 284–89.

Glaser, Barney, and Anselm Strauss. 1967. *The Discovery of Grounded Theory: Strategies for Qualitative Research*. Hawthorne, UK: Aldine de Gruyter.

Goshgarian, Gary. 2015. *Exploring Language*. Boston: Pearson.

Guerra, Juan. 1997. "The Place of Intercultural Literacy in the Writing Classroom." In *Writing in Multicultural Settings*, ed. Carol Severino, Juan Guerra, and Johnnella Butler, 248–60. New York: Modern Language Association.

Guerra, Juan. 2015. *Language, Culture, Identity, and Citizenship in College Classrooms and Communities*. London: Routledge.

Guix, Juan G.L. 2007. "The Translator in Aliceland: On Translating Alice in Wonderland into Spanish." In *The Translator as Writer*, ed. Susan Bassnett and Peter Bush, 95–105. London: Continuum.

Hadi-Tabassum, Samina. 2006. *Language, Space, and Power: A Critical Look at Bilingual Education*. Clevedon, UK: Multilingual Matters.

Hall, Jonathan. 2009. "WAC/WID in the Next America: Re-thinking Professional Identity in the Age of the Multilingual Majority." *WAC Journal* 20: 33–47.

Hannam, Kevin, Mimi Sheller, and John Urry. 2006. "Editorial: Mobilities, Immobilities, and Moorings." *Mobilities* 1 (1): 1–22.

Hannerz, Ulf. 2003. "Being There . . . and There . . . and There! Reflections on Multi-Site Ethnography." *Ethnography* 4 (2): 201–16.

Harwood, Nigel, and Gregory Hadley. 2004, "Demystifying Institutional Practices: Critical Pragmatism and the Teaching of Academic Writing." *English for Specific Purposes* 23 (4): 355–77.

Hesford, Wendy, Edgar Singleton, and Ivonne M. García. 2009. "Laboring to Globalize a First-Year Writing Program." In *The Writing Program Interrupted*, ed. Donna Strickland and Jeanne Gunner, 113–25. Portsmouth, NH: Boynton/Cook.

Hibbard, Laura. 2012. "Wisconsin Student Punished for Using Native Tongue." *Huffington Post*, March 2. https://www.huffpost.com/entry/miranda-washinawatok-student-receives-apology-from-school_n_1316407.

Hirsch, Marianne. 2012. *The Generation of Postmemory: Writing and Visual Culture after the Holocaust*. New York: Columbia University Press.

hooks, bell. 1981. *Ain't I a Woman: Black Woman and Feminism*. Boston: South End.

Hopper, Paul. 1998. "Emergent Grammar." In *The New Psychology of Language*, ed. Michael Tomasello, 155–75. Mahwah, NJ: Lawrence Erlbaum.

Hornberger, Nancy. 1990. "Bilingual Education and English-Only: A Language-Planning Framework." *Annals of the American Academic of Political and Social Science* 508: 12–26.

Hornberger, Nancy, and David Cassels Johnson. 2007. "Slicing the Onion Ethnographically: Layers and Spaces in Multilingual Language Education Policy and Practice." *TESOL Quarterly* 41 (3): 509–32.

Horner, Bruce. 1999. "Re-thinking the 'Sociality' of Error: Teaching Editing as Negotiation." In *Representing the "Other": Basic Writers and the Teaching of Basic Writing*, ed. Bruce Horner and Min-Zhan Lu, 139–65. Urbana, IL: National Council of Teachers of English.

Horner, Bruce. 2001. "'Students' Right,' English Only, and Re-Imagining the Politics of Language." *College English* 63: 741–58.

Horner, Bruce. 2002. "Critical Ethnography, Ethics, and Work: Rearticulating Labor." *Journal of Advanced Composition* 22 (3): 561–84.

Horner, Bruce. 2011. "Relocating Basic Writing." *Journal of Basic Writing* 30 (2): 5–23.

Horner, Bruce. 2016. *Rewriting Composition: Terms of Exchange*. Carbondale: Southern Illinois University Press.

Horner, Bruce, and Min-Zhan Lu. 2007. "Resisting Monolingualism in 'English': Reading and Writing the Politics of Language." In *Rethinking English in Schools: Towards a New and Constructive Stage*, ed. Viv Ellis, Carol Fox, and Brian Street, 141–57. London: Continuum.

Horner, Bruce, Min-Zhan Lu, and Paul Matsuda, eds. 2010. *Cross-Language Relations in Composition*. Carbondale: Southern Illinois University Press.

Horner, Bruce, Min-Zhan Lu, Jacqueline Royster, and John Trimbur. 2011. "Language Difference: Toward a Translingual Approach." *College English* 73 (3): 299–317.

Horner, Bruce, Samantha NeCamp, and Christiane Donahue. 2011. "Toward a Multilingual Composition Scholarship: From English Only to a Translingual Norm." *College Composition and Communication* 63 (2): 269–300.

Horner, Bruce, and Cindy Selfe. 2013. "Translinguality/Transmodality Relations: Snapshots from a Dialogue." *The Working Paper Series on Negotiating Differences in Language and Literacy*. Louisville, KY: University of Louisville.

Horner, Bruce, and Laura Tetreault. 2016. "Translation as (Global) Writing." *Composition Studies* 44 (1): 13–30.

Horner, Bruce, and Laura Tetreault. 2017. *Crossing Divides: Exploring Translingual Writing Pedagogies and Programs*. Logan: Utah State University Press.

Horner, Bruce, and John Trimbur. 2002. "English Only and US College Composition." *College Composition and Communication* 53 (4): 594–630.

House, Juliane. 2003. "English as a Lingua Franca: A Threat to Multilingualism?" *Journal of Sociolinguistics* 7 (4): 556–78.

House, Juliane. 2012. "Review: *Translation in Language Teaching*." *Applied Linguistics* 33 (2): 216–19.

House, Juliane. 2016. *Translation as Communication across Languages and Cultures*. London: Routledge.

Hrach, Susan. 2013. "Translation and the Future of Early World Literature." *Pedagogy* 13 (3): 453–67.

Hymes, Dell. 1973. "Speech and Language: On the Origins and Foundations of Inequality among Speakers." *Daedalus* 102 (3): 59–85.

Inoue, Asao. 2017. "Writing Assessment as the Condition for Translingual Approaches." In *Crossing Divides: Exploring Translingual Writing Pedagogies and Programs*, ed. Bruce Horner and Laura Tetreault, 119–34. Logan: Utah State University Press.

Irvine, Judith. 1989. "When Talk Isn't Cheap: Language and Political Economy." *American Ethnologist* 16: 248–67.

Irvine, Judith, and Susan Gal. 2000. "Language Ideology and Linguistic Differentiation." In *Regimes of Language: Ideologies, Polities, and Identities*, ed. Paul Kroskrity, 35–83. Santa Fe, NM: School of American Research Press.

Isaacson, Walter. 2011. *Steve Jobs*. New York: Simon and Schuster.

Ivanič, Roz. 1998. *Writing and Identity: The Discoursal Construction of Identity in Academic Writing*. Amsterdam: John Benjamins.

Ivanič, Roz, Richard Edwards, David Barton, Marilyn Martin-Jones, Zoe Fowler, Buddug Hughes, Greg Mannion, Kate Miller, Candice Satchwell, and June Smith. 2009. *Improving Learning in College: Rethinking Literacies across the Curriculum*. London: Routledge.

Janks, Hilary. 2004. "The Access Paradox." *English in Australia* 139: 33–42.

Jeha, Shafik. 2004. "English as the Teaching Language." In *Darwin and the Crisis of 1882 in the Medical Department: And the First Student Protest in the Arab World in the Syrian Protestant College*. Beirut: American University of Beirut Press.

Jenkins, Jennifer. 2014. *English as a Lingua Franca in the International University: The Politics of Academic English Language Policy*. London: Routledge.

Jenkins, Jennifer. 2015. *Global Englishes*. London: Routledge.

Jerskey, Maria. 2013. "Literacy Brokers in the Contact Zone, Year 1: The Crowded Safe House." In *Literacy as Translingual Practice: Between Communities and Classrooms*, ed. Suresh Canagarajah, 197–206. New York: Routledge.

Johns, Ann. 2005. "Guest Editor's Introduction" [Special Issue: The Linguistically-Diverse Student: Challenges and Possibilities across the Curriculum]. *Across the Disciplines* 2. https://wac.colostate.edu/atd/special/lds.

Johnson, David Cassels. 2013. *Language Policy*. Basingstoke, UK: Palgrave Macmillan.

Johnson, Eric, and David Cassels Johnson. 2015. "Language Policy and Bilingual Education in Arizona and Washington State." *International Journal of Bilingual Education and Bilingualism* 18 (1): 92–112.

Jordan, Jay. 2012. *Redesigning Composition for Multilingual Realities*. Urbana, IL: National Council of Teachers of English.

Jordan, Jay. 2015. "Material Translingual Ecologies." *College English* 77 (4): 364–82.

Kapp, Rochelle. 2012. "Students' Negotiation of English and Literacy in a Time of Social Change." *Journal of Advanced Composition* 32 (3–4): 591–614.

Kells, Michelle Hall, Valerie Balester, and Victor Villanueva, eds. 2004. *Latino/a Discourses: On Language, Identity, and Literacy Education.* Portsmouth, NH: Boynton/Cook.

Khubchandani, Lachman. 1998. "A Plurilingual Ethos: A Peep into the Sociology of Language." *Indian Journal of Applied Linguistics* 24 (1): 5–37.

Kilfoil, Carrie. 2015. "Beyond the 'Foreign' Language Requirement: From a Monolingual to a Translingual Ideology in Rhetoric and Composition Graduate Education." *Rhetoric Review* 34 (4): 426–44.

Kirsch, Gesa, and Joy Ritchie. 1995. "Beyond the Personal: Theorizing a Politics of Location in Composition Research." *College Composition and Communication* 46 (1): 7–29.

Kloss, Heinz. 1998. *The American Bilingual Tradition.* Washington, DC: Center for Applied Linguistics and Delta Systems.

Kramsch, Claire. 1998. "The Privilege of the Intercultural Speaker." In *Foreign Language Learning in Intercultural Perspective*, ed. Michael Byram and Michael Fleming, 16–31. Cambridge: Cambridge University Press.

Kramsch, Claire. 2006. "The Traffic in Meaning." *Asia Pacific Journal of Education* 26 (1): 99–104.

Kramsch, Claire. 2009. *The Multilingual Subject.* Oxford: Oxford University Press.

Kroskrity, Paul. 2000. *Regimes of Language: Ideologies, Polities, and Identities.* Santa Fe, NM: School of American Research Press.

Kroskrity, Paul. 2004. "Language Ideologies." In *A Companion to Linguistic Anthropology*, ed. Alessandro Duranti, 496–517. Malden, MA: Blackwell.

La France au Liban "Taxi." 2010. YouTube video, 0:26. Posted by Laser Films. Accessed March 11, 2015. https://www.youtube.com/watch?v=UzoDp6JciM4.

Laviosa, Sara. 2014. *Translation and Language Education: Pedagogic Approaches Explored.* London: Routledge.

Lee, Jerry Won. 2016. "Beyond Translingual Writing." *College English* 79 (2): 174–95.

Lefevere, André. 1992. *Translation, Rewriting, and the Manipulation of Literary Fame.* London: Routledge.

Leonard, Rebecca Lorimer. 2013. "Traveling Literacies: Multilingual Writing on the Move." *Research in the Teaching of English* 48 (1): 13–39.

Leonard, Rebecca Lorimer. 2014. "Multilingual Writing as Rhetorical Attunement." *College English* 76 (3): 227–47.

Leonard, Rebecca Lorimer, and Rebecca Nowacek. 2016. "Transfer and Translingualism." *College English* 78 (3): 258–64.

Leonard, Rebecca Lorimer, Kate Vieira, and Morris Young. 2015. "Special Editors' Introduction." *Literacy in Composition Studies* 3 (3): vi–xii.

Leung, Constant, Roxy Harris, and Ben Rampton. 1997. "The Idealised Native Speaker, Reified Ethnicities, and Classroom Realities." *TESOL Quarterly* 31: 543–75.

Leung, Constant, and Brian Street, eds. 2012. *English: A Changing Medium for Education.* Bristol, UK: Multilingual Matters.

Lewis, Anthony. 2005. "Language and Translation: Contesting Conventions." In *In Translation*, ed. Paul St-Pierre and Prafulla Kar, 15–24. Amsterdam: John Benjamins.

Lewis, Cynthia, Patricia Enciso, and Elizabeth Birr Moje. 2007. *Reframing Sociocultural Research on Literacy: Identity, Agency, and Power.* Mahwah, NJ: Erlbaum.

Lillis, Theresa. 2009. "Bringing Writers' Voices to Writing Research: Talk around Texts." In *Why Writing Matters*, ed. Awena Carter, Theresa Lillis, and Sue Parkin, 169–89. Amsterdam: John Benjamins.

Lillis, Theresa, and Mary Jane Curry. 2010. *Academic Writing in a Global Context: The Politics and Practices of Publishing in English.* London: Routledge.

Lillis, Theresa, and Carolyn McKinney. 2013. "The Sociolinguistics of Writing in a Global Context: Objects, Lenses, Consequences." *Journal of Sociolinguistics* 17 (4): 415–39.

Lu, Min-Zhan. 1994. "Professing Multiculturalism: The Politics of Style in the Contact Zone." *College Composition and Communication* 45 (4): 442–58.

Lu, Min-Zhan. 2004. "An Essay on the Work of Composition: Composing English against the Order of Fast Capitalism." *College Composition and Communication* 56 (1): 16–50.

Lu, Min-Zhan. 2009. "Metaphors Matter: Transcultural Literacy." *Journal of Advanced Composition* 29: 285–93.

Lu, Min-Zhan. 2010. "Living-English Work." In *Cross-Language Relations in Composition*, ed. Bruce Horner, Min-Zhan Lu, and Paul Matsuda, 42–56. Carbondale: Southern Illinois University Press.

Lu, Min-Zhan, and Bruce Horner. 2012. "(Re)Writing English: Putting English in Translation." In *English: A Changing Medium for Education*, ed. Constant Leung and Brian Street, 59–78. Bristol, UK: Multilingual Matters.

Lu, Min-Zhan, and Bruce Horner. 2013. "Translingual Literacy, Language Difference, and Matters of Agency." *College English* 75 (6): 586–611.

Lu, Min-Zhan, and Bruce Horner. 2016. "Introduction: Translingual Work." *College English* 78 (3): 207–18.

Luke, Allan. 1996. "Genres of Power? Literacy Education and the Production of Capital." In *Literacy in Society: Language Description and Language Education*, ed. Ruqaiya Hasan and Goeffrey Williams, 308–38. New York: Longman.

Lundsford, Karen. 2012. "Conducting Writing Research Internationally." In *Writing Studies Research in Practice*, ed. Lee Nickoson and Mary Sheridan, 220–30. Carbondale: Southern Illinois University Press.

Maalouf, Amin. 2008. *Origins: A Memoir*. Trans. Catherine Temerson. New York: Farrar, Straus, and Giroux.

Makoni, Busi, and Sinfree Makoni. 2010. "Multilingual Discourses on Wheels and Public English in Africa: A Case for 'Vague Linguistique.'" In *Routledge Companion to English Language Studies*, ed. Janet Maybin and Joan Swann, 258–270. London: Routledge.

Makoni, Sinfree, and Pedzisai Mashiri. 2007. "Critical Historiography." In *Disinventing and Reconstituting Languages*, ed. Sinfree Makoni and Alastair Pennycook, 62–89. Clevedon, UK: Multilingual Matters.

Makoni, Sinfree, and Alastair Pennycook, eds. 2007. *Disinventing and Reconstituting Languages*. Clevedon, UK: Multilingual Matters.

Malagon, Helen, and Alma Chacon. 2009. "Washington State Transitional Bilingual Instruction Program Guidelines." Olympia, WA: Office of Superintendent of Public Instruction, Migrant and Bilingual Education.

Malagon, Helen, Paul McCold, and Julie Hernandez. 2012. "Educating English Language Learners in Washington State, 2010–2011." Olympia, WA: Office of Superintendent of Public Instruction, Migrant and Bilingual Education.

Mangelsdorf, Kate. 2010. "Spanish as Alternative Discourse: Working against Language Demarcation." In *Cross-Language Relations in Composition.*, ed. Bruce Horner, Min-Zhan Lu, and Paul Matsuda, 113–26. Carbondale: Southern Illinois University Press.

Mangelsdorf, Kate. 2017. "Language Difference and Translingual Enactments." In *Crossing Divides: Exploring Translingual Writing Pedagogies and Programs*, ed. Bruce Horner and Laura Tetreault, 199–206. Logan: Utah State University Press.

Marcus, George. 1995. "Ethnography in/of the World System: The Emergence of Multi-Sited Ethnography." *Annual Review of Anthropology* 24: 95–117.

Martins, David. 2015. *Transnational Writing Program Administration*. Logan: Utah State University Press.

Matsuda, Paul Kei. 2006. "The Myth of Linguistic Homogeneity in US College Composition." *College English* 68 (6): 637–51.

Matsuda, Paul Kei, Michelle Cox, Jay Jordan, and Christina Ortmeier-Hooper. 2011. *Second-Language Writing in the Composition Classroom: A Critical Sourcebook*. Boston: Bedford/St. Martins.

Menard-Warwick, Julia. 2014. "'Tiffany Does Not Have a Solid Language Background, as She Speaks Only English': Emerging Language Ideologies among California Students." *Critical Inquiry in Language Studies* 11 (2): 75–99.

Miller, Catherine, and Dominique Caubet. 2010. "Arabic Sociolinguistics in the Middle East and North Africa (MENA)." In *Sociolinguistics around the World: A Handbook*, ed. Martin Ball, 238–56. London: Routledge.

Miller, Laura, and Ralph Ginsberg. 1995. "Folklinguistic Theories of Language Learning." In *Second Language Acquisition*, ed. Barbara Freed, 293–315. Amsterdam: John Benjamins.

MLA Ad Hoc Committee on Foreign Languages. 2007. "Foreign Languages and Higher Education: New Structures for a Changed World." *Profession* 12: 234–45.

Monroe, Kristin. 2016. *The Insecure City: Space, Power, and Mobility in Beirut*. New Brunswick, NJ: Rutgers University Press.

Moore, Daniel, and Laurent Gajo. 2009. "Introduction—French Voices on Plurilingualism and Pluriculturalism: Theory, Significance, and Perspectives." *International Journal of Multilingualism* 6 (2): 137–53.

Mukherji, Sujit. 1994. *Translation as Discovery and Other Essays on Indian Literature in English Translation*. New Delhi: Allied.

Müller, Martin. 2007. "What's in a Word? Problematizing Translation between Languages." *Area* 39 (2): 206–13.

New London Group. 1996. "A Pedagogy of Multiliteracies: Designing Social Futures." *Harvard Educational Review* 66 (1): 60–92.

Ninnes, Peter, and Meeri Hellstén. 2005. *Internationalizing Higher Education: Critical Explorations of Pedagogy and Policy*. Hong Kong: University of Hong Kong.

Nuñez, Elizabeth. 2000. "Writing for Effect." In *Language Crossings: Negotiating the Self in a Multi-Cultural World*, ed. Karen Ogulnick, 40–45. New York: Teachers College Press.

Ogulnick, Karen. 2000. *Language Crossings: Negotiating the Self in a Multi-Cultural World*. New York: Teachers College Press.

Ortmeier-Hooper, Christina. 2008. "English May Be My Second Language, but I'm Not 'ESL.'" *College Composition and Communication* 59 (3): 389–419.

Paikeday, Thomas. 1985. *The Native Speaker Is Dead: An Informal Discussion of a Linguistic Myth with Noam Chomsky and Other Linguists, Philosophers, Psychologists, and Lexicographers*. Toronto: Paikeday.

Parakrama, Arjuna. 1995. *De-hegemonizing Language Standards: Learning from (Post)Colonial Englishes about "English."* Hampshire, UK: Macmillan.

Park, Joseph Sung-Yul, and Lionel Wee. 2012. *Markets of English: Linguistic Capital and Language Policy in a Globalizing World*. London: Routledge.

Paz, Octavio. 1992. "Translations of Literature and Letters." In *Theories of Translation: An Anthology from Dryden to Derrida*, ed. Rainer Schulte and John Biguenet, 152–63. Chicago: Chicago University Press.

Pedersen, Anne-Marie. 2010. "Negotiating Cultural Identities through Language: Academic English in Jordan." *College Composition and Communication* 62 (2): 283–310.

Peng, Jian-E. 2011. "Changes in Language Learning Beliefs during a Transition to Tertiary Study." *System* 39 (3): 314–24.

Pennycook, Alastair. 1997. "Vulgar Pragmatism, Critical Pragmatism, and EAP." *English for Specific Purposes* 17 (1): 253–70.

Pennycook, Alastair. 2001. *Critical Applied Linguistics: A Critical Introduction*. Mahwah, NJ: Erlbaum.

Pennycook, Alastair. 2007. *Global Englishes and Transcultural Flows*. London: Routledge.

Pennycook, Alastair. 2008. "English as a Language Always in Translation." *European Journal of English Studies* 12 (1): 33–47.

Pennycook, Alastair. 2010. *Language as a Local Practice*. London: Routledge.

Pennycook, Alastair, and Emi Otsuji. 2015. *Metrolingualism: Language in the City*. London: Routledge.
Perry, Theresa, and Lisa Delpit, eds. 1998. *The Real Ebonics Debate: Power, Language, and the Education of African-American Children*. Boston: Beacon.
Pratt, Mary Louise. 1987. "Linguistic Utopias." In *The Linguistics of Writing*, ed. Nigel Fabb, Derek Attridge, Alan Durant, and Colin MacCabe, 48–66. Manchester, UK: Manchester University Press.
Pratt, Mary Louise. 2002. "The Traffic in Meaning: Translation, Contagion, Infiltration." *Profession*: 25–36.
Pratt, Mary Louise, Birgit Wagner, Ovidi Carbonell i Cortés; Andrew Chesterman, and Maria Tymoczko. 2010. "Translation Studies Forum: Cultural Translation." *Translation Studies* 3 (1): 94–110.
Prendergast, Catherine. 2008. *Buying into English: Language and Investment in the New Capitalist World*. Pittsburgh: University of Pittsburgh Press.
Preston, Dennis. 1991. "Language Teaching and Learning: Folk Linguistic Perspectives." In *Roundtable on Languages and Linguistics*, ed. James Alatis, 583–603. Washington. DC: Georgetown University Press.
Preto-Bay, Ana Maria, and Kristine Hansen. 2006. "Preparing for the Tipping Point: Designing Writing Programs to Meet the Needs of the Changing Population." *WPA: Writing Program Administration* 30 (1–2): 37–57.
Prinsloo, Mastin. 2012. "What Counts as English." In *English: A Changing Medium for Education*, ed. Constant Leung and Brian Street, 22–41. Bristol, UK: Multilingual Matters.
Putman, John. 2008. *Class and Gender Politics in Progressive-Era Seattle*. Reno: University of Nevada Press.
Py, Bernard. 2004. "Pour une Approche Linguistique des Représentations Sociales." *Languages* 154: 6–19.
Ramanathan, Vaidehi. 2006. "Of Texts AND Translations AND Rhizomes: Postcolonial Anxieties AND Deracinations AND Knowledge Constructions." *Critical Inquiry in Language Studies: An International Journal* 3 (4): 223–44.
Reiff, Mary Jo, Anis Bawarshi, Michelle Ballif, and Christian Weisser. 2015. *Ecologies of Writing Programs: Program Profiles in Context*. Anderson, SC: Parlor.
"Report on Enrollment, Retention, and Graduation." 2012. Office of Minority Affairs and Diversity. Accessed March 5, 2017. http://www.washington.edu/diversity/files/2013/03/Report-on-Enrollment-Retention-Graduation.pdf.
Ricento, Thomas. 2006. "Americanization, Language Ideologies, and the Construction of European Identities." In *Language Ideologies, Policies, and Practices: Language and the Future of Europe*, ed. Patrick Stevenson and Clare Mar-Molinero, 44–57. Hampshire, UK: Palgrave Macmillan.
Rubdy, Rani, and Mario Saraceni. 2006. *English in the World: Global Rules, Global Roles*. London: Continuum.
Rubdy, Rani, and Peter Tan. 2008. *Language as Commodity: Global Structures, Local Marketplaces*. London: Continuum.
Rugh, Douglas, Bell Dorman Rugh, and Alfred Howell. 1994. *Daniel Bliss: Letters from a New Campus*. Beirut: American University of Beirut Press.
Saarinen, Taina, and Tarja Nikula. 2013. "Implicit Policy, Invisible Language: Policies and Practices of International Degree Programs in Finnish Higher Education." In *English-Medium Instruction at Universities: Global Challenges*, ed. Aintzane Doiz, David Lasagabaster, and Juan Manuel Sierra, 131–50. Bristol, UK: Multilingual Matters.
Salameh, Franck. 2010. *Language, Memory, and Identity in the Middle East: The Case for Lebanon*. Lanham, MD: Lexington Books.
Saraceni, Mario. 2010. *The Relocation of English*. Hampshire, UK: Palgrave Macmillan.
Saussure, Ferdinand. 1959. *Course in General Linguistics*. New York: Philosophical Library.

Schatzki, Theodore. 2001. "Introduction: Practice Theory." In *The Practice Turn*, ed. Theodore Schatzki, Karin Knorr-Cetina, and Eike von Savigny, 1–14. London: Routledge.

Schaub, Mark. 2003. "Beyond These Shores: An Argument for Internationalizing Composition." *Pedagogy* 3 (1): 85–98.

Schieffelin, Bambi, Kathryn Woolard, and Paul Kroskrity. 1998. *Language Ideologies: Practice and Theory*. New York: Oxford University Press.

Schiffman, Harold. 1996. *Linguistic Culture and Language Policy*. London: Routledge.

Schroeder, Christopher, Helen Fox, and Patricia Bizzell, eds. 2002. *ALT/DIS: Alternative Discourses and the Academy*. Portsmouth, NH: Boynton/Cook.

Schwantes, Carlos. 1998. *The Pacific Northwest: An Interpretive History*. Lincoln: University of Nebraska Press.

Seidman, Steven. 2012. "The Politics of Cosmopolitan Beirut." *Theory, Culture, and Society* 29 (2): 3–36.

Severino, Carol, Juan Guerra, and Johnnella Butler. 1997. *Writing in Multicultural Settings*. New York: Modern Language Association.

Shaaban, Kassim. 2005. "English Language Teaching in Lebanon: Challenges for the Future." In *Teaching English to the World: History, Curriculum, and Practice*, ed. George Braine, 103–13. Mahwah, NJ: Erlbaum.

Shaughnessy, Mina. 1977. *Errors and Expectations: A Guide for the Teacher of Basic Writing*. New York: Oxford University Press.

Sheller, Mimi, and John Urry. 2006. "The New Mobilities Paradigm." *Environment and Planning A* 38 (2): 207–26.

Shuck, Gail. 2006. "Combating Monolingualism: A Novice Administrator's Challenge." *WPA: Writing Program Administration* 30 (1–2): 59–82.

Silva, Tony, Ilona Leki, and Joan Carson. 1997. "Broadening the Perspective of Mainstream Composition Studies: Some Thoughts from the Disciplinary Margins." *Written Communication* 14 (3): 398–428.

Simon, Sherry. 1999. "Translating and Interlingual Creation in the Contact Zone: Border Writing in Quebec." In *Post-Colonial Translation: Theory and Practice*, ed. Susan Bassnett and Harish Trivedi, 58–74. London: Routledge.

Sims, Michael. 2012. "Some Book." *New York Times*, April 22.

Singh, Rajendra. 1998. *The Native Speaker: Multilingual Perspectives*. New Delhi: Sage.

Slevin, James. 2001. *Introducing English: Essays in the Intellectual Work of Composition*. Pittsburgh: University of Pittsburgh Press.

Smitherman, Geneva. 1996. *Talkin and Testifyin: The Language of Black America*. Detroit: Wayne State University Press.

Smitherman, Geneva, and Victor Villanueva, eds. 2003. *Language Diversity in the Classroom: From Intention to Practice*. Carbondale: Southern Illinois University Press.

Sonntag, Selma. 2015. "State Tradition and Language Regime in the United States: Time for Change?" In *State Traditions and Language Regimes*, ed. Selma Sonntag and Linda Cardinal, 44–61. Quebec: McGill Queen's University Press.

Spack, Ruth. 1997. "The Rhetorical Construction of Multilingual Students." *TESOL Quarterly* 31: 765–74.

Spolsky, Bernard. 2004. *Language Policy*. Cambridge: Cambridge University Press.

Statistical Abstract of the United States. 2011. Languages Spoken at Home by State. Accessed March 5, 2017. http://ftp.census.gov/library/publications/2010/compendia/statab/130ed/tables/11s0054.pdf.

Stephens, Crissa, and David Johnson. 2015. "'Good Teaching for All Students': Sheltered Instruction Programming in Washington State Language Policy." *Language and Education* 29 (1): 31–45.

Stevenson, Patrick, and Clare Mar-Molinero. 2006. *Language Ideologies, Policies, and Practices: Language and the Future of Europe*. Hampshire, UK: Palgrave Macmillan.

Straus, Jane, Lester Kaufman, and Tom Stern. 2015. *The Blue Book of Grammar and Punctuation*. San Francisco: Jossey-Bass.

Stroud, Christopher, and Mastin Prinsloo. 2015. *Language, Literacy, and Diversity: Moving Words*. London: Routledge.

Tardy, Christine. 2011. "Enacting and Transforming Local Language Policies." *College Composition and Communication* 62 (4): 634–61.

Tardy, Christine. 2017. "Crossing, or Creating Divides? A Plea for Transdisicplinary Scholarship." In *Crossing Divides: Exploring Translingual Writing Pedagogies and Programs*, ed. Bruce Horner and Laura Tetreault, 181–89. Logan: Utah State University Press.

Taylor, Shelley, and Kristin Snoddon. 2013. "Plurilingualism in TESOL: Promising Controversies." *TESOL Quarterly* 47 (3): 439–45.

Thaiss, Christopher, and Terry Zawacki. 2006. *Engaged Writers and Dynamic Disciplines: Research on the Academic Writing Life*. Portsmouth, NH: Boynton/Cook.

Trask, Haunani-Kay. 1999. *From a Native Daughter: Colonialism and Sovereignty in Hawai'i*. Honolulu: University of Hawai'i Press.

Trimbur, John. 2000. "Composition and the Circulation of Writing." *College Composition and Communication* 52 (2): 188–219.

Trimbur, John. 2008. "The Dartmouth Conference and the Geohistory of the Native Speaker." *College English* 71 (2): 142–69.

Trimbur, John. 2016. "Translingualism and Close Reading." *College English* 78 (3): 219–27.

Tsagari, Dina, and Georgios Floros. 2013. *Translation in Language Teaching and Assessment*. Cambridge: Cambridge Scholars Publishing.

"2017–2021 Diversity Blueprint." Office of Minority Affairs and Diversity. Accessed March 5, 2017. https://www.washington.edu/diversity/files/2017/01/17_DiversityBlueprint-010917.pdf.

Tymoczko, Maria. 2006. "Translation: Ethics, Ideology, Action." *Massachusetts Review* 47 (3): 442–61.

van Lier, Leo. 2004. *The Ecology and Semiotics of Language Learning: A Sociocultural Perspective*. Boston: Kluwer Academic.

Varghese, Manka, Suhanthie Motha, Gloria Park, Jenelle Reeves, and John Trent,. 2016. "Language Teacher Identity in Multilingual Education" [Special Issue]. *TESOL Quarterly* 49 (1): 219–20.

Venuti, Lawrence. 1996. "Translation and the Pedagogy of Literature." *College English* 58 (3): 327–44.

Venuti, Lawrence. 1998. *The Scandals of Translation: Towards an Ethics of Difference*. London: Routledge.

Vertovec, Steven. 2007. "Super-Diversity and Its Implications." *Ethnic and Racial Studies* 30 (6): 1024–54.

Walters, Keith, and Michal Brody. 2005. *What's Language Got to Do with It?* New York: W. W. Norton.

Weinberger, Eliot. 2000. "Anonymous Sources: A Talk on Translators and Translation." *Encuentros* (Cultural Center, International Development Bank) 39: 1–13. Accessed September 20, 2016. http://www.iadb.org/exr/cultural/documents/encuentros/39.pdf.

Wible, Scott. 2009. "Composing Alternatives to a National Security Language Policy." *College English* 71 (5): 460–85.

Wible, Scott. 2013. *Shaping Language Policy in the US: The Role of Composition Studies*. Carbondale: Southern Illinois University Press.

Widdowson, Henry. 2003. *Defining Issues in English Language Teaching*. Oxford: Oxford University Press.

Wiley, Terrence. 2000. "Continuity and Change in the Function of Language Ideologies in the United States." In *Ideology, Politics, and Language Policies*, ed. Thomas Ricento, 67–85. Amsterdam: John Benjamins.

Williams, Joseph. 1981. "The Phenomenology of Error." *College Composition and Communication* 32 (2): 152–68.

Williams, Raymond. 1973. *The Country and the City*. Oxford: Oxford University Press.

Wittman, Emily, and Katrina Windon. 2010. "Twisted Tongues, Tied Hands: Translation Studies and the English Major." *College English* 72 (5): 449–69.

Woolard, Kathryn. 1998. "Language Ideology as a Field of Inquiry." In *Language Ideologies*, ed. Bambi Schieffelin, Kathryn Woolard, and Paul Kroskrity, 3–47. New York: Oxford University Press.

Woolard, Kathryn. 2004. "Is the Past a Foreign Country? Time, Language Origins, and the Nation in Early Modern Spain." *Journal of Linguistic Anthropology* 14 (1): 57–80.

Woolard, Kathryn, and Bambi Schieffelin. 1994. "Language Ideology." *Annual Review of Anthropology* 23: 55–82.

Yancey, Kathleen Blake. 2001. "WPA Outcomes Statement for First-Year Composition." *College English* 63: 321–25.

Yildiz, Yasemin. 2012. *Beyond the Mother Tongue: The Postmonolingual Condition*. New York: Fordham University Press.

Yngve, Victor. 1996. *From Grammar to Science: New Foundations for General Linguistics*. Amsterdam: John Benjamins.

Young, Vershawn Ashanti, Rusty Barrett, and Y'Shanda Young-Rivera. 2014. *Other People's English: Code-Meshing, Code-Switching, and African American Literacy*. New York: Teachers College Press.

ABOUT THE AUTHOR

Nancy Bou Ayash is an associate professor of language and rhetoric at the University of Washington. She has taught previously at the University of Louisville, the American University of Beirut, and Notre Dame University–Louaize, Lebanon. She studies the workings and effects of language politics in higher education on academic writing experiences and practices in transnational contexts. She has published in *College English*, the *Writing Program Administration Journal*, and numerous edited collections. She is the winner of the James Berlin Award (2014).

INDEX

AAVE. *See* African American Vernacular English
Abad, Pacita, 127, 128
academics, 5; English literacy, 87–88, 174; and language policy, 73–74; rule enforcement in, 57–58
academic writing: at Beirut University, 63–66, 74–77; language "error" in, 55–56; personal pronoun use in, 153–56
accuracy, 33
activism, 11, 21; in translingualism, 18, 170–71, 185
Adler-Kassner, Linda, 165–66
advertising, 4, 201(n1)
African American Vernacular English (AAVE), 124–25, 133
agency, 21, 27, 55, 165–66; and identity, 125–26; linguistic structure and, 59–60; student, 88–89, 95–96, 124–25
Ahmad, Dohra, *Rotten English*, 35
Ain't I a Woman (hooks), 34
Anzaldúa, Gloria, 127, 128, 130; *Borderlands/La Frontera*, 34; "How to Tame a Wild Tongue," 111
Apple, *Think Different* slogan, 3–4
Arabic, 206(n10); and academic literacies, 97–98, 188; Lebanese, 67–68, 72, 82–83
archipelagos, in language use, 29–31
Arnoldi, Jakob, 162
assessment, in translingual setting, 182
authority, and personal pronoun use, 154–55

bahasa rojak, 118, 119
Baker, Mona, 152
Banyan tree model, 44–45, 143
Bassnett, Susan, 34, 143–44
Bawarshi, Anis, 131
Beirut, 46, 63, 174, 206(n2); language use in, 67–71, 206(n4); overhead electricity cables, 47–48; sociolinguistic landscape, 136–37; student agency in, 95–96
Beirut University (BU), 7, 10, 23, 207(n11); academic literacy at, 87–88, 97–98; English monolingualism at, 98–99; ethnography, 186–94; FYW

program, 74–78, 86–87, 138; graphic design/communication arts, 83–86; language policies at, 72–74, 206(n10); language use at, 63–65, 79–81, 89–94, 136; multilingualism at, 81–82; translation at, 100–101, 145–46, 209(n7)
Bernabé, Jean, 49
bilingual education, 107, 207(n2)
bilingualism, in Lebanon, 72, 73
Blommaert, Jan, 53, 190
Borderlands/La Frontera (Anzaldúa), 34
border-making decisions, 32
Brody, Michal, *What's Language Got to Do with It?*, 35
brokering, language ideologies, 103, 207(n12)
Butler, Judith, 99
Byram, Michael, on intercultural communicative competence, 126–27

Calvet, Louis-Jean, 21, 42, 65, 138, 181
Canagarajah, Suresh, 36, 52, 162
CCCC Statement on Second-Language Writing and Writers, 110
Chamoiseau, Patrick, 49
Chinese students, FYW class, 148–64
Chomsky, Noam, 27
citizenship, 177
civic engagement, and translation, 156–57
Civil Rights Movement, 132
code-islands, 30–31, 33
code-meshing, 14, 35, 78, 137, 157–58
code mixing, multilingual, 34–35
code switching, 35, 124–25
Cofer, Judith Ortiz: "May He Be Bilingual," 75; "Volar," 74
collaborative hybridization, 134
colloquialism, 4, 125
commodity, English as, 178
communicative contexts, 55
competence: intercultural communicative, 126–27; language, 51–52, 203–4(n10)
composition classes, 179; translingualism, 166–67
Confiant, Raphaël, 49
contestation, language, 132–33
Council of Writing Program Administrators (CWPA), 148

230 INDEX

counterhegemonic engagement, 10
co-writer-reader-ship, 60
Cronin, Michael, 142
cross-disciplinary dialogue, 101
cross-language work, 127–28, 145, 208(n15); negotiation in, 158–59
culture, 3, 5, 123, 168; and language identity, 129–30; and language use, 156–58
curricula, 8, 34, 192
CWPA. *See* Council of Writing Program Administrators

Dasgubta, Probal, 45
data: analyses of, 17–18, 190–94; collection of, 10–11, 190–94
difference, 33, 62; language, 73–74, 76, 110–11, 142; language and cultural, 35, 123, 125–26; and translation, 164, 165
discourse, 204(n14); academic, 171–72
Diva, 78, 95, 137, 176, 180, 195; in FYW class, 91–92; multilingualism of, 89–91; translingual literacy, 96–97
diversity, 62, 107, 108, 128; and difference, 62, 111; and internationalization, 108; in Lebanon, 70–71; language and sociocultural, 7, 14, 26; of meaning, 50; under multilingualism, 31; responses to, 75, 110–111, 135; in rhetoric and composition, 39; student participants, 187; under translingualism, 49; University of Seattle, 108; in Washington state, 107
Dobrin, Sidney, 179
Donahue, Christiane Tiane, 10, 95, 135
Dryer, Dylan, 182

EAE. *See* Edited American English
eclecticism, 118
ecology, ecologies, 77, 90, 174; and infrastructures of writing programs, 136-7, 174, 190; language and writing, 94, 138; institutional, 110, 179; socialization, 101, 123; writing assessment, 182
Edited American English (EAE): at Beirut University, 79–80; punctuation rules, 56–57
educational system, in Lebanon, 71–72
Elbow, Peter, 34
electricity cables, in Beirut, 47–48
electronic translation technologies, 168
ELF. *See* English as a lingua franca
ELL. *See* English Language Learners
Enlightenment, 26
English, 79, 121, 169, 177, 184, 208(n10); at Beirut University, 63–64; in Lebanon, 67–68, 72; Malaysian, 117–18; as pluralistic, 123–24; and social identity, 160–61
English as a lingua franca (ELF), 57, 208(n10)
English as a second language (ESL): University of Seattle, 108, 110; usage of, 23–24
English Language Learners (ELL), 110
English-only ideology, 27–28, 73
English Plus resolutions, 107
English writing, 5; academic, 27–28; monolingualism, 27–28
"errors," 113, 205(n7); and academic rules, 57–58; language, 55–56; punctuation, 56–57
ESL. *See* English as a second language
ethnography, 184, 186; critical, 8–12, 201(n3); data collection and analysis, 190–93; interviews, 193–94, 196–99; participants, 187–89
Exploring Language (Goshgarian), 35

fawda, 102
first-year writing (FYW) programs, 125, 167, 170–71, 183; and academic literacy, 87–88, 98, 176; at Beirut University, 74–78, 96–97; code mixing in, 34–35; educational landscape of, 135–36; English as translation in, 88–94; ethnography of, 186–94; as isolating, 86–87; language representations, 175, 184–85; students' language resources in, 137–38; and translation, 144, 168–69; at University of Seattle, 103, 110–14, 115–16, 120, 146, 148–64
Firth, Alan, 52
fixity: language, 128–29, 133; social contexts of, 119–20
flexibility, language practice, 122–23
FLL. *See* foreign language learning
fluency, 33, 51, 52
fluidity, 4; of language, 117–18
foreign language learning (FLL), 22
Foskett, Nick, 108
French language, 63; learning, 120–22; in Lebanon, 67–68, 71, 72, 206(nn8, 9)
From a Native Daughter (Trask), 34–35, 148

Gajo, Laurent, 100
Gal, Susan, 26
García, Ofelia, 44, 107
gatekeeping, 46; academic, 65, 76, 125
Ghaith, Ghazi, 71–72
Giddens, Anthony, 54
globalization, 7, 13, 53
glossodiversity, 49

good citizenship, 26
Goshgarian, Gary, *Exploring Language,* 35
graduate teaching assistants (GTAs), in University of Seattle study, 111–14, 189
grammar, 4, 54
grammatical correctness, Apple slogans, 3–4
graphic design, and language use, 83–86, 98
grounded theory, 210–11(nn6, 7)
GTAs. *See* graduate teaching assistants
Guerra, Juan, 138–39

Hadi-Tabassum, Samina, 32
Halliday, Michael, glossodiversity, 49
Herderian triad, 26
heterogeneity, of Malaysian vernacular English, 118
higher education, diversity in, 108
home languages, 32; and standard written English, 33–34
hooks, bell, *Ain't I a Woman,* 34
Hopper, Paul, 54
Horner, Bruce, 29, 52, 59, 141; *College English,* 60–61; on translinguality, 36–37
"How to Tame a Wild Tongue" (Anzaldúa), 111
hybridity, 32, 118; of language practice, 122–23
hybridization, collaborative, 134
Hymes, Dell, 41, 205(n1)

identity, identities, 4, 44, 127, 168, 177, 210(n4); and agency, 125–26; language, 83, 128, 129–30; language resources, 181–82; self-, 161–62; social, 160–61
individuality, 59
information brokers, 11
Inoue, Asao, 182
institutional language policies, 18
intelligibility, of translations, 151–52
internationalization, 109
international students, at University of Seattle, 115–16, 148
interrogation, of monolingualism, 182
intervention, 21
interviews, 192–94, 206(n5); protocol for, 196–99
island-hopping pedagogies, 33
isolationism, language, 133
Ivanič, Roz, 81; *Writing and Identity,* 149

Jenkins, Jennifer, 57, 109
Jobs, Steve, *Think Different* slogan, 3–4, 6
Johnson, David Cassels, 108

KAPPA, 78, 95, 137, 176, 180–81, 195; on FYW classroom, 93–94; *modo di dire,* 92–93; translingual literacy, 96–97
knowledge, 66, 88; flows of, 9–10
Kramsch, Claire, 47

laborers, language and literacy, 53
landscaping, sociolinguistic, 136–37, 190–91, 210(n3)
language, 4, 6, 36, 43, 59, 66, 86, 132, 173; fixity of, 119–20; fluidity of, 117–18; form of, 21–22; identity and culture, 129–30; landscapes of, 104; learning, 66, 120–22; Lebanese educational system, 71–74; ownership of, 24; rights to, 33; social and networked location of, 99–100; territorialization of, 29, 51
language difference. *See* difference
language ideologies, 5–7, 16, 20–21, 77, 103, 108, 165, 171, 175, 191, 202(n1), 207(n12); monolingual, 26–28; multilingual, 28–35, 112; translingual, 35–38
language policies, 8, 35, 176, 177, 191, 192, 204(n17); at Beirut University, 72–74, 206(n10); University of Seattle, 108–9, 113–14; in Washington state, 107–8
language representations, 16–17, 21–22, 42, 66, 67–71, 97–98, 135, 171, 174–75, 203(nn5, 6); ethnography of, 186–94; fluidity of, 177–78; and linguistic insecurity, 22, 65, 79, 97, 102; local, 184, 202(n3); multiple, 114–15; and practices, 140, 184; Seattle, 104–6; translingual, 101–2, 142–43, 180–81
language use, 55, 124, 133–34, 206(n7); at Beirut University, 63–66, 72–78, 79–80, 87–94, 99; and culture, 156–58; in graphic design, 83–86; as learning, 52–53; in Lebanon, 67–71, 206(nn4, 9); in Malaysia, 116–20; monolingual, 26–27; multilingual, 81–82; in Seattle, 104–6; and social identity, 160–61; stakeholders and, 175–76
languaging, 43, 45
learning, 10; foreign language, 120–22; as language use, 52–53; resources to, 107–8
Lebanon, 74, 92; language policies, 72–73, 191; language use, 67–72, 206(nn4, 9)
Lefevere, André, 143
Leonard, Rebecca Lorimer, 23, 101
Lewis, Anthony, 143
Lillis, Theresa, 9, 13, 99, 201, 207, 210
Li Ming, 133, 176, 180, 181, 195; cross-language work of, 127–28, 208(n15);

and language fixity, 128–29; and language identity, 129–30; language use by, 134, 137; multiple literacies of, 126–27; translation choices of, 130–31
"Lingua Franca" (Sante), 75
linguistic landscaping, texts for, 190–91, 210(n3)
linguistics, 5, 17; alignments, 63, 64–65; of community, 27; of contact, 14; ideological orientation 8; utopias, 27, 31
listening, active, 10
literacy, literacies, 95, 134; academic, 65, 87–88, 97–98, 130, 167, 174, 184–85; in Lebanese educational system, 7, 71–74, 115, 119; monolingual, 26–27; translingual, 96–97
Lu, Min-Zhan, 34, 57, 104; *College English*, 60–61
Lucas, 78, 97, 176, 195; academic literacy, 87–88, 98; agency, 95, 96; language use, 63–64
Lundsford, Karen, 11

Ma Boulangerie, 104–5
Makoni, Busi, 68
Makoni, Sinfree, 44, 66, 68, 141
Malaysia, 176; English in, 117–19; language varieties in, 116–17
Malika, 137, 176, 195; code switching by, 124–25; on English pluralism, 123–24; foreign language learning by, on 120–22; language contestation by, 132–33, 134; linguistic resources of, 178–79; maintaining agency and identity, 125–26
Mandarin, multiple literacies in, 126, 127, 148
Mangelsdorf, Kate, 101
Mashiri, Pedzisai, 44
Matsuda, Paul Kei, 115
Mateo, 165, 176, 195; code-meshing by, 157–58; cross-language negotiation of, 158–59; language use by, 156–57, 159–60; social identity of, 160–62
"May He Be Bilingual" (Cofer), 75
meaning, 126, 205(n8); construction of, 59–60; textual and visual production of, 105–6
meaning-making practice, 45, 78; translation as, 149–50, 169
mediational means, 22
meso-political action, 36, 59, 147(fig.)
meso-spaces, 183
missionaries, 71
MLA Ad Hoc Committee on Foreign Languages, 141, 166

mobility, 4, 44, 80; and immobility, 45-46; politics of, 46
Modern Standard Arabic, 67, 83
modo di dire, 92–93
monolingualism, 13, 25(table), 51, 58–59, 95, 102, 107, 108, 134, 138, 140, 182, 183–84, 191, 203(nn8, 9); Beirut University, 75–76, 86–87, 98–99; dominance of, 33–34, 39; as language ideology, 6, 8, 26–28; and multilingualism, 28–29, 31–32; standards and rules, 53–54
Moore, Daniel, 100
"Mother Tongue" (Tan), 148
moving traffic model, 45–47
Mukherji, Sujit, 143
multilingualism, 39, 110, 112, 138, 204(nn12, 13), 206(n1); academic, 126–27; archipelagos/code-islands in, 29–31; code-mixing in, 34–35; home languages in, 32–33; as language ideology, 13–14, 25(table), 28; in Lebanon, 67, 92; maintaining, 81–82; of students, 89–91
multimodal literacies, 111

narrative theory, 152
Naser, 78, 176, 178, 180, 195; agency, 95, 96; Arabic language use, 82–83; communication arts, 83–86; and English academic literacies, 97–98; English learning, 86–87
Nathalie, 78, 97, 178, 195; agency, 95, 96; English usage, 79–82, 175–76; linguistic alignments, 64–65
National Council of Teachers of English (NCTE), 148
National Writing Project (NWP), 148
nation-state language policies, 18
Native English speaker (NES), 52, 205(n6); as standard, 51, 74, 109
NCTE. *See* National Council of Teachers of English
negotiation, 7, 5, 44, 52, 58, 59–60, 103, 113, 123, 126; cross-language, 158–59; over language resources, 96, 125; of monolingualism, 39, 182; in translation, 152, 168–69; translation classes, 145–46
neologisms, 12–13
NES. *See* Native English speaker
Nikula, Tarja, 109
non-native English speakers (NNES), 64, 109
Nowacek, Rebecca, 101
Nuñez, Elizabeth, 24
Nur, 195; on Malaysian language use, 116–20; language use, 133–34, 176
NWP. *See* National Writing Project

opacité, 140
Other, students as, 168
overhead electricity cables model, 47–48

paratexts, 171
Park, Joseph Sung-Yel, 176
Paz, Octavio, 173
Pennycook, Alastair, 5, 36, 66, 49, 141, 142
performances, compartmentalization of, 88
Persepolis (Satrapi), 148–49
personal pronoun, use of, 153–56
pluralism, 123–24
plurality, 32
policies: language, 8, 10, 18, 107; at University of Seattle, 108–9
politics, language, 107; meso-, 36, 59, 147(fig.)
postmonolingualism, 8, 15–16, 78, 139, 166, 171; language ideology and, 134–35
power, 33, 120, 132, 165; language as, 162–63
practice(s), 16–17, 21, 60, 124, 203(n4); flexibility and hybridity, 122–23; language, 42, 67–71, 174, 184; representational, 42, 135, 140, 186–94
Pratt, Mary Louise, 27
prestige, Standard Written English, 33
proficiency, 51, 52
pronoun usage: personal, 153, 154; second-person singular, 161–62
punctuation, EAE rules of, 56–57
purity, language, 133

Ras Beirut, 206(n3); superdiversity of, 67–68
readability, in translations, 151–52
reader-writer relationships, 5
reading, 60, 93
Reiff, Mary Jo, 183
relationships, in translingual writing, 56
representations. *See* language representations
rereadings, 146; and translation, 150–51
research design, as critical ethnography, 8–9
resistance, from students, 167–68
resources, 53; and identity, 181–82; language, 89–91, 118–19, 133, 137–38, 178; for writing students, 37–38
responsibility, 55
retranslations, 146
rewriting, 146, 147(fig.), 150, 151
rhetorics, 6; of translation, 143–44
rojak English, 118
Rotten English (Ahmad), 35

Ruijia, 165, 176, 195; on nonstandardized language, 3, 5, 6; translation work, 162–64
rules, 152; academic enforcement of, 57–58; monolingualism, 53–54; personal pronoun use, 153–56; punctuation, 56–57
Ryan, 195; on agency and voice, 165, 176; translation work of, 153–56, 168

Saarinen, Taina, 109
Said, Samad, 117
Sante, Luc, "Lingua Franca," 75
Satrapi, Marjane, *Persepolis*, 148–49
Saussure, Ferdinand, 27
Schatzki, Theodore, 36
Seattle, 7, 174, 207(n1); language use in, 104–6; sociolinguistic landscapes in, 136–37. *See also* University of Seattle
second language acquisition (SLA), 22; learners and, 52–53
security/insecurity, of language form, 21–22
sedimentation, 54
Seidman, Steven, 71
self-identity, selfhood, 161–62, 177
self-referencing, in writing, 153–54
semiodiversity, 49
serendipity, 60
Shaaban, Kassim, 71–72
SLA. *See* second language acquisition
slang, 124
Smitherman, Geneva, *Talkin and Testifyin*, 34
social engagement, and translation, 156–57
socialization, 130; language, 77, 81, 123, 175, 179
sociocultural relations, 15, 98
sociolinguistics, 10, 17, 18
sojourner, 126–27
sovereignty, 27
Spanish: code-meshing, 157–58; use and literacies, 158, 159
stakeholders, language use and, 175–76
Standard English, 124, 203–4(n10); mastery of, 132–33
standards, 6, 23, 37, 52; monolingualism, 53–54
Standard Written English (SWE), 23, 27, 30, 125, 176; at Beirut University, 75, 99; and home languages, 33–34
structuralism, 27
structure: and agency, 58–59; dynamism of, 50–51; provisional and negotiable, 54
students, 24, 165; agency of, 58, 88–89, 95–96; and FYW ethnography, 186–94;

interview protocol for, 196–97; language resources for, 37–38, 137–38; language use of, 70–71; resistance of, 167–68; at University of Seattle, 115–16; in writing classrooms, 138–39
subjectivity, 44
superdiversity, 13, 115; of Beirut, 67–68; and sociolinguistic landscapes, 136–37, 174; urban landscapes, 45–46
SWE. *See* Standard Written English
symbiotic intermingling, 45
synergy, 60

Talkin and Testifyin (Smitherman), 34
Tan, Amy, "Mother Tongue," 148
taxi-lingua culture, 68
taxis, in Beirut, 68–70, 206(n7)
TBIP. *See* Transitional Bilingual Instruction Program
teachers, 5; FYW, 189–90; interview protocol, 198–99; professional development and preparation of, 179–80
teaching, 101; translingual ideology, 36–37, 39–40
territorialization, of languages, 29, 51
textual analysis, 10
Thoreau, Henry David, 149
tolerance, 33
tourism, and Lebanese language use, 68–71
traffic movement, 45–47
transcentricity, 49, 50, 61
transdirectionality, 49, 50, 61
Transitional Bilingual Instruction Program (TBIP), 107
translation, 5, 33, 61–62, 64, 140–41, 158, 208–9(nn1, 2, 6); at Beirut University, 75, 88–94, 100–101, 145–46, 209(n7); choices in, 130–31; critical, 143–44, 181–82; cross-language work, 127–28; English as, 88–94; language as power, 162–63; meaning making in, 149–50; process of, 168–70; readability and intelligibility, 151–52; rereading and, 150–51; as rewriting, 143; self-referencing in, 153–54; social and civic engagement in, 156–57; social identity in, 160–62; writing pedagogies, 172–73
translingualism, 6, 8, 12, 14–15, 17, 25(table), 35, 38, 52, 56, 60, 91, 100, 115, 165, 182, 202(nn10, 11); activism in, 18, 170–71, 185; Banyan tree model, 44–45; in composition work, 166–67; language representation, 101–2, 180–81; literacy, 96–97; meaning making in, 149–50; moving traffic model, 45–47; negotiability in, 54–55; overhead electricity cables model, 47–48; representational practices, 42, 142–43; in Seattle, 104–6; writing and teaching, 36–37, 39–40
translingual activism. *See* activism
transversality, 50, 52, 62
Trask, Haunani-Kay, *From a Native Daughter*, 34–35, 148
trilingualism, 72
Trimbur, John, 51, 58, 59
Trivedi, Harish, 34; on critical translation, 143–44

University of Seattle, 7, 103, 110, 138; academic literacies and, 126–27; data collection at, 10–11; ethnography, 186–94; graduate teaching assistants in, 111–13; international students at, 115–16; language difference and, 136–37; language policies, 108–9, 113–14; translation-oriented class at, 146–64
urban landscapes, 202(n9); superdiversity of, 45–46

Venuti, Lawrence, 173
Vertovec, Steven, 13
voice, 165, 204(n13)
"Volar" (Cofer), 74

Wagner, Johannes, 52
Walden (Thoreau), 149
Walters, Keith, *What's Language Got to Do with It?*, 35
Washington (state), 115, 208(n7); language policy, 107–8
Wee, Lionel, 176
Weber, Max, 88
What's Language Got to Do with It? (Walters and Brody), 35
Wible, Scott, 9, 107, 180
Williams, Joseph, 55–58
WPA Outcomes Statement for First-Year Composition, 148
writing, 78, 93; at Beirut University, 74–77, 207(n11); internationalized instruction, 9, 95; as *translation*, 144, 172–73, 181–82; translingual ideology, 36, 39–40, 101, 180–81
Writing and Identity (Ivanič), 149
writing center, Beirut University, 80–81

Xun Lu, 163

Yildiz, Yasemin, 8, 15–16, 26, 130
Yuran, 169

www.ingramcontent.com/pod-product-compliance
Ingram Content Group UK Ltd.
Pitfield, Milton Keynes, MK11 3LW, UK
UKHW042122200326
4879IPUK00002B/24